W9-DBP-813

Understanding Criminal Justice

Understanding Criminal Justice:
Sociological Perspectives

Philip Smith and Kristin Natalier

SSAGE Publications
London • Thousand Oaks • New Delhi

SAGE Publications Ltd
1 Oliver's Yard
55 City Road
London EC1Y 1SP

SAGE Publications Inc.
2455 Teller Road
Thousand Oaks, California 91320

SAGE Publications India Pvt Ltd
B-42, Panchsheel Enclave
Post Box 4109
New Delhi 110 017

British Library Cataloguing in Publication data

A catalogue record for this book is available from
the British Library

ISBN 0-7619-4031-6
    0-7619-4032-4

Library of Congress control number available

Typeset by C&M Digitals (P) Ltd., Chennai, India
Printed in Great Britain by The Cromwell Press Ltd, Trowbridge, Wiltshire

Contents

Acknowledgements   *ix*

INTRODUCTION   1

The Sociological Imperative   1
What this Book Does and Doesn't Do   4
The Structure of the Book   6

1   THEORETICAL APPROACHES TO LAW
AND CRIMINAL JUSTICE   8

Introduction   8
Social Order and Modernity   9
Contract Theory   12
Emile Durkheim   13
The Marxist Tradition   19
Symbolic Interactionism and Labelling Theory   26
Poststructuralism   28
Postmodern Approaches   32
Weberian Approaches   36
Norbert Elias and the Civilizing Process   37
Feminist Perspectives   39
The Relevance of Theory   42
Study Questions   42
Glossary of Key Terms   43
Suggested Further Reading   45
Suggested Websites   46

2   THE LAW   47

Introduction   47
Legal Systems   47
Liberal Legal Philosophy   50
Law and Norms   51
Past Processes: The Emergence of Law   52

Current Questions: Law, Postmodernity and Globalization   55
Jurisprudential Approaches to the Law   57
Equality   62
Objectivity   64
Public/Private Dichotomy   69
Rights   72
Conclusion   78
Study Questions   79
Glossary of Key Terms   79
Suggested Further Reading   81
Suggested Websites   81

3   THE POLICE   83

Introduction   83
The History of Policing   84
Police Culture   88
The Police World-view and Behaviour   89
Routine Policing   91
Styles of Policing   95
Policing and Politics   103
The Policing of Minorities   104
Police Deviance   107
Reforming the Police   108
Other Enforcement Agencies   110
Private Policing   112
Police and the Media   115
Conclusion   117
Study Questions   118
Glossary of Key Terms   118
Suggested Further Reading   119
Suggested Websites   120

4   COURT PROCESSES AND PERSONNEL   121

Introduction   121
The Role of the Courts   121
Language and Power   125
Sentencing   128
Ethnicity   129
Gender   133
Minimizing Discretion in Sentencing   136

Judging Victims: Rape, Gender Stereotypes and Victims of Crime   139
Key Courtroom Players – Lawyers, Judges, Juries   142
Alternative Adjudication   154
Media Representations of Law   159
Conclusion   163
Study Questions   163
Glossary of Key Terms   164
Suggested Further Reading   166
Suggested Websites   166

5   PUNISHMENT   167

Philosophies of Punishment   167
Prisons   169
The History of the Prison   169
Do Prisons Work?   172
Prison Populations   175
The Experience of Prison and Prison Culture   178
Prisons as a Negotiated Order   182
Women in Prisons   183
Intermediate Sanctions   185
The Death Penalty   188
New Initiatives in Punishment   189
Conclusion   192
Study Questions   192
Glossary of Key Terms   193
Suggested Further Reading   194
Suggested Websites   194

6   CONCLUSION   196

Law, Criminal Justice and the Sociological Perspective   196
Study Questions   206
Glossary of Key Terms   206
Suggested Further Reading   206

BIBLIOGRAPHY   207

INDEX   221

Acknowledgements

This book originated in our teaching experience in the program in Criminology, Criminal Justice and Legal Studies at the University of Queensland. Thanks are due to undergraduate and postgraduate students in those programs for asking the right questions. Our colleagues John Western and Paul Mazzerolle deserve special mention for their support. Jim Davidson of Sage Publications prompted us to write the initial proposal. Thanks are due to Jim, and also to Miranda Nunhofer, Caroline Porter and Ian Antcliff at Sage for overseeing this project. We also extend our deep appreciation to Philippa Smith, for her assistance in proofreading the manuscript. We thank Richard Collier for detailed comments on the draft manuscript.

This book is dedicated to John Western in recognition of his remarkable contribution to the teaching and research of criminology and sociology in Australia.

Introduction

The Sociological Imperative

Why study law and criminal justice? Answering this question is at the core of this text. By the end of this book the reader will have come to understand the myriad paths through which these social institutions come to play a vital, if contested, role in our society. We can begin by pointing to just some of the simple ways that they impact upon social life. The legal and criminal justice systems soak up a large proportion of the budget in all nations. They are a political hot potato that can win and lose elections. They also provide material for the media. Every newspaper and television news bulletin will contain stories about crime and punishment. There are also impacts at the level of our daily lives, even if we think of ourselves as a law-abiding citizen. Who among us has not scanned the roadside for a speed camera or radar gun, reported a theft to the police, restrained ourselves from committing some act for fear of legal consequences or felt the prickle of anxiety as we took the risk? For those more intimately involved with the criminal justice system, its significance is direct and ongoing. It can be a source of income and career identity for some, such as police officers and lawyers, and for others, like the long-term prisoner, it is inescapable, controlling every aspect of their daily life. Put in these common-sense terms, law and criminal justice are self-evidently important. They are a brute social fact of peculiar empirical weight. But accepting the significant social role of legal and criminal justice institutions does not mean that we must believe they are an unmitigated good. Some people see them as inherently oppressive institutions that offer 'peace' and stability through perpetrating injustice upon marginalized or oppressed groups. Others broadly endorse their goals and actions.

We have probably all been involved in debates and arguments with our friends and family over things such as the treatment of refugees, whether the police are racist, or whether a particular court judgment just reported in the newspaper is biased. Having opinions on such issues may be demanded of us as students but it is also important beyond the academic realm. Engaging with the questions surrounding the law and the criminal justice system is a sign of responsible and active citizenship. To do this we need to go beyond knee-jerk reactions and views derived second-hand from the media or first-hand from our own, probably narrow and limited, experiences. We see this book as presenting a series of discussions from a critical and questioning perspective. It offers the tools to be stronger students and more effective citizens, and encourages readers to make their judgments from a firmer and more informed footing.

How do we study the law and the criminal justice system from a sociological perspective? Sociology is fundamentally the study of human behaviour and human groups. It demands a critical appraisal of the familiar – of what we consider to be no more than common sense. It enables us to step back from what happens to us and locate our experiences – and those of any other individual – within the broader social and historical context. C. Wright Mills (1975) referred to this as 'the sociological imagination', the ability to link the biography, experiences and concerns of any one person into the over-arching patterns of the society in which they live. It looks at the way in which individuals and institutions are connected through sets of relations – of dependence, of power, of identity – and considers the implications of these connections. In so doing, a sociological perspective investigates the intersection of structure and agency. To varying degrees, sociologists try to understand the world in terms of the relationships between people's choices (including the meanings they ascribe to behaviours or artefacts, for example) and the structures that constrain and create the decisions and opportunities available to them. Thus, sociology grounds the study of any particular issue in the empirical world, but moves beyond simple reportage. It examines and explains the regularities and differences that are evident in society, patterns that may be either manifest or latent. Sociology offers the potential for a more nuanced and sophisticated understanding of the social world and our own life and others' lives.

From our own experiences around dinner tables, in corridors, over coffee and in front of the television, it seems that the world is full of potential social scientists. Concern or debate might be sparked by what seems to be a legal or perhaps moral issue but often even the most informal discussion will show the glimmerings of a sociological approach. Rather than a narrow commentary on, or interpretation of, strict law, our everyday thinking incorporates questions of power, difference, interaction, practice and ideology. Most people do not use these terms to name them, but they are emergent in how we see the world.

A sociological perspective is particularly useful when studying law and criminal justice because these are products of human action and human thought. It is important not to reify the law, to remember that it does not and cannot exist independently of the people who argue about it, formulate it, apply it, and those who are subject to it. The same is true of the criminal justice system, perhaps more obviously so. Sociology provides the tools for a more rigorous, systematic and confident understanding of law and the criminal justice system. Roger Cotterrell (1998: 183) identifies three key elements to a sociological approach to these institutions. First, a sociological perspective conceptualizes the law as social, bound up in a web of relations, interactions, beliefs and institutions, rather than transcending them. Second, law is empirical, not theoretical – it plays out in observable and material ways. Third, it is important to approach the study of law systematically. To be sure, being on the receiving end of prosecution for having a faulty tail light or watching a news story on police racism provides some insight into the issues at stake. But these are isolated episodes from which it would be dangerous to generalize. When we think more closely about the three dimensions, we might find that our long-held presumptions start to crumble. This can be disconcerting but the payoff is a stronger, more accurate and relevant appreciation of what goes on around us.

In this book we facilitate a deeper understanding through two key strategies. First, we foreground social theory. Approaching the law and criminal justice systems from a theoretically informed angle allows us to attain a critical distance from our own lifeworld and ask bigger, and perhaps more telling questions. In other words, theory enables us to tune up our intellects and become smarter thinkers. Second, we summarize and make use of data and the cumulative results of social science research throughout this book. Researching law and criminal justice in a methodologically sound way is a time-consuming and challenging task, but for this reason the results are more valid and easily generalizable than those derived from our own experience. With a century or so of quality research behind us, we are now in a position to point to broad generalities that have arisen from research efforts as well as to ongoing debates where outcomes are less certain. By referring to this rich history of research we are able to provide a substantial empirical foundation from which more informed views can be formulated.

At the core of this book are three simple questions:

- *Why do the legal and criminal justice systems take the form they do?* In answering this we will point in particular, but not exclusively, to their ties to modernity and the various theoretical accounts that have attempted to explain this association.
- *What are the implications of the legal and criminal justice systems for matters of social exclusion and inequality?* Our response here focuses in particular on themes relating to class, race and gender. We also point to the diverse paths by which such inequality can be produced, often in unexpected ways that would not have occurred to us without the benefit of theory and research.
- *What is the relationship between the organization of legal and criminal justice system institutions and the culture, practices and ideologies of their members, and what are the consequences of these?* Sociologists argue that it is important to move beyond individual psychology or idiosyncrasies. We discuss the diverse lifeworlds, value systems and institutional forms that exist and the ways that these produce consequences that often undermine formal institutional goals and social expectations.

To reiterate our earlier points, as sociologists we approach these questions with reference to the role of culture and social structure and their place in the organization of social life within modernity and postmodernity. In other words, we understand law and criminal justice as something intimately caught up with the rest of social life and as themes in a wider heritage of sociological thinking. From such an angle it is mistaken to study these institutions without also having in the frame an image of the organization of society as a whole, whether through functionalism, Marxism, feminism, poststructuralism or any other available model. This is because of the issue of social control (see next chapter pp. 9–11). The criminal justice system can be understood as enforcing social control so that human actions accord with prevalent goals, structures and agendas. Once we have an idea what these might be, we can begin to interpret the workings of law and criminal justice with reference to our big picture model of society.

The position taken here broadly opposes two trends in the study of criminal justice. The first is towards an understanding of criminology as an isolated discipline marked by its own insular concerns, middle-range theories and technical accomplishments often oriented around the control of particular social or administrative problems. In the extreme, this leads to an empiricist programme simply involving the collection of facts. Such research can make a valuable contribution to social policy, but does not really engage with the history of social thought or the diversity of perspectives that can generate deeper reflexivity about the goals and methods of criminal justice. We do, however, refer to much of this literature in the course of this book precisely because it has provided answers to a number of compelling short- and middle-range questions. These might be on issues as diverse as resistance to community policing, the rationale behind restorative justice and the impact of gender on sentencing decisions. The second tradition in the criminal justice literature involves a vocationally oriented perspective towards law, policing or corrections. Many textbooks, such as those on 'Justice Administration' and 'Legal Process' can be found that subscribe to this camp. They tend to be full of dry descriptions of rules and procedures, 'best practice', court hierarchies, duties and obligations of diverse personnel, and so forth. Our argument is that this approach too often takes the object of study for granted and fails to step back and ask more fundamental questions. In other words, it describes what is the case rather than asking why it is like it is, and, just as importantly, how it could be different. Put simply, it is too close to an insider's perspective. By contrast, this book is all about asking challenging questions, adopting a critical perspective and the thinking outside the square.

This book also deviates from the jurisprudential tradition that for a very long time dominated the study of law. Jurists and legal scholars have expended gallons of academic blood, sweat and tears in the service of defining and legitimating the bases and proper scope of laws and legal decisions, and their proper relationship to each other. The focus of the exchanges is philosophically interesting and intellectually and morally challenging but ultimately deficient from a social scientific perspective. They are expressed through what often amounts to an asocial framework, or one that at best incompletely recognizes the social context of law and its related institutions, and fails to link theory and empirical research. We briefly overview the defining characteristics of major jurisprudential approaches but we are not aiming to untangle their intricacies. Instead, they stand as examples of the need to acknowledge the constructed nature of our laws and legal system.

What This Book Does and Doesn't Do

This all said, we are now in a position to avoid disappointing readers and to flag up front what can be expected from this book. So, let's be clear, this book is not about crime and deviance. We do not discuss crime rates, theories of why people commit crimes, the lived experience of criminality, and so forth. There are plenty of good books out there that will do this for you. Ours is about formal *responses to crime* and *efforts to regulate crime* through law, courts, policing and corrections and it provides resources for thinking about these sociologically. A further feature of the book is that we focus on the intersection of law and criminal justice. While these are often treated separately, we suggest it is often more useful to explore the ways that they are inter-related. After all, the criminal justice system generally comes into play only once the law has been broken, and a legal system without a criminal justice system would be little more than a set of toothless rules in dusty books. We have already emphasized that this is not a handbook for practitioners but rather a resource for critical thinkers. Yet we do not intend this to be a dull study in philosophy. On the contrary, we refer continually to empirical materials and to studies on criminal justice institutions, many of these fascinating examples illustrate the complexity of social life. Hence by the end of this book you will have not only a repertoire of theoretical skills, but also a good knowledge of the basic contours of current social research on the law, prisons, courts and the police. To fulfil this objective, we have not as a rule entered into the intricacies of all legal and sociological debate. We note the existence of general points of contention but do not offer an exhaustive step-by-step account of the ins and outs of each matter. In effect, this book will get the reader 'up to speed' in very short order and provide a platform for further, more advanced study.

In writing this book we have included a number of features that will assist readers. Key terms are highlighted in **bold**. These are recapitulated in a glossary at the end of each chapter. Familiarity with these will be of great benefit in studying criminal justice. Study questions have been provided to assist students in their revision strategies. We have also listed further readings. Many of these are the seminal studies that we refer to in the text. There is often no substitute for reading a great author in the original. Other suggested further readings are texts that deal with a particular theme in more detail than we have space for in this book. Finally, we have included a list of useful websites and a brief evaluation of them. It should be remembered that websites can be problematic. Some are by and large public relations tools; this is often the case with those run by police departments. Others, particularly those of governmental research agencies, offer data that will assist in developing a picture of current trends, budgets and policies. It is, however, remarkably difficult to locate sites that engage with core theoretical issues and for this reason websites are generally better seen as sources of information and food for thought. Please remember that web addresses can change and websites come and go, so you might have to use your own initiative or skills with a search engine to locate the sites we mention or others like them. We generally find academic journals and books to be more worthwhile than the Internet. For the most part, the items we cite or discuss will prove valuable as a next stop – after all, this is why we used them in putting this book together. We also recommend using the CD-ROM *Sociological Abstracts*, which is available through most university libraries. This lists articles in refereed academic journals from throughout the social sciences. By using the correct search terms you are almost certain to encounter original research on the topic that you are investigating.

The Structure of the Book

Turning to the structure of this book, Chapter 1 outlines the dominant theoretical perspectives on law and criminal justice. We document the contributions of classical social theory as well as more recent developments. A number of themes recur throughout the chapter: the consequences of the arrival of modernity, and the centrality of power and culture in shaping the targets and the style of the criminal justice process. The major contention is that law and criminal justice today have to be understood as the product of a historically specific set of institutions and cultural codes. The remaining four chapters continue this thread, but although we refer back to major paradigms, more attention is given to middle-level findings from contemporary social research than to blue sky thinking. In this way the chapters also operate to inform the reader of the basic contours of particular research fields.

In other books the criminal justice system is frequently described as a set of interlocking institutions which combine to 'process' a hypothetical offender as they break a criminal code, get caught by the police, go to court and then on to prison. Our chapters are organized to follow this sequence, although we do not share this vision of a smoothly integrated system. We start with the law in Chapter 2, asking where it comes from and why we have it. Although we often think of the law as something that is dry, abstract, rarified and codified, we emphasize here the ways that it is tied to society through interests and values. The law is not something outside of society – on the contrary, it is a strategic research site that crystallizes in its prescriptions and stuffy tomes the very essence of our social order and our cultural values. The secret for the researcher is learning how to extract this gem of meaning from a mountain of dross. We illustrate this possibility with particular reference to feminist critiques of legal reasoning and legal categories. Chapter 3 deals with the police – an institution charged with the enforcement of the law. The contemporary police force is shown to be a response to problems arising with the arrival of urban modernity but we suggest that it is riven by a number of flaws and confronted by a number of challenges. In outlining contemporary policing, an emphasis is given to informal 'police culture' and the obstacle this presents to reform, even as we outline and critique a number of important new directions in policing, such as community policing and private policing. Chapter 4 looks at the courts. Although these are supposed to be impartial, a number of factors have been argued to impact upon the fair administration of justice. We explore these, looking in particular at the role of culture and power in the courtroom setting and the varied ways that these can work to tip the scales of justice against certain groups. Chapter 5 investigates corrections. Here our major focus is on the prison. After looking at the history of prisons, we explore prison culture and the impact this has on inmate life. The chapter also outlines alternatives to prison and discusses the contemporary trend towards privatization within the corrections industry. Chapter 6 provides the conclusion.

In sum, this book aims to provide a series of tools that encourage a critical and informed approach to some of the most important and prevalent institutions in contemporary life. Throughout, discussion focuses on the empirical nature of law and criminal justice, their presence and effects in the 'real world', rather than the possibilities they offer when 'on the books'. Further, we emphasize the ways in which both laws and the systems through which they are implemented are the products of human actions and meaning making, with all the contingencies and imperfections this entails. Fundamentally, laws and the criminal justice system are not hermeneutically sealed from their broader contexts; they can only be understood with reference to them.

1 Theoretical Approaches to Law and Criminal Justice

Introduction

From the perspective of sociology, the analysis of law and criminal justice is not only an empirical issue. We can never understand what is going on simply by collecting and sifting through more and more facts, statistics, policy evaluations and accounts. What are also required are theoretical frames. Only when we have these can we move beyond the study of disconnected specifics towards a big picture understanding of law and criminal justice as social institutions embedded in culture, history and a wider social structure. Some thirty years ago the noted theorist Alvin Gouldner observed that 'all studies of crime and deviance, however deeply entrenched in their own technical traditions, are inevitably grounded in larger, more general social theories which are always present, even as unspoken silences' (1973: ix). This point still holds today. Theoretical awareness is urgently needed so researchers can uncover the hidden presuppositions behind their work and realize a broader and more powerful vision in their research enterprise. Reflexive and careful attention to questions of social theory will allow us to develop abstract and generally applicable models that help us to think about law, punishment and regulation in a more comprehensive and critical way. By critical we do not necessarily mean making criticisms or challenging the status quo, but rather moving beyond common-sense thinking. Consequently, in this chapter we will be asking, and perhaps answering, the following questions:

- What is the purpose of the criminal justice system?
- How do law and criminal justice fit with the wider organization of modern society?
- Whose interests are served by legal codes and institutions?
- How does our broader culture and system of beliefs influence the administration of justice?

The major approaches to these questions have conventionally been divided into two camps: those influenced by **consensus theory** and those espousing **conflict theory**. The arguments of the former generally stress the benefits of law and criminal justice for society in bringing order and stability. They see them as underpinned by widely shared values and as an expression of common sentiments. By contrast, conflict arguments claim that legal and justice systems favour the interests of dominant groups. The focus in this perspective tends to be on the repressive dimensions of power and its exercise. In recent years this kind of binary classification of theories has become less common. A greater emphasis is now placed on pivotal concepts and middle-level theory rather than sweeping debates and denunciations – a result reflected, for example, in the rise of left realism (see pp. 24–25). Since the 1970s influences from feminism and post-structuralism have also complicated the picture. Although positioned on the 'conflict' side of the field, they have suggested that the image of the powerful and powerless needs to be revised in decisive ways from that advocated by classical Marxist criminology with its emphasis on a binary class struggle. In the remainder of this chapter we unpack the chest of theoretical tools that sociologists have been using to make sense of law and criminal justice. Our major concern here, of course, is not to advocate any one position as superior, but rather to provide a balanced summary and appraisal of core thinkers and approaches. We will look at a range of theories, some concerned more with law, others with criminal justice issues and some with both. By the end of the chapter the reader will have acquired an intellectual foundation that will enable them to engage with the subsequent, more empirical material in this book with greater sophistication and insight.

Social Order and Modernity

In order to start our journey in this chapter we need to introduce the **problem of social order**. This refers to the requirement that all societies have to ensure a basic level of stability, to maintain peace and to 'function' in a more or less efficient way so that basic human needs can be met. A society that cannot solve this problem will soon cease to exist. It will descend into anarchy and be unable to reproduce itself day after day, year after year. In general, social order is maintained through culture and power. Culture allocates roles and identities, provides motivations and expectations, and sets out norms and boundaries that mark out acceptable and non-acceptable behaviours. Power provides enforcement mechanisms that can be brought into play against those breaking cultural rules. **Positive sanctions** are sets of rewards that operate as inducements to conform. These can include things like social approval, a pay rise or a medal from the Queen. Likewise **socialization** contributes to social order. From the day we are born, our identities are shaped by our culture. We internalize shared value patterns and norms so that we know right from wrong (as our culture defines these); we acquire motivations as to what we want out of life and we acquire expectations about appropriate ways to behave. The vast bulk of the work involved in maintaining social order in everyday life is carried out by positive sanctions and socialization. For the most part, most people conform most of the time and are mostly happy to do so.

Deviant acts are those that offend against norms and are held to threaten the maintenance of social order. If detected, these incur **negative sanctions** that are intended as a punishment and to act as a deterrent. Most deviant acts are dealt with by small-scale, informal negative sanctions such as ostracism by the group or a critical comment by a friend. Think, for example, of what happens if someone cheats at Scrabble or breaks wind in the car or stubs their toe and swears in church. More serious, though less common, are infractions against the social order that lead to formal negative sanctions. These involve the summoning of authority, the invocation of written rules and the handing out of clearly specified punishments. This book is essentially about these formal, negative sanctions in the contemporary social world – more specifically, those regulated and administered by the state. We explore their nature, ask how they are changing, investigate how they are influenced by culture and serve particular social interests – in short, we provide a theoretical and empirical account of a set of institutions pivotal to social control today.

In order to fully understand what is unique or interesting about this object of inquiry, it is useful to turn towards findings from the discipline of anthropology and gain some perspective. For much of human history we have lived in small-scale band societies. Evidence from these suggests that social order is maintained through informal means or with reference to supernatural powers rather than through differentiated and secular mechanisms for adjudication and enforcement. In his study of the Mbuti pygmies, who live in the rainforests of equatorial Africa, Colin Turnbull discusses the existence of a spontaneous and collective form of justice. Within the face-to-face group 'everything settles itself with apparent lack of organization' (1961: 115). The group as a whole exercises sanctions such as ostracism, gossip, beatings and ridicule to bring offenders back into line and to demonstrate public disapproval. According to Turnbull, the Mbuti are of a sociable disposition and fear of contempt and isolation keeps most of them in line. They have a precarious existence where survival depends on collective hunting strategies and close cooperation, so unity is a key social value. This helps explain why 'disputes are generally settled with little reference to the alleged rights and wrongs of the case, but more with the sole intention of restoring peace to the community' (ibid.: 110). Such a system places an emphasis on the rapid resolution of disputes and maintenance of group solidarity. There are clear affinities between this way of maintaining social order and contemporary initiatives such as 'alternative dispute resolution' and 'reintegrative shaming' (see pp. 154–159 and 189–190).

Another African culture, that of the Azande of the Southern Sudan, can be used to illustrate the centrality of supernatural powers and divination to the maintenance of social order in traditional societies. Within this society, oracles are part of the self-help system of village justice. They are believed to be able to reveal the truth and are consulted by individuals to find out the causes of their misfortune. For example, one might use the oracle to check up on suspected adultery, to discover the identity of the witch bringing sickness or to find out who has been stealing from a granary. The most important of these investigative tools is the poison oracle. This consists of strychnine being given to a chicken. As this is done, questions are asked about what has been happening. The survival or death of the fowl provides a 'yes' or 'no' answer accordingly. As the anthropologist E.E. Evans-Pritchard (1976: 124) puts it, the oracle 'was itself the greater part of what we know as the rules of evidence, judge, jury and witnesses'. Although such a system might seem to an outsider to be unfair or liable to be quickly discredited by contradictory results, Evans-Pritchard reports that this is not the case. The Azande have an elaborate network of beliefs that allows them to account for inconsistencies in the oracle (the question was not phrased correctly, a witch has tampered with the poison, etc.) and prefer using it to the European justice alternative introduced by the colonial British.

These anthropological studies point to the role of what generally is referred to as 'non-legal social control'. This persists in complex societies in the myriad ways that individuals, communities and organizations investigate and punish wrongs and try to resolve their disputes without involving state authorities or invoking the law. Governmental systems of social control have been superimposed upon this but have not fully replaced it. Donald Black (1976) has proposed a theory of the relationship between these two systems, asserting that the law and governmental intervention are more likely where other forms of control and self-help are weak. These include not only customs and traditions, but also bureaucracies and professions that have formal systems for self-regulation. This theory looks attractive but has some problems (Roach Anleu, 2000: 141–2). Studies of 'collective efficacy' suggest that strong communities are more likely to organize themselves against wrong doing *and* work with law enforcement than those where 'nobody cares'. The major variable predicting whether individuals or organizations report crime is the seriousness of the offence, not the strength of their community ties or self-help mechanisms. Black is nothing if not a positivist, so consideration of how individuals interpret events, think of the police and the law and decide what steps to take is precluded from his rather mechanistic analysis. Clearly these have to come into the frame with phenomena such as sexual assault or victimless crime or in situations where there is community suspicion of the justice system. But we are getting away from our main point. This is that rational, bureaucratic, secular legal social control by the state is just one of the many possible solutions to the problem of social order. For most of human history, communities have used informal 'non-rational' means to ensure conformity and have done so quite successfully. Even today legal social control exists alongside a raft of alternatives. In explaining how it came onto the scene in the first place, we need to think about the rise of modernity. The shift from a rural agricultural, local, religious society towards an urban, industrial, state-regulated, secular one had profound implications for the emergence of contemporary forms of social control. Social theorists were one group of people to engage in this task. The political philosophers of the seventeenth and eighteenth centuries were another, and it is to them that we turn next.

Contract Theory

Contract theory provided the first developed set of conceptual tools for thinking through the relationship between the rise of modernity and the emerging rule of law. Appearing in the seventeenth century following the collapse of the medieval world-view, contract theory was very much concerned with providing a philosophical foundation for the existence and power of the modern state (Held, 1984). Contract theorists argue that the state is necessary to protect the interests of its subjects and maintain social order. Without an over-arching authority things would be very unpleasant, or as Thomas Hobbes put it in *Leviathan* (1991 [1615]), a 'warre of everyone against everyone' in which the typical life was 'nasty, brutish and short'. The **social contract** was the term used to describe the arrangement whereby individuals gave up some of their liberties and powers to the state (or sovereign monarch) in return for physical security. The state would offer protection to all, operate justly and maintain peace by the impartial administration of the law and the enforcement, if need be, of order. In this vision the law was to regulate the relationship of citizens towards each other as well as the tie between citizens and the state. Over time the Hobbesian version of the social contract gave way to the subtly different liberal world-view of John Locke. This gave the state a role as the preserver of 'natural rights' to life, liberty and property and placed an even stronger emphasis on consent as the foundation of the legitimate power. According to Locke (1936 [1690]), the law was essential for democracy and free association among people, famously writing that 'Wherever Law ends Tyranny begins'. For Locke, then, law and criminal justice are seen as more than just necessary for peace. They are also essential for maintaining basic human freedoms. The work of Jean-Jacques Rousseau in *The Social Contract* (1968 [1762])pushed this line of thinking even further, suggesting that (in the ideal case at least), laws were the expression of a 'general will' arrived at through public debate and eventual agreement. The overall picture of contract theory, then, is of law and criminal justice as a form of social regulation that provides common social goods and has broad popular consent. It is important, however, to observe that there are subtle differences between each theory, reflecting the fact that they emerged in different historical epochs. Hobbes gives an emphasis to questions of peaceful coexistence, reflecting the fact that he was writing during the transition from an unruly medieval epoch. Locke's main concern seems to be property rights – an issue pivotal to an era of mercantile expansion and its growing middle class. Rousseau links the social contract to popular sovereignty – a concern of republican thinking during the Enlightenment.

Contract theory has been particularly important in the field of political science and has been nearly as influential for theoretical discussions of the law within jurisprudence. Such writings often revolve around concepts such as freedom, democracy, consent and the state. Nevertheless the approach has not been without its critics and, indeed, much of the literature today seems to be devoted to spelling out just what is wrong with contract theory. Many suggest it is hopelessly naïve on matters of power. The state might better be seen as imposing laws on behalf of certain social groups (or even itself) rather than expressing a popular will. Marxism, for example, understands the state as operating in the interests of the ruling class (see pp. 19–24). Moreover, we never really see people entering into a 'contract'. Indigenous peoples and right-wing separatist extremists alike have found that as citizens we have little choice but to accept the laws of the state in which we are born. There is no real chance of opting out or refusing the contract, setting up our own laws and defining our own independent territories. In effect, then, the social contract is a philosophical and ideological fiction, not something that has ever really existed. Critics have also suggested that contract theorists were products of their time and consequently more interested in justifying the privileges of free men rather than those of slaves and dependent women. In effect, the contract was a deal struck between affluent men – a masculine ideology that served to reinforce their power and exclude minorities from political and economic participation. Notwithstanding these criticisms, or perhaps because of them, contract theory does have the merit of drawing our attention to the question of popular consent for the law and its administration. It also highlights the fact that a specifically *political* process is at the heart of law and criminal justice in modern societies with the state and state power at its core. For all these virtues, contract theory has had a limited impact in sociology and mainstream criminology. In these disciplines the most significant thinker to paint the criminal justice system in a positive light was Emile Durkheim.

Emile Durkheim

As we approach the centenary of his death, Emile Durkheim has become increasingly acknowledged as one of the most profound thinkers on the law, justice and punishment. A founder of sociology, Durkheim (1858–1917) lived and worked in France. Capable of brilliant twists of counter-intuitive thinking, Durkheim saw that in order to truly understand criminal and legal process we have to view it as intimately tied up with morality, sentiment and emotion and as reflecting the wider organization of society. Durkheim's writing on these topics is mostly to be found in his work from the 1890s, especially his doctoral dissertation *The Division of Labour in Society* (1984 [1893]) and in *Moral Education* (1973).

At the core of Durkheim's thinking is **functionalism**. This argues that we have to understand society as a system. Its constituent elements, whether they are roles, institutions, patterns of activity, values or individuals, need to be read in terms of their relation to that system and the contribution they make to its survival and stability. Ideas taken from biology have often proven central to this model. The component parts of society are thought to support the whole, just as the various organs and muscles of an animal enable it to survive. Each contributes something indispensable to the whole and this function explains its existence. Pivotal to Durkheim's functionalist view of society was the idea that it was held together primarily by shared sentiments known as the **collective conscience**. He saw feelings of morality and belonging as a core feature of human beings in society. Crime, according to Durkheim, is an activity that confronts and transgresses the collective conscience and generates intense emotions such as outrage. Consequently, the law could be understood as a 'visible symbol' (1984: 24) of the collective conscience and punishment as 'an act of vengeance, since it is an expiation. What we are avenging, and what the criminal is expiating, is the outrage to morality' (ibid.: 47). Such a definition places collective meanings at the centre of our understanding of social responses to crime.

Perhaps surprisingly, given these views, Durkheim's view of crime was not entirely negative. Indeed, he argues with great consistency that crime was sometimes good for society. First, he pointed out that many reformers, such as the Greek philosopher Socrates, had been considered to be criminals. Durkheim suggested that in contexts such as this, crime had helped innovation and change to take place by pushing moral boundaries and enabling new understandings to be established. Without such crime we would have a static and inflexible society. More important, however, was a second argument. In Durkheim's view, crime was a good thing because it entailed punishment, and punishment, in turn, had beneficial social consequences. Durkheim argued that by denouncing crime and criminals in punishment activity, society was able to reaffirm and make concrete diffuse ideas about morality. Through such action the collective conscience could be strengthened and individuals reminded of their shared obligations and sentiments. Durkheim even went so far as to say that crime would have to be invented if it did not exist. Hence deviance arises due to social needs and the level of perceived deviance tends to remain constant. Thus, in a monastery, he notes, events that are trivial can be elevated to the status of major sins because even here moral boundaries need to be ritually established.

Of course there were limits to how far Durkheim was prepared to advocate deviance as a social good. He distinguished between normal and pathological deviance. The former made a positive net contribution to society and was not too extensive while the latter was fundamentally threatening to the social order. Indeed, pathological deviance could be an indicator of **anomie** – a situation in which the moral regulation of society had broken down.

One of Durkheim's major contributions was to provide a detailed account of the historical evolution of legal regulations and punishment and to point to the ties between the emergence of modernity and the forms of contemporary criminal justice. In his view, the 'law reproduces the main forms of social solidarity' (1984: 28) and could be used to explore how this solidarity had changed over time. He argued that 'primitive' societies had almost no division of labour – people did the same jobs such as hunting and collecting. As a result, he (wrongly) believed members all thought the same way. This meant there was little tolerance for diversity – a situation Durkheim thought of as **mechanical solidarity**. Offending was met with harsh, retributive punishments. By contrast in complex (i.e. modern) societies there were specialized tasks, people were more individualized and, as a result, the collective conscience had developed a greater tolerance for difference. Durkheim describes this as **organic solidarity**. This is because social cohesion is ensured by the components of society working together like the organs of the body. In such a situation punishments tended to be restorative – that is to say, they try to reintegrate people into the community. Durkheim tried to demonstrate this shift by looking at legal codes as these had changed over history, for example, those described in the Bible or those among the Romans. Although his account is plagued by nineteenth-century evolutionist thinking and has been shown by anthropological research to be empirically wrong ('primitive' societies tend, in fact, to be quite forgiving), it is a pioneering effort. Notably it suggests that punishment shifts over time need to be understood in a context of wider social (differentiation and complexity) and cultural (collective conscience) change. Here, then, is the core of a strongly sociological explanation of law and justice. To summarize, what lessons about law and criminal justice can we distil from Durkheim's work?

- We need to think about the criminal justice system in terms of its contribution to the wider problem of social order and its location in an encompassing social system. It is a serious mistake to take law and criminal justice as autonomous spheres of life that go their own merry way without inputs from broader shifts in culture and society. This important point, we suggest, holds whether or not one subscribes to Durkheim's functionalist world-view and, indeed, alternative accounts on this theme will be provided in the rest of this chapter.
- The law and criminal justice system can be thought of as products of a collective conscience and as underpinned by moral codes and emotions. Because they reflect deeply held beliefs and values, it is a mistake to see laws and punishments only as the dry product of cool and calculating reason. Certainly, we have to pay attention to the way that public opinion and wider social values have determinate impacts upon what goes on.
- In the process of marking out the good from the bad, processes of punishment become symbolic. They have ritual properties and are directed to the wider citizenry, not just the individual criminal. In a sense, they are semiotic or signalling activities in which a message about, say, justice and morality is spelled out. In Durkheim, then, we find the germ of a strongly cultural understanding of punishment. Only in recent years have we begun to pay attention to this dimension of his work.

Having acknowledged these benefits, there are clearly a number of problems with Durkheim's work. He often assumes rather than demonstrates a social consensus. Indeed, some critics argue that modern societies cohere without consensus rather than because one is present. Themes of power and inequality are also notably absent from his work. Crime seems to be punished simply because society feels outraged. There is no awareness that criminal justice might not be a level playing field with dominant groups advantaged at the expense of others. There are also serious problems when it comes to issues of causality. Durkheim's functionalist position sees criminals punished and laws enacted because of abstract social needs and the diffuse swirling sentiments of the collective conscience. Many argue that this is too vague a conceptualization of how things really happen and that an adequate explanation needs to be able to identify real actors who make real decisions. Finally, we note that only some crimes and criminal justice actions fit Durkheim's model very well. Popular responses towards paedophiles and serial killers, for example, clearly demonstrate that collective morality and emotions are at play. Similarly, executions match broadly with Durkheim's understanding of punishment as a kind of ritualized morality lesson. In other cases his template does not seem so applicable. Nobody seems to care very much about parking tickets, speeding or tax evasion. Contrary to Durkheim's emphasis on punishment as a public display of outrage, many punishments are conducted without an audience and without any obvious public lesson being drawn. Prisons, for example, are shut off from wider society and few people particularly care what goes on there. This reality confronts Durkheim's understanding of punishment as a dramatic display of law and morality and suggests there might be a dull, instrumental reason that drives its implementation – perhaps power, perhaps simply inertia.

Elaborations from Durkheim

Durkheim's thinking that cultural forces drive the criminal justice system has been elaborated in a number of ways. Some have looked at his ideas on the links between the collective conscience and the identification of deviance within a functionalist framework. The book *Wayward Puritans* by Kai Erikson (1966) is probably the best-known work in this genre. Erikson looked at three 'crime waves' and responses to these in the criminal justice system of the colony of Massachusetts during the seventeenth century. The first of these involved attacks on a minority religious sect, the second the persecution of Quakers, and the third the famous Salem witch trials. Erikson argues that the deviance was to all intents and purposes invented. Often there was no evidence of serious wrongdoing. Witches, for example, were identified on the basis of testimony from a group of hysterical girls or from confessions derived under torture. In other cases, the Puritan majority became obsessed with trivial differences from the norm. Hence Quakers were prosecuted for having long hair. Using Durkheim's ideas, Erikson suggests that a process of **boundary maintenance** was at work. In order to define who they were and what their mission was, the Puritans had to act against deviance – even if it was an imagined or exaggerated rather than a real threat. Such a finding is consistent with Durkheim's observation, mentioned on a previous page, that deviance might need to be invented, even in a monastery.

Erikson believes that a broader climate of social change was behind the various 'crime waves'. The moral boundaries of the Puritan settlement were under threat not so much because of the activities of deviants, but rather because of the unfolding of culture and history. Wider contexts included the loss of political support from English Puritans, internal fighting over land, the migration of non-Puritans into the colony and a declining sense of mission among the settlers. Erikson sees the episodes he identifies as having some socially beneficial effects – for the wider community if not for the victims. They provided ground rules for living and enabled the colony to retain and develop a sense of purpose in this changing world. Such ideas are similar to those on moral panics that we review later in this chapter, in that social responses to deviance are taken to be driven by factors that have little to do with crime and punishment narrowly conceived. However, the moral panics literature tends to have a more negative view of such episodes. Erikson, by contrast, takes a lead from Durkheim's belief that the identification and punishment of deviants reaffirm the collective conscience.

It is instructive to compare *Wayward Puritans* with Stanley Cohen's (1973) *Folk Devils and Moral Panics*, which was written around the same time. Very loosely and indirectly influenced by Durkheim, this text also drew upon labelling theory and critical criminology (see pp. 26–27) to explore societal reactions to crime, and especially the media treatment of criminality. The issue in focus was a series of seaside disturbances in Britain during the 1960s. These involved motorbike-riding youths, fighting and vandalism. Cohen noted an exaggerated response to these events, with sensationalist newspaper coverage, television debates and questions in Parliament following hot on the heels of what was really a very minor crime episode. Cohen designated the event a **moral panic**. When this occurs: 'A condition, episode, person or group of persons emerges to become defined as a threat to societal values and interests; its nature is presented in a stylised and stereotypical fashion by the mass media, the moral barricades are manned by editors, bishops, politicians and other right thinking people' (1973: 9). Like Erikson, Cohen observes the disproportionate nature of the response to crime, but he does not have a functionalist logic to his inquiry. Cohen's interest is more in middle-range institutional responses to crime in the media, politics and the criminal justice system as well as themes related to elites and power. His text was to provide an important resource for later, more Marxist accounts of moral panics as well as subsequent work looking at the role of the media in framing crime and delinquency (see pp. 23–24).

More recently, discussions on the ritual and dramaturgical dimensions of punishment have also started to come out of the Durkheimian stable. These have been influenced by his last major work *The Elementary Forms of Religious Life*, where Durkheim (1968 [1912]) noted the centrality of ritual and the sacred to social life. Current work has fused this model with his earlier work on law, crime and justice. Responding to criticisms about idealism and conservatism, these more recent Durkheimian analyses have tended to move away from the functionalist thinking of *The Division of Labour in Society*. The judicial process is seen as a contested signifying act in which themes of morality, the sacred and profane are at stake within a wider political environment where power and control are also at play. The work of one of the authors of this book falls into this camp and can serve as an illustration. Philip Smith (1996) looked at the history of public executions and understands them as a ritual event in which dominant elites attempted to transmit moral codes.

During the eighteenth century it was hoped that the execution would be a kind of morality play in which the evil of the criminal was exposed and the power of the state dramatized. Accounts of executions, especially at Tyburn in London, indicated that things were not working out as planned. Victims died in diverse ways that undermined the official narrative. Some were highly religious and looked like martyrs in the face of death. Others showed bravado and cracked jokes, thus expressing contempt for the law. The audience for such events was usually drunk, bawdy or engaged in petty crime, looking upon the whole episode as an excuse for a riotous day out. For elites, such behaviour suggested their ritual was failing as a form of civic education – to the contrary, it seemed to be encouraging crime and dissent. Using pamphlets and other documents published by reformers at the time Smith is able to show that the subsequent movement of executions from a public to a hidden arena was a damage control exercise – in effect, an attempt to patch up a ritual that had gone badly wrong.

Finally, it is worth noting the movement of Durkheim's legal theory into twentieth-century structural functionalism. In the systems theory of Talcott Parsons (1970), society was made up of subsystems (the economy, politics, etc.), which each contributed in a specific and positive way to its overall needs. The law was the subsystem allocated the task of ensuring social integration by regulating and preventing conflict. Within this vision the law was invested with a general moral authority and served, in turn, to ensure that the values and needs of the wider community were upheld by other subsystems and their actors. In common with Durkheim's perspective in *The Division of Labour in Society*, that of Parsons points usefully to the fact that the law is more than a bunch of formal rules and regulations that are just a nuisance or simply expressions of power; it has ties to wider symbolic and cultural patterns. In our society, for example, there is a strong emphasis placed on highly abstract values such as universalism (everybody should be treated equally), freedom and achievement because these are core aspects of modernity. Legal codes are expected to uphold these values, in effect, translating them into more concrete codes for human action as 'an integrated system of universalistic norms' (1967: 510). Evidence for this cultural foundation to the law can be seen in the fact that statutes which appear to violate our core values are denounced as unfair by those on the left and right alike.

Drawing on Weber (see pp. 36–37), Parsons also pointed to the ties between the law and modernity from a more historical perspective. These views are best expressed in an essay called 'Evolutionary Universals in Society' (Parsons, 1967). Here, he suggests that by promoting universalism, the law had provided the basis for the calculability and social stability that sustained entrepreneurial attitudes, investment and innovation. Hence he remarks that: 'The development of the English Common Law ... not only constituted the most advanced case of universalistic normative order, but probably was decisive for the modern world ... it is no accident that the Industrial Revolution first occurred in England' (1967: 514). Importantly, the law had autonomy from other social systems and was 'relatively independent of both religious agencies ... and vested interest groups.' This structural location ensured the law had broad support, would be free from capricious interference and could serve as a platform for democracy and the emergence of modern ideas about rights and citizenship. The law, then, helps us to maintain a form of social order consistent with our value patterns and organization. Some scholars argue this emphasis on the positive contribution of the law to social life is mistaken. They suggest, contra Parsons, that it is controlled by certain groups and that its universalism is a cloak for power. We move on to explore these arguments in the next sections as we shift from consensus to conflict theories of law and criminal justice. In the next chapter we look in more detail at arguments that specifically attack universalistic ideas of reason and justice as these are embodied in the law.

The Marxist Tradition

Surprisingly the great philosopher, political economist, historian and founder of communism Karl Marx (1818–1883) did not write much about crime or criminal justice in his major works such as *Das Kapital* (1962 [1867]). Nevertheless his broader perspective has proven to be highly influential. Before moving on to specifics relating to law and criminal justice, we need to briefly review the Marxist vision of social life. Durkheim, as we have seen, asserted that society was a broadly cooperative enterprise held together by common sentiments and moral codes. For Marx, by contrast, conflict is at the heart of the social order. Struggles exist between classes and are driven by inequalities. Hence Marx's vision of social life privileges economic life. Indeed, the economy (base) broadly determines whatever else goes on in politics or culture (superstructure) – a position sometimes thought of as **economic determinism** or the **base/superstructure model**.

According to Marx, every society, to put it simply, is divided into two classes. In the contemporary world the owners of property, or bourgeoisie, are the **dominant class** and control the 'means of production' (factories, farms, etc.) while workers are the **subordinate class** and can sell only their labour power. The interests of owners and workers are always at odds. The former want more profit and the latter more wages. Conflict is inevitable, leading to a society where order is primarily maintained by power and force, supported by **ideology**. This term refers to the system of ideas that masks inequality and justifies forms of social organization associated with oppression. Over the years the Marxist model has undergone considerable elaborations and refinements with an increasing emphasis placed on the role of ideology in sustaining a capitalist society that is in permanent 'crisis'. However, the core argument has remained that we live in a world based on injustice and power and that dominant groups exploit subordinate groups. The Marxist approach to law and criminal justice builds on this platform, suggesting that they are two among many instruments through which the state works to support the interests of the dominant class. Pivotal functions include allowing economic exploitation, legitimating the use of force in controlling political dissent and protecting the property of the rich.

We can see the basics of such an approach in fragments written by Marx and his collaborator Friedrich Engels. Hence in *The German Ideology*, Marx and Engels (1964 [1846]) have a discussion of the relationship between property, the state and the law. In contrast to theorists of the social contract (see pp. 12–13) who took the state to represent universal interests, Marx and Engels describe it as 'nothing more than the form of organization which the bourgeois necessarily adopt both for internal and external purposes, for the mutual guarantee of their property and interests' (ibid.: 79). Consequently, they assert that the idea that the law is based upon the general will or a popular mandate is simply a juridical illusion. To the contrary, because 'civil law develops simultaneously with private property' and 'the state mediates in the formation of all common institutions' (ibid.: 80), both are better understood as partners in a process of domination, in this case, ensuring the property rights of the dominant class.

It is all too easy to imagine the state writing whatever laws it wishes to blatantly support the interests of the powerful. However, Marx and Engels suggested that the relationship of law to economic and political life is not as straightforward as we might think. The need for the law to be internally non-contradictory and to appear universalistic (in effect, to exhibit the characteristics identified by Parsons, above) means legal codes reflect the class system in subtle and indirect ways. These might elude common sense and a routine, uncritical jurisprudential analysis. Hence in his letter of 27 October 1890, to Conrad Schmidt, Engels argued that: 'In a modern state law must not only correspond to the general economic condition and be its expression, but must also be an internally consistent one' (1969: 442). Consequently it rarely 'happens that a code of law is the blunt, unmitigated, unadulterated expression of the domination of a class – this in itself would offend the "conception of right"' (ibid.: 442–3).

Developments within the Marxist Tradition

Today the majority of Marxist criminologists and legal theorists follow this line in deciphering the subtle ways in which the law operates as an instrument of political and ideological control. However, the most important early work tied criminal justice to a broadly orthodox Marxian political economy. *Punishment and Social Structure* (1939) by Georg Rusche and Otto Kirchheimer attempted to show how forms of punishment were related to the need for labour. They identified three ways in which this took place. First, prisoners could be workers when required by the capitalist system. According to this position, executions were common when there was a surplus supply of person power. During a period of pre-capitalist expansion in the Early Modern period, however, there was a labour shortage. Consequently, punishments often took forms such as transportation to plantations or a spell as a galley slave. Second, punishments could help to train labour for capitalists by teaching skills and discipline. Third, the criminal justice system could serve to encourage people to work by making non-productive alternatives (e.g. begging or stealing) illegal or unattractive. Here Rusche and Kirchheimer point in particular to anti-vagrancy laws. These made it illegal for people to wander the countryside begging. Building on this logic they suggest that conditions in prisons and poor houses would necessarily be worse than the least attractive job. If life in penal institutions improved too much, then working might not seem such a good idea! A similar argument was made by William Chambliss (1964) a few decades later. He agreed that anti-vagrancy laws passed in the previous centuries were designed to force vagabonds to settle down and work for a living. He writes 'these statutes were designed for one express purpose: to force labourers ... to accept employment at a low wage' (ibid.: 69). This kind of legislation, he asserts, was also tied to the growth of trade in the early stages of capitalist modernity because vagrants were seen as potential predators on passing mercantile traffic.

Particularly during the 1970s a new field of Marxist theory emerged associated with books such as *The New Criminology* by Ian Taylor, Paul Walton and Jock Young (1973) and *Class, State and Crime* by Richard Quinney (1977). This style of work is often called **radical criminology** and sometimes 'critical criminology'. It showed less interest in issues of labour supply and a greater concern with questions of social control over marginal and oppressed populations. A central role was given to the state, which was seen as a front for ruling-class interests and a selective enforcer of the law (e.g. Chambliss, 1975). Radical criminology also suggested that crime patterns reflected social inequality, exclusion and blocked social mobility. Hence Chambliss (1975: 168) writes: 'crime becomes a rational response of some social classes to the realities of their lives. The state becomes an instrument of the ruling class enforcing laws here but not there, according to the realities of political power and economic conditions.'

In recent years a number of lines of argument have developed in this tradition, which we can briefly summarize here:

- Attention is given to **criminalization**. In the Marxian context, this usually means the way that laws are framed by the state to reflect the needs of the ruling class. Chambliss (1975: 154) writes that: 'without doubt the single most important force behind criminal law creation is doubtless the economic interest and political power of those social classes which either (1) own or control the resources of the society, or (2) occupy positions of authority in state bureaucracies.' Legislation on strikes and industrial regulation, for example, might be framed to help maximize profits and prevent industrial unrest. A variant on this position is to suggest that laws reflect the morals and values of the middle class. Policies on prostitution and drugs, according to some Marxist theorists, fall into this category.
- The centrality of discretion within the criminal justice system (see pp. 83, 94, 124) means that members of the dominant class can break the law with impunity. Criminality is really a matter of labelling (see pp. 26–27), with the label sticking only to those who are powerless. What Quinney (1977) calls 'crimes of domination' are rarely punished. These might include things like illegal industrial activities, health and safety violations and toxic waste dumping.

- The criminal law and its application in crime control activity serve to limit unrest arising from social inequality. In effect, the criminal justice system works to make protest and revolution more difficult and is a form of political control. An example of this is the role of policing in strike-breaking activity or dealing with urban unrest.
- Crime, especially as it is represented in the media, has an ideological role. Crime imagery is used in populist ways to divert attention from enduring social inequality, or used as a label to make political protest look illegitimate. For example, Marxist scholars have suggested that urban discontents are often framed as 'riots' when really they are 'rebellions' or even 'revolutions' against poverty, racism and injustice.
- The law and criminal justice systems are underpinned by major capitalist enterprises. These seek to increase profits by expanding the scope of their activity and encouraging new initiatives in the law and order field. In the United States, for example, there has been concern about the rise of the so-called 'prison-industrial complex' which makes money from the provision of labour, equipment and services in the corrections area.
- Many crimes are indeed committed by the working class, such as theft and drug dealing. These are a response to inequality and social exclusion, in effect, a reasonable action in a survival situation. We should not understand such crimes as the action of losers and failures, but rather as a creative and imaginative response to powerlessness that can be thought of as 'resistance'.

Although framed with reference to issues of class, since the 1980s these kinds of arguments have been transplanted and applied to a range of other dimensions of inequality such as race, gender, sexual orientation and age. As Marxism weakens in theoretical influence, the case is increasingly being put that the law and the criminal justice system reflect not only specifically class interests and moralities, but also those of whites, heterosexuals, males, older people, and so forth. Hence feminists might speak of the law and law enforcement operating in the interests of males, queer theorists talk of the heterosexual bias in the criminal justice system and experts on race criticize the racist dimensions activities such as policing. Nevertheless the Marxian position should not be written off. It remains capable of formidable insights into how culture and power are linked as demonstrated in Box 1.1.

Box 1.1   Douglas Hay: Court Process as Ideology in the Eighteenth Century

In recent decades neo-Marxist historians have provided some of the most interesting work looking at the ideological role of the criminal justice system. A fascinating and classic study is Douglas Hay's (1975a) exploration of criminal justice in eighteenth century England. Hay's essential premise was that the ruling class constructed an ideology that enabled them to dominate a much larger class of the poor and marginal.

He writes that: 'Loyalties do not grow simply in complex societies – they are twisted, invoked and often consciously created' (ibid.: 62). Hay notes that large numbers of offences, many of them quite trivial, carried a potential death penalty. However, relatively few people who were found guilty were actually given a death sentence. Why was this? Hay suggests that the answer lies in the ideological function of criminal justice. Court sessions, called assizes, were held every few months in country towns. These had ritual and theatrical characteristics, such as pomp and ceremony, and thereby drew attention to the majesty of the law. Periodic and well-publicized executions of affluent people suggested that the law was impartial. Most important of all, judges were able to show mercy by handing down sentences that fell short of death. Hay argues these three features had ideological foundations. They dramatized the power and universalism of the law, indicated that the rulers were merciful and obscured the fact that the legal system worked to protect the property and interests of a numerically small dominant class. His conclusion is that in the eighteenth century, England was 'a society with a bloody penal code, an astute ruling class who manipulated it to their advantage and a people schooled in the lessons of Justice, Terror and Mercy' (ibid.: 62–3).

How does Hay's approach compare with those of other Marxist traditions?

One of the more important studies of recent decades where the diverse themes of radical criminology come together is in the work of Stuart Hall and his colleagues in a book entitled *Policing the Crisis* (1979). Drawing on the work of Marxist theorists of ideology, Gramsci and Althusser, and combining this with influences from Stanley Cohen (see p. 17), the book argues that ideologies surrounding crime and criminal justice can play a key role in holding society together at times when capitalism is on the rocks. Hall et al. (1979) suggest that a moral panic arose in Britain during the 1970s over the crime of mugging. Young, urban, working-class Afro-Caribbean and Asian youth were the folk devils allegedly responsible for the rise in this kind of crime. Although objectively measured, mugging rates remained much the same, the media, politicians, 'experts' and the courts spoke in emotive terms of a society where crime was out of control in the streets. These institutions were also 'active in defining situations, in selecting targets, in initiating campaigns, in structuring these campaigns' (ibid.: 52). There was widespread support for tough action from the criminal justice system (see also p. 103). The real dynamic behind this moral panic, Hall et al. argue, lay in a crisis of the capitalist system, widening class divides and resulting urban unrest. The general, society-wide sense of anxiety and unease created by these developments was displaced onto minority youth and prevented the unification of the working class. The forces of capital were able to mobilize racism to 'defeat attempts to construct, at the political level, organisations which do in fact adequately represent the class as a whole' (1979: 395). Meanwhile, repressive policies of law enforcement were enacted by the state and justified with reference to street crime. As a result, the capitalist system was able to stumble on despite growing crisis tendencies in British cities.

The Critique of the Marxist Position

Marxist analyses of law and criminal justice have always looked strongest when critiquing legal regulation of inherently controversial activities such as drugs or homelessness, or attacking paramilitary crime control strategies and official inactivity on issues such as corporate and environmental crime. In these contexts a case can often be made that particular definitions of 'problems' have prevailed and that specific populations have been targeted by dominant groups. The approach seems less successful when it comes to explaining the legal regulations and law enforcement directed against crimes that almost everyone agrees are wrong: incest, child abuse, murder, rape, and so forth. A Durkheimian view of a collective conscious seems to do a much better job here with its argument that there is a shared morality embodied in the law. There are also enduring issues related to causality. There is more than a whiff of conspiracy theory about much Marxist criminology – the image arises of ruling elites getting together in secret rooms, deciding what is in their best interests and cooking up laws and crime control strategies. If we reject this image, the alternative which grounds causality in the system rather than in individual actors, is scarcely less appealing. Marxist criminological thinking about this kind of issue was strongly influenced by the work of Louis Althusser (1971) and other political theorists who argued that the state operated in the 'long-term interests of capital' even if members of the dominant class were ignorant of the best course of action. There is a kind of functionalist logic at play here with the state propping up the capitalist social system and doing whatever is necessary to maintain order and boost profits. In the context of crime control, for example, the state might implement a tough new policy for clamping down on strikes and a weak new policy of environmental regulation. Yet just how the state 'knows' what to do is a mystery. We can see this problem of agency in looking back at the work of Douglas Hay or Stuart Hall discussed earlier. Just how did the needs of a dominant class get refracted into sentencing decisions by specific judges? Why did a panic arise just when it was required by a capitalist system in crisis?

A final problem with Marxist approaches – at least in their more fundamentalist guise – comes from an inability to propose what the mainstream might see as sensible crime control policies. In *The New Criminology*, Taylor, Walton and Young had argued that 'for crime to be abolished ... social arrangements themselves must also be subject to fundamental social change' (1973: 282). In the 1970s and the 1980s less cautious left-wing criminologists converted this rather coded remark into vocal claims that wholesale transformation to socialism was required. This would lead to a removal of the inequalities that generated crime and place the state under the control of the people, thus preventing it from acting as an agent for dominant class interests. Many saw such a proposition as simply laughable, given the reality of state oppression in the nominally socialist Soviet bloc. After all, dissidents such as Alexander Solzhenitsyn had pointed to the Soviet criminal justice system (with its KGB, Gulags, etc.) as a key tool of oppression, not workers' liberation. The fall of European Communism in 1989 made extremist Marxist arguments appear as instantly and hopelessly outdated as that fad of 1975, the pet rock. A lack of realism had opened the floodgates for the criminal justice policy agendas of neo-liberals on the political Right. What was perceived by some as the harping tendency of neo-Marxists to tirelessly denounce routine reforms as pointless had simply led to their exile and irrelevance. The later work of Jock Young (1986) and the new paradigm of **left realism** can be seen very much as a response to these issues as radical criminologists woke up and smelled the coffee burning.

The position of left realism recognized that much earlier work within the Marxist tradition was unrealistic and idealistic. Young argues that by explaining away crime as a state- and media-sponsored myth, the approach had failed to come to terms with it as a real problem. In so doing it had trivialized the experiences of the victims of illegal acts – many of them among society's most disadvantaged groups. Feminist work played a major role in the transition to this new perspective. This had continually documented the experiences of women and children as victims of domestic violence and sexual assault, suggesting that there was a major problem that needed urgent action if social justice was to be attained. Left realism also acknowledged that much radical criminology had managed to antagonize major players in the criminal justice system such as the police by suggesting, in effect, they were simply the goon squad of the bourgeois state.

In advocating left realism, Jock Young demanded that left-wing criminology become more sensitive to empirical realities and popular concerns. For example, working-class people should not be seen as Robin Hoods robbing the rich to feed the poor – they overwhelmingly victimize other working-class people. For left realists crime now could be seen as a real issue for working-class people and something that should be addressed by the authorities. Earlier Marxist work, such as that of Hall et al. (1979), discussed earlier (see pp. 23–24), seemed to imply that policing action was inherently oppressive. By and large, then, marginal people would be better off if the state simply left them alone. Left realism argued to the contrary that not enough was being done by the police to protect working classes and minorities. Consequently, during the 1990s radical criminologists began to conduct work on the problem of crime as it was experienced by the working classes, and lobby for a fair share of governmental resources. This meant criminologists working to address a crime problem rather than pretending that it didn't exist or was simply a phantasm constructed by the media. The new perspective also demanded a concerted effort to uncover real patterns of crime as these affected marginal populations and a suspicion of official statistics as under-estimates (in contrast to the moral panic work arguing they were exaggerations). The result was a practical, policy-oriented, empiricist agenda aimed at documenting crime and victim experiences among working-class people, women and minorities and implementing crime reduction strategies to confront these.

Today the main significance of the Marxist analysis of law and justice lies in the fact that it moved issues of power onto the agenda in a theoretically sophisticated way. As an engine of conceptual innovation, however, it has now probably been overtaken by poststructural, postmodern and feminist approaches or by pragmatic policy research influenced by left realism. Important themes introduced or made salient by neo-Marxists such as those on criminalization, differential law enforcement and media influence continue to exist, but they are frequently combined with poststructural theory or applied to social categories other than class, such as age, race or gender. We return to this issue later in this chapter.

Symbolic Interactionism and Labelling Theory

Contrasting with more structural approaches to the analysis of the criminal justice system, such as those of Durkheimian functionalism and Marxism, are those that place a greater emphasis on the creativity and agency of humans. According to this tradition, large-scale empirical regularities arise not so much from external and constraining social facts but rather as an aggregate of individual actions. So far as the study of law and criminal justice is concerned, **labelling theory** represents the greatest contribution to this tradition. The emphasis here is on the ways that law and the criminal justice system operate to ascribe a deviant or criminal identity onto offenders. Howard Becker's (1973) book *Outsiders* remains the standard text here. According to Becker, there is no such thing as deviance *per se*. Rather, there are acts that are labelled as deviant by (some parts of) society. The criminal justice system can be understood as a set of institutions whose job is to apply the label of 'deviant'. Inquiry informed by this perspective can look at:

- the process of labelling. (e.g. rituals, legal procedures and statutes);
- the role of discretion in deciding who is labelled (e.g. police decisions whether to caution or arrest);
- the links between labelling and social inequality (e.g. the fact that minorities are more likely to be successfully labelled than members of the middle classes).

For Becker, exploring labelling was all about asking, 'Who can ... force others to accept their rules and what are the causes of their success? This is, of course, a question of political and economic power' (ibid.: 17). Here Becker is pointing to the process of **criminalization** whereby particular activities are made illegal and the individuals who do them labelled as deviant. He suggests that influential groups and institutions can play a major role in this process. Becker considers the case of marijuana, which was generally legal in the United States in 1930, but was banned within the space of a few years. He suggests that this was the result of an initiative by the Federal Bureau of Narcotics, which was seeking to increase its own power, authority and funding in the era after the prohibition of alcohol had been repealed.

This organization provided information to the media and lobbied in Washington and elsewhere in order to have the drug banned. This brings us to Becker's argument that it is useful to think about the fact that 'rules are the products of someone's initiative' and he goes on to claim 'we can think of the people who exhibit such enterprise as **moral entrepreneurs**' (ibid.: 147). These can be classified into two types. Rule creators can be thought of as 'crusaders' fighting to get an issue onto the agenda, while rule enforcers are groups that take responsibility for ensuring an existing law is upheld. Becker's ideas about labelling and moral crusades were to later filter through to the work on moral panics that we have already reviewed (see pp. 17, 23–24).

Becker shared with other interactionists a concern with the self and pointed out that the label of 'deviant', once successfully applied, is a **master status**. This means that it trumps other forms of identity such as those related to kinship (e.g. 'mother') or occupation (e.g. 'electrician'). As such, it is extremely powerful and can lead to continuing social exclusion. The result can be a vicious circle in which the 'deviant' comes to adopt and identify with the deviant label. Here, then, is a theory that argues that the criminal justice system can help to create crime in the very act of controlling it.

This concern with the deviant self was also central to the work of Erving Goffman, writing on the ways in which individuals respond to encounters with the criminal justice system and other institutions of social control. His most influential text of this genre was *Asylums* (Goffman, 1968). This study was based on participant observation of a mental hospital in the United States. Goffman pointed out that the asylum, like the prison, was a **total institution**. These are cut off from the outside world, marked by a hierarchical division of staff and inmates and feature a tight control of everyday life via rules and regulations. Goffman suggested that, on entry, the newcomer 'begins some radical shifts in his moral career, a career composed of the progressive changes that occur in the beliefs that he has concerning himself and significant others' (ibid.: 24). They are stripped of their outside identity and given an inmate identity by procedures such as showering, having their hair cut and being given a number and uniform. Drawing on the work of the anthropologist Arnold van Gennep, he referred to this as a **rite of passage**, in effect, a ritual in which identity change is effected and managed. Within the asylum, policies of reward and punishment continue this task. They encourage conformity and the normalization of deviance with eventual release the final prize for those who change in the appropriate ways. Hence he argues that we can understand total institutions as 'forcing houses for changing persons; each is a natural experiment on what can be done to the self' (ibid.: 22). Despite these efforts at control, Goffman shows that inmates have strategies of resistance through which they maintain an autonomous identity. These include unauthorized uses of equipment, activities such as smoking and gambling, and playing along with the rules of the game without undergoing internal change.

Critics of the symbolic interactionist perspective acknowledge that it offers valuable insights into process, but suggest that it lacks a systematic account of the wider social order. Goffman, for example, cannot account for the existence of the asylum whereas Foucault (see below) is able to connect it to the rise of new forms of power under modernity. In this respect, radical criminology is more satisfying in its treatment of labelling and criminalization precisely because it is able to marry them to a big picture theory of society and history – Marxism. Labelling theory, by contrast, tends to take a more pluralist view with criminal justice agendas rising and falling according to contingent struggles between diverse interested parties. From another angle, however, the tradition is vulnerable to the same critique as radical criminology. There is an equivalent tendency in symbolic interactionist work to side with the underdog or celebrate the perspective of the deviant. This is epitomized by Becker's (1967) famous article entitled 'Whose Side are We On?' Here he suggests that as most criminological research was conducted by those in power, often on behalf of official agencies, the perspective of the deviant had been overlooked. Consequently the sociologist should balance the account by explaining criminality 'from below'. Critics suggest that this compensation has often gone too far, with the symbolic interactionist romanticizing the deviant and becoming blind to the darker sides of criminality and subcultural life such as violence, sexism and racism (see p. 40).

Poststructuralism

In the past 20 years poststructuralist approaches have provided an important alternative to neo-Marxism. Much of the appeal lies in the fact that they enable critical perspectives to be generated, but in a way that does not give primacy to capitalism and to class relations. The origins of this approach largely hang on the work of one scholar, Michel Foucault (1926–84) and, so far as the study of criminal justice is concerned, just one text: *Discipline and Punish* (1975). In this book Foucault suggests that the form of power that organizes criminal justice has substantially changed over the past few centuries. This is allied to wider social shifts associated with the rise of modernity, in particular, a growing concern with the regulation and control of populations.

Discipline and Punish begins with the graphic description of the torture and execution in the mid-eighteenth century of Damiens, a man who had attempted to kill the French king. Foucault reproduces a gruesome account of the slow and systematic dismemberment of his body as it is attacked with red hot pincers, as his limbs are broken, and as he is cut open and pulled apart by a team of horses. The whole process lasted several hours. Next Foucault presents a prison timetable from some 80 years later. This details procedures in a model prison with minute precision. The entirety of the book can be thought of as an attempt to analyse and explain this dramatic transformation. By the end of the journey Foucault has arrived at some startling conclusions about the ways that power works in the modern world. Most notably he suggests we should rewrite the history of criminal justice. Rather than understanding the prison as a humanitarian invention that does away with barbarism, he suggests that it represents a new and even more insidious form of power.

Foucault suggests that **sovereign power** was at play in the case of Damiens. This was associated with the absolutist monarchies of Early Modern times. Here power worked directly upon the body, but only did so intermittently. It was often symbolic or allegorical in form and was directed towards an audience as a public display of the power of the king. By the nineteenth century this had been largely replaced with **disciplinary power**. This involved changing the soul of the deviant and making them self-regulate their behaviour so that they would be normalized. Pivotal in this process was the construction of a **docile body**. Foucault writes that in engaging with the prison: 'The human body was entering a machinery of power that explores it, breaks it down and rearranges it' (ibid.: 138). Technologies such as treadmills, dull repetitive work and 'discipline produces subjected and practised bodies, docile bodies' (ibid.). In exploring the production of these bodies Foucault says we need to look at the **microphysics of power**. Rather than accounting for power through the study of the large-scale and abstract (e.g. as expressed in the doctrines of contract theory, Marxism, etc.), Foucault wants to see how power permeated down to the routine, small-scale and everyday. He is especially concerned with how it impacted upon the body via systems of regulation and desire. This has also been thought of as a 'capillary' understanding of power – power can be likened to the circulatory system as it branches out into smaller and smaller channels of control. The overall image Foucault advocates is of people caught up in intricate webs of power, which define their identities and activities. Such an approach differs from those of classical political theory or even Marxism. These see one actor A, having power over another actor, B. Foucault suggests, by contrast, that both A and B are caught up in a system of power. Hence, for example, both the prison administrator and the prisoner are part of an over-arching and controlling system of disciplinary power. Looking at how they are both constituted by this web of power relations is more useful than looking at the power the official has over the inmate.

The novelty of Foucault's position is the centrality in his theoretical framework of architectural and spatial innovations and the ways that these allowed the surveillance of populations. Emblematic in this respect was the **panopticon**. This was a device that had been advocated by the eighteenth-century philosopher, Jeremy Bentham. It consisted of a central tower surrounded by prison cells. A single guard in the tower could look into the cells, but the prisoners could not tell if they were subject to the gaze of the guard. Foucault and Bentham believed prisoners would come to self-regulate their behaviour, given this situation of uncertainty. Each prisoner would become their own jailer 24 hours a day as they tried to ensure that their behaviour could withstand scrutiny. Foucault writes: 'the major effect of the Panopticon: to induce in the inmate a state of conscious and permanent visibility that assures the automatic functioning of power' (ibid.: 201).

It is vital to realize Foucault insists that the forms of power manifested in the prison have to be understood within the context of wider social changes. Other institutions were also involved in creating docile bodies – he points in particular to the military and its use of repetitive drill exercises. Techniques involving control through surveillance were also common in schools, hospitals and factories. The prison, then, only shows in a heightened form the ways that power works in modernity through regulating bodies and populations and by shaping the self. He also argues that the prison was not a stand-alone institution (as common sense tells us) but rather part of a **carceral continuum**. It was merely the last of a long line of sanctions and institutions aimed at controlling deviance and reforming the self. He identifies asylums, borstals, courts, hospitals, reformatories and schools as part of this chain of interconnected sites where power is reproduced in modernity and suggests that we can map these throughout the geography of the **carceral city**. In his later work on *The History of Sexuality*, Foucault (1990) was to add the idea of **biopower** to his conceptual arsenal. This consisted of a series of discourses in the areas of health and psychiatry aimed at promoting, monitoring and controlling human reproduction and desire. Again the image is of proliferating institutions and knowledges that regulate, define and even invent human subjects. Hence Foucault sees biopower, like disciplinary power, as inherently productive rather than negative or repressive. He writes that: 'Power would no longer be dealing simply with legal subjects over whom the ultimate dominion was death, but with living beings … it was the taking charge of life, more than the threat of death, that gave power its access even to the body' (ibid.: 143). This vision contrasts with those that see power over sexuality and the body as simply as a series of legal prohibitions and informal taboos.

One final element of Foucault's analysis of power and punishment is his idea of **discourse**. This is a system of ideas through which knowledge and power are reproduced. He stresses the fact that all discourses are supported by and make possible expert professions, each with access to a corpus of information and know-how. According to Foucault, the arrival of modernity was characterized by a rapid growth in the human sciences – forms of knowledge aimed at defining, understanding and controlling populations. In the case of criminal justice, relevant experts might be prison reformers, architects, psychologists and criminologists. Foucault does not suggest that the discourses professed by these groups are simply part of a cynical bid for power. Rather, he suggests that both 'experts' and 'deviants' are created and defined by the discourses they use. This emphasis on the power of ideas to classify the world and structure action shows the enduring legacy of **structuralism** on Foucault. This, in part, was the view that argued that humans do not have ultimate freedom but rather are created and influenced by relatively autonomous cultural systems. But equally significant to Foucault were the ideas of the nineteenth-century German philosopher, Friedrich Nietzsche, and his belief that history can be understood as a 'will to power'. The centrality of thinking about power/knowledge to Foucault can be interpreted as the fusion of these two traditions, one looking at the form of ideas and the other at their role in the struggles in social life. Foucault is often thought of as a key figure in **poststructuralism** because of this intellectual perspective.

Foucault's ideas have proven to be hugely influential for criminology. There are a number of positives that we can recapitulate quickly:

- He has focused attention on the *how* of power. This directs our attention to matters of historical detail and calls for efforts to explore the precise technologies and systems of ideas through which power is constructed and reproduced.
- His ideas about the power of discourse enable us to think about criminal justice in a strongly cultural way. Arguably, only the Durkheimian tradition can offer a similarly rich account of the interactions between meaning and action in the interpretation of punishment.
- This stress on the significance of discourse has enabled a critical theory of punishment to emerge that is free from the Marxist baggage of economic determinism, opening up a space for thinking about the autonomy of culture. In a similar way, his interest in professions and institutions has enabled ideas about class to be displaced from the centre of critical inquiry into powerful social groups.
- Even Foucault's detractors believe him to be an innovative thinker who is always exciting and provocative.

Having acknowledged all this, Foucault has not been without his critics. Historians have suggested that the transformation that he traces took place over several centuries and not several decades (Spierenburg, 1984). Certainly the physical cruelty of punishments had begun to decline much earlier than the late eighteenth century. Perhaps it is also the case that the symbolic dimensions of punishment have changed less than Foucault states in describing the transition from sovereign to disciplinary power. For Foucault modern punishment is a machine-like and Kafkaesque process that is without the rich symbolic textures that it had in the past. It is a brute but dull fact driven by cultural frames organized around power and rationality. This claim probably exaggerates a general trend, for it can be argued that even today punishment retains a symbolic component. The death penalty, for example, has a theatrical aspect and many punishments continue to express and generate powerful popular sentiments, most notably the executions of notorious criminals. And as one of the authors of this book has argued, punishment technologies and punishment places can be understood in Durkheim's terms as richly loaded cultural symbols in a differentiated collective conscience rather than as simply instruments for the rational control of bodies and administration of power as Foucault contends. Thus, Smith (1999, 2003) shows how the prison of the Bastille, France, and the technology of the guillotine have been narrated and contested through history as sacred and profane. The Bastille carries an iconic loading within French culture, thanks to its place in the mythology of the French Revolution, while the guillotine has been variously seen as spooky, barbaric and holy, as well as simply efficient.

From a methodological perspective, Foucault has a worrying tendency to confuse levels of analysis and to read off real-world effects from the study of discourses. For example, he might take a document on how to run a prison and how to reform prisoners and then treat this as if it is evidence of what really happened. In truth, the real-world ability of prisons to 'normalize' people is limited. Hence recidivism data (see p. 175) suggests that most prisoners are not made docile by the prison – on the contrary, it seems to help push some into a life of crime. Ideas about resistance to power are likewise notoriously under-theorized. Foucault mentions here and there that power always throws up some forms of resistance but unlike Goffman in *Asylums* (see pp. 27–28), he never really explains why this is the case or what the bases for this resistance might be.

Postmodern Approaches

Perhaps better described as poststructural, Foucault's work with its focus on power and discourse has fed through to a raft of postmodern approaches to law, crime and criminal justice. **Postmodernism** is a complex field, perhaps better appreciated as a collection of ideas and methods rather than a bounded theoretical perspective. It was developed in part as a reaction to the intellectual failures of structuralism, in part as a critique of modernist social thinking and the project of the Enlightenment. Postmodernism as a perspective has come to shape the study of multiple aspects of social life: literature, architecture, art and more latterly, law. In many other disciplines postmodernists refer to the existence of a new, or at least emerging era, in which social structures and relationships are claimed to be markedly different to those of modernity. However, in the investigation of law, these debates about epochs of social evolution have taken a back seat. The extent to which law and its associated institutions have been transformed in recent decades plays a lesser role than the philosophical critique of its modernist claims and the deconstruction of its theoretical and epistemological foundations (Hunt, 1990: 516). In studies of the criminal justice system, ideas about an emerging 'risk society' seem to have gained more traction than those of a nascent postmodern epoch (see pp. 204–205).

To appreciate the characteristics of postmodernism, it is useful to briefly reconsider the modernist concept of law. Many of the presumptions of modernity have been distilled in the claims made for law: the possibility of reason, objectivity, rationality, and the existence and identification of a singular truth. It has been assumed that striving for and achieving these ideals will benefit all people. This assumption was part of a broader claim that particular forms of knowledge would lead to social progress (Lyotard, 1984). Law has been celebrated for and judged upon its conformity to these universalistic standards. Postmodern approaches to law and the criminal justice system challenge this reading. At one level it is argued that claims about the value-neutral characteristics and emancipatory potential of the law are myths. We have already noted critical perspectives, such as Marxism and labelling theory, which highlight how value judgements and biases shape the law and its application. Hence laws and the criminal justice system have manifestly not always been sources of protection – they have been used to oppress and exclude particular groups, often with devastating consequences (Conley and O'Barr, 1990). Postmodernists go further and suggest that identifying the empirical failings of law is not the only game in town for critical theory. Rather than measuring the performance of the law against a yardstick of modernist beliefs, we need to rethink the ways that legal categories and legal reasoning are flawed. Alan Hunt (1990: 509) comments that:

> [the problem] is not so much that modernism has arrived at the wrong answers, but that its questions were unanswerable: they have been too broad, too abstract, riddled with a distinctive mix of naïve humanism, an unwarranted faith in science and an over-optimistic view of the capacity of language to capture and share knowledge.

Postmodernism's alternative starting point for inquiry is grounded in a post-positivist world-view that sees language as constitutive of reality rather than as simply describing it (Yeatman, 1994: 13–14). Any legal reasoning, or the study of that reasoning, ultimately says more about the ways in which meaning is constructed and represented than it does about the thing allegedly under consideration. Although there is no final 'truth' that language can uncover, postmodernists recognize that there exists a range of competing discourses that make claims to truth (Patterson, 2003). The aim of research should be to map these, and to investigate and recover the multiple realities through which people understand the social world, rather than uncover general principles, an over-arching order (Bauman, 1987) or a definitive account of the role of law, its basis, usefulness or effects. This emphasis reflects the broader concern of postmodernists, one that extends beyond issues of law and the criminal justice system: the focus shifts from 'reality' to the text itself, which constructs that reality through its representation (R.H. Brown, 1994: 229). The law, whether in legal proceedings, written judgments or any other form, does not – indeed cannot – uncover some pre-existing reality; it creates that reality through its linguistically mediated work of representation and interpretation.

In arguing the absence of any foundational truth, postmodernists also reject the possibility of adopting an objective and disinterested perspective on the world and any particular event or idea that occurs within it (Feldman, 2001: 2362). Within postmodernism, any knowledge is contingent, localized and incomplete, the product of interpretation and consensus rather than a disinterested report on reality (Bauman, 1992: 102; Yeatman, 1994: 1). In light of this realization, no one version of the world can claim to be true to the exclusion of others, or more worthy of being imposed. For this reason, postmodern approaches see legal texts as an influential way in which reality is constructed, but reject the idea that there can be a single correct interpretation of these. According to Hunt (1990: 513), 'the question is no longer how to interpret the text; rather, it is about the legitimacy of legal discourse as a mechanism of power disguised as the pursuit of interpretive truth'. It is claimed that recognizing this can have an emancipatory effect. Space is opened up to incorporate the voices and experiences of groups who have traditionally been excluded from the interpretation, development and practice of law – those whose perspectives have been defined as deviant, untrue or otherwise problematic. In practice, this can often take the form of presenting narratives and stories, emphasizing the uniqueness of individuals, rather than only describing structures and groups

(Calavita and Seron, 1992: 766). By including these stories, theorists can provide a more complete and dialogic – but not necessarily truer – version of experiences in a particular realm of social life.

And so it is that 'difference' becomes a key analytic touchstone. **Difference** means more than dissimilarity: relations of power are intrinsically bound up with its construction and effects. Power comes not from brute force, but through the ability of language to define and categorize individuals and groups and, in so doing, construct their position relationally (Hutchinson, 1992). However, power is never simply imposed upon people. They are still able to contest the ways in which they are represented, through recourse to alternative discourses. Nor is power absolute. Recognizing the significance of difference creates a mandate to focus on the experiences of minority groups, the marginal and oppressed and to explore how they have been disadvantaged by dominant discourses even as they are 'invented' and defined by these. Groups and their experiences do not exist outside of the discourses that are applied to them. This in turn has implications for the traditional legal subject, an abstract entity who, although constructed through legal reasoning, has very real consequences. The legal subject is used as the standard against which the actions and omissions of citizens were measured. Postmodern approaches recognize not only the fiction of this character, but the ways in which it pushes alternative world-views to the margins. Further, the legal subject presents a singular, bounded identity. This fails to gel with the postmodern notion of identities as fractured and multiple (Boyle, 1998).

The preoccupations and claims of postmodern approaches on discourse, difference and representation have contributed to a literature that is often focused on texts rather than data collection in the 'real world'. Such texts might be derived from the media, government policy documents, written judgments, architectural plans, written official records or even criminology books and journals. The postmodern agenda here is to interrogate and 'deconstruct' key concepts and categories, showing how they invent and frame what they purport to describe or how their categories are unstable.

The reader should be able to see clear affinities between some aspects of the postmodern approach and symbolic interactionism, labelling theory, neo-Marxist criminology and even old-fashioned Chicago School ethnography. These perspectives emphasize the significance of processes of definition and collective meaning making in the imposition of law and criminal justice system, and people's responses to them. Moreover, all have been focused on the experiences of groups that do not enjoy institutionalized positions of power. Postmodern theory differs from these more modernist views in that it problematizes the idea of an ultimate truth. As we have already noted, it claims that all aspects of the social world are constructed rather than simply discovered. This destabilizing stance contrasts with the more conventional attempt to explain how the world – in this case, the legal and criminal justice systems – actually is. A second major point of divergence is the relative sophistication of postmodern approaches in their application of cultural theory. Influences from structuralism, poststructuralism, semiotics and psychoanalytic theory have been combined into a style of work which is often abstruse and sometimes has a stronger resemblance to philosophy and avant-garde literary criticism than to mainstream sociological writing on law and justice.

The most common critiques of postmodernism revolve around the charge of 'relativism', a philosophical position which avoids judgements on what is right and what is wrong. Hunt (1990: 524) terms this 'the big fear', a 'catastrophic scenario in which any concession to contingency or any retreat from the objectivity of knowledge-claims necessarily leads, via the associated imagery of the "slippery slope", unwittingly, but unavoidably towards the abyss of relativism and its even more dangerous associate, nihlism' (see also Arrow, 1997; Nussbaum, 1994). Some commentators have argued that this potential position has adverse ethical and political implications. It denies the possibility of moral judgements as anything more than an assertion of subjective values, mere preference or consensus. It further means that the insights of any person are as valid as those of someone who has spent their years studying legal principles and applying them. If we are all experts now, then why go to law school, or, for that matter, listen to a postmodern legal scholar?

Margaret Davies (2002: 304) offers the rejoinder that postmodernism is useful because in rejecting traditional modes of legitimation it demands an interrogation of how we judge the true and the real. We are asked to reconsider any 'natural' connection between language and what it signifies, and the 'natural' and intuitive legitimacy of particular concepts (see also Feldman, 2001). In other words, postmodernism makes a net positive contribution to reflexivity. However, Davies' argument does not address a further concern. Critics suggest that poststructural and postmodern approaches have limited policy applicability even if they are intellectually worthwhile as a reflexive activity (Handler, 1992; cf. MacKinnon, 2000). As with radical criminology (see pp. 24–25), policy relevance has been an enduring problem, with postmodernists usually positioning themselves as outsiders to dominant structures. A compounding factor here has been the postmodern/poststructural emphasis on the impossibility of attaining truth – the criminologist and their subject alike are caught up in what Nietzsche called the 'prison house of language' and positioned by institutional and political realities. In contrast to the realist ontology of radical criminology, this epistemological position sees knowledge becoming perspective, and social life a battle of these for authority. While postmodern theorists are often directly concerned with social justice (e.g. Delgado and Stefancic, 1992; Lopez, 1994), their approach does not appeal to bureaucrats and policy analysts who inhabit a different intellectual paradigm, believing we need to collect facts and objective knowledge in order to have a sensible administration of criminal justice. Critics on the left have also suggested that the relativistic stance of postmodernism threatens to undermine concepts such as 'equality' and 'rights' by arguing that these are simply discursive constructions. This is worrying because these have historically been the basis of moral arguments for progressive reform. Notwithstanding such critique postmodern approaches to the law and criminal justice have been influential in stimulating theoretical renewal, particularly in the area of critical legal studies which we investigate in the next chapter (see pp. 61–77).

Weberian Approaches

Foucault's work, as we have seen, pointed to the growth of formal regulation and control in the administration of criminal justice. An important precursor to this perspective, albeit one seemingly ignored by Foucault himself, was the German theorist Max Weber (1864–1920). Weber's (1978) major life work was concerned with explaining the rise of modernity in the West. He pointed to social trends towards social rationalization and bureaucratization within a broader context of state formation. The Weberian world-view is one wherein haphazard but meaningful forms of traditional social organization and culture have been replaced by systematic but meaning-empty administrative alternatives, creating what he once termed the 'iron cage' of modernity.

As might be expected, Weber's writings on the law document this narrative. He succinctly asserts 'our interest is centred on the ways and consequences of the rationalisation of the law' (1978: 775–6). His historical research showed how the diverse, often competing legal traditions of the Middle Ages (including the sacred codes of religious law) and forms of justice that depended upon the caprice of rulers were gradually replaced by the systematic, predictable and universal rule of law. This was tied in turn to the growth of the state. The state, Weber noted, claimed a monopoly over the legitimate use of violence within a territory. It put an end to feuds and conflicts between warlords, but at the price of an increasing centralization of administrative and military power. Weber also paid considerable attention to the growth of the legal profession as an inevitable consequence of legal rationalization. He wrote 'the increased need to specialised legal knowledge created the professional lawyer' for whom 'rational training is an ineluctable requirement' (ibid.: 775). We discuss Weber's vision of the evolution of the law in more detail in the next chapter (see pp. 54–55).

Weber's approach influenced Talcott Parsons (see pp. 18, 54–55) and the early work of Anthony Giddens (1981). In his book *The Nation State and Violence*, Giddens explores the ways that the state progressively eroded individual liberties, taking control of the administration of justice and monopolizing the use of force. He sees the emergence of the prison, for example, as part of a growing network of functions organized around social control and the pacification of populations internal to the state. In the Middle Ages the state was not much more than a loose affiliation of nobility in a territory surrounded by an unruly frontier. With the arrival of the Early Modern period (the sixteenth, seventeenth and eighteenth centuries) came what was known as 'absolutist monarchy' and things slowly changed. More contemporary ideas of sovereignty developed along with administrative systems, fixed national borders and concepts of citizenship. Legal codes adjusted in response to this new reality. They became more formal and less particularistic. Hence, Giddens writes: 'The promulgation of abstract codes of law, which apply to the whole population of a state, is again closely connected with the notion of sovereignty' (ibid.: 98).

Giddens notes three important changes to the law and criminal justice in the shift away from the medieval world. First, the law became more impersonal and a greater emphasis was given to inalienable private property rights, in part through a rediscovery of Roman Law. This was associated in part with the growth of commercial and mercantile interests (these also influenced John Locke's version of contract theory, see p. 12). Second, we find rational, bureaucratic carceral institutions taking over from the barbaric and haphazard punishments delivered by the regional warlord, in his dungeon or the town square. Third, sovereignty theory, with its emphasis on the king as direct ruler of a fixed territory, encouraged the 'centralisation of methods of law enforcement' (1981: 151) as the emerging nation state took control of social order away from local powers and imposed unified national systems of criminal justice administration. Ideas of the 'social contract' that we have already discussed are consistent with this new ideological and political environment (see pp. 12–13). In combination, these developments saw power and the legitimate use of force, which nominally belonged to the king, concentrated in the hands of the bureaucratic and institutional apparatus of the state.

In summary, the work of both Weber and later, Giddens, describes a series of historical changes to the law. They track the gradual rationalization of the set of rules used to govern people and the centralization of authority, processes linked to the rise of the state. The strength of this approach lies in the recognition that the ordering and logic of legal systems are as significant an indication of the structure of society as their content, that is, the individual rules of which they are constituted. Like many of the other theoretical frameworks we have so far discussed, Weberians emphasize the appropriateness of studying the law and criminal justice systems within their particular social and historical contexts. That said, the perspective is not without problems. It tends to over-emphasize rationalization, coordination and centralization of control. As we have seen, much of the work of maintaining social order is still conducted at local levels in everyday life. Moreover the operation of the criminal justice system depends heavily on non-rational, non-codified inputs such as rules of thumb in judicial discretion or informal expectations in police work (see pp. 89–95, 128–136). Finally, the extent to which the various armatures of law and criminal justice really are centralized and coordinated is open to debate. There are good grounds for thinking of them as weakly and minimally integrated rather than as a machine-like system of interlocking gears.

Norbert Elias and the Civilizing Process

A figure who needs to be discussed in this chapter but who does not fit into any easy narrative or classification is Norbert Elias (1897–1990). In his work, *The Civilising Process*, Elias ([1939] 1978) provides an account of the emergence of modern sensibilities that has applications to the field of criminal justice. Looking at books on manners and etiquette, Elias observed that over the centuries these became increasingly prescriptive, with the body regulated more and more closely. For example, a text from the Middle Ages might instruct a person not to spit into the communal soup bowl, while one from the eighteenth century might tell them how to hold a knife and fork when eating peas. Elias notes a growing obsession with self-control and a tendency to hide from public view the spontaneous expression of emotion as well as basic biological activities such as sex and defecation. The exhibition of such animalistic activities began to cause anxiety and was seen as uncivilized.

Elias links these changes in the regulation of the self to a broader social transformation revolving around the movement towards modernity. Gradual redefinition of manners mirrored the shift from a lawless and violent medieval world to a 'court society' where social advancement came through demonstrating social refinement among fellow nobility. There was a related transformation of the self with freedom of spontaneous emotional expression replaced by another kind of freedom, that of greater control over the self. Central to this were reflexivity and self-monitoring, with mental and physical life subject to self-imposed constraint. New behavioural norms about politeness and dignified comportment gradually filtered down to other classes from the court society.

But what has any of this to do with criminal justice? The perspective developed by Elias helps us to understand two things: first, why punishments became less brutal and barbaric and, second, why those we still have are hidden rather than public spectacles. In contrast to the situation in the Middle Ages, blood and pain are found offensive to contemporary 'civilized' norms. They speak of barbarism not civilization. Punishment is generally seen as an expression of something uncivilized and therefore we no longer wish to see it. We hide it away behind walls – just as we do with other brute facts of life such as death, illness and sex. By associating the arrival of modernity with shifts in the self, emotional life and attitudes to violence, Elias provides the potential for a data-grounded alternative to Foucault and Durkheim in explaining why we have moved from public torture to the prison. It is a potential realized, for example, in the studies of Pieter Spierenburg discussed in Box 1.2.

Box 1.2   Pieter Spierenburg: The Spectacle of Suffering

Perhaps the best application of Elias' approach has been by the historian Pieter Spierenburg (1984) in his book *The Spectacle of Suffering*. He looked at executions in Holland over several centuries. Drawing on archival sources, he noted a general decline in the display of violence and a reduction in the level of brutality over this period. Looking at diaries and other accounts from a few centuries ago, he is able to document growing revulsion at the violent punishments. An activity such as branding was seen as normal at the start of the period but as disgusting at the end. As predicted by Elias's emphasis on the court society as the source of new norms,

Spierenburg found that new emotional responses started in the higher classes and then worked their way down to lower social groups. He was able to trace changes in law and punishment practice to these emerging sensibilities, suggesting that there was a growing 'aversion to the sight of physical punishment and a consequent criticism of the penal system among certain groups from the aristocracy and bourgeoisie' (ibid.: 204). The shift towards modernity was implicated in the change, with spectators having an increasing identification with sufferers thanks to increasing 'mutual dependence between social groups' in the Early Modern period. This position is also consistent with Durkheim's views on organic solidarity in modernity, which we have already discussed (see pp. 14–15).

Locate some contemporary commentary (media reports, political speeches, press releases, polls, etc.) on punishment issues. Do they support Spierenburg's basic thesis that themes of empathy and sensibility are pivotal today?

Feminist Perspectives

In the past three decades feminist theorists have contributed a good proportion of the truly ground-breaking work on law and criminal justice. Indeed, feminism must be understood as one of the most dynamic areas within criminology as a whole. Feminist approaches gained momentum during the 1960s and become a major force in criminology and legal studies by the 1980s, thanks to the work of scholars such as Pat Carlen, Catherine MacKinnon, Martha Minow, Ngaire Naffine, Jocelyn Scutt and Carol Smart. Foundational is the view that that society is organized around the rule of men (**patriarchy**), with culture and social structure serving to marginalize women, regulate their bodies and exclude them from full civic participation. Before dealing with the diversity of approaches within this basic framework, it is useful to begin with commonalities and points of broad agreement. Central to the broad agenda of feminist research on law and justice are a set of claims and research questions. We outline these below:

- How does the law and criminal justice system reflect patriarchal realities? In other words, how do they work to exclude and regulate women? How are they informed by underlying masculine assumptions and prejudices about women? Central to this agenda are themes relating to the regulation of sexuality and the body and the idea that the 'social contract' (see pp. 12–13) is really a *patriarchal* social contract (see, for example, Pateman, 1988). Such analyses might look at either sexist legal statutes or specific contexts in which the law was applied, such as routine policing or the operation of the courts. Rape provides a good example of this. Feminist research on rape demonstrates the patriarchal nature of legal and popular definitions of rape and the ways that these impact upon criminal justice process, such as judicial reasoning or police discretion (see pp. 139–144).

- The experiences and exclusion of women in the criminal justice system whether as policewomen, lawyers, victims or offenders. The focus here is often on adaptation to institutional and professional realities that have been constructed around male power and interests such as sexist occupational cultures or gendered occupational expectations. These issues are discussed in further detail later in this book (see pp. 144–149). Much of this work has involved confronting the belief that women are relatively advantaged. For example, there has long been a belief that female offenders are advantaged by a **chivalry effect** (p. 134) and that the discretion of male police officers and judges works in their favour. Some feminists have argued to the contrary that conventional sexual and family ideologies can work against women. Those who transgress mainstream norms are punished.

- There has also been a substantial genre of reflection on the treatment of women in criminological theory itself. Scholars such as Naffine (1997) have argued that mainstream criminological theory can be taken to reflect the wider patriarchal order. Women have been ignored, marginalized, stereotyped and trivialized in diverse ways. Studies here often engage in close readings of 'malestream' classics and indicate the ways in which they exhibit ignorance or prejudice. For example Naffine (1997: 40–1) points to the ways that Howard Becker's *Outsiders* (see pp. 26–27) reproduces and tacitly endorses the sexist perspective of his male research subjects. Consistent with his principles of recording the perspective of the underdog, Becker conducted participant observation with marijuana smoking jazz musicians. In his writings about them, however, Naffine claims that women are depicted as nagging 'drudges of domesticity who fail to appreciate the artistic calling of the musician husband' and as sex objects 'shaking their asses [to the music] but having nothing to say on their own behalf'.

- Some feminists have debated the existence of a distinctive 'female' way of approaching legal issues, for example, ideas about justice or approaches to interaction during policing. The argument has been made that women enter into situations with different criteria and patterns of behaviour and that these may be beneficial in many contexts. For example, it has been suggested that women are less adversarial or confrontational than men (pp. 146–149).

Engagement with this broad range of issues draws upon a range of philosophical and epistemological positions (Naffine, 1997). Speaking very broadly, **liberal feminists** are mostly concerned with attaining equal opportunity and equal treatment for women. Their concern is to document inequality, double standards and legislative or substantive exclusion. This is probably the dominant position. It is closely tied to policy-relevant research and operates with the assumption that the status quo should be reformed but not overturned. **Radical feminists** are less optimistic. They emphasize the ubiquity of male power and the dominance of men as a class over women as a class. They suggest the need for fundamental changes that establish alternative, more women-centred realities and values. Radical feminism is often associated with pro-lesbian and separatist agendas. **Socialist feminism**, as the name suggests, comes from an intersection of Marxism and feminism and has a focus on class and gender as dual systems of oppression. Although this perspective often teams up with radical feminism, there is a stronger emphasis on economic inequality whereas radical feminism tends to foreground themes related to body, identity and sexuality. To Naffine's list we can add **postmodern feminist** perspectives (see above pp. 32–35). These focus on issues of discourse and cultural representation, often working to deconstruct the idea of 'woman' as established by other feminisms as essentialist. They insist instead that there are multiple and overlapping dimensions of oppression (race, class, gender, disability, sexual orientation, developing world, etc.), each sustained by a particular pattern of discourse. These position women with respect both to each other and to patriarchal systems of power.

We can also detect methodological differences between feminists. Some work centres on collecting information and data to document oppression or misguided views on women (e.g. statistics on female under-representation in senior management in the police force, evidence showing women are as effective as men in police work). This is known as **feminist empiricism** and is the dominant approach of liberal feminism. Ngaire Naffine (1997: 30–1) writes that this perspective 'points out the crude stereotyping that has represented the official wisdom on women in criminology and in the criminal justice system. It raises objections to the empirical claims made about women when those claims are based on meagre evidence, with a good sprinkling of prejudice.' By contrast, the position of **standpoint feminism** rejects the norms of science and reason as inherently patriarchal and suggests that researchers should retrieve women's experiences and realities. In its more extreme formulation, the argument is made that the experience of oppression gives privileged access to knowledge. Therefore the stories and narratives provided by women afford a more accurate insight into the structures of power than those of men. Such a perspective is understandably pivotal to much radical feminism and overlaps in complex ways with more postmodern and poststructural feminist agendas. These set about attacking the idea of truth and seek instead to document the discourses and narratives through which power and identity are constructed and maintained in a kind of cultural critique. A major focus here is on avoiding simplicities and instead deconstructing universalistic claims to reason. The literature is often highly reflexive and philosophical, frequently making use of postmodern cultural theory to critique core concepts. As we have already mentioned, even the idea of 'woman' has come under attack, with women of colour and lesbians, for example, asserting that they experience problems and realities that are not shared by all other women. The argument is made that the majority of feminist research reflects the experiences of heterosexual, white, middle-class women (many of them academics) and that this is a relatively privileged group. Hence political questions arise about 'who shall speak' on behalf of women as well as more empirical issues such as the extent to which findings derived from one study can be applied to other women.

Debates between these various positions can be fierce. Radicals and poststructuralists suggest that liberal and empiricist feminists have some complicity with a patriarchal system, in effect, they are wrong to try to pull down the master's house with the master's own tools (science, positivism, etc.). The more orthodox feminists retort that their work can have direct policy relevance because, unlike abstruse and perhaps unrealistic radical alternatives, they can engage with the rules of dominant institutions and discourses and make practical suggestions that can best improve the life chances of women.

The Relevance of Theory

In this chapter we have briefly reviewed a number of theoretical approaches to law and criminal justice. The material presented here has documented not only diversity, but also the benefits that come from critical and creative thinking. Social theory helps us to broaden our perspective and move away from a narrow, empirical, data-driven and descriptive approach to law and justice driven by common sense, insider perspectives and immediate policy needs to ask bigger questions and find unexpected answers. These relate to the role of culture, modernity, power and inequality and their various intersecting contributions to ways in which social order is maintained. In the following chapters we will see these themes returning time and again as we engage in more focused, middle-range discussions of the law, policing, courts and corrections.

Study Questions

1   How has modernity influenced the shape of law and criminal justice?
2   Outline the ways in which contending social theories explain the gradual reduction of the levels of violence used in punishment.
3   Identify and contrast the diverse understandings of culture and punishment outlined in this chapter.
4   Briefly outline the major themes in feminist theory of law and criminal justice.
5   How does Foucault's approach differ from that of radical criminology?
6   Consider the theoretical approaches described in this chapter. Can you make a judgement as to which has the most explanatory power? Which has most practical use as a tool for social change? Is there a relationship between explanatory power and usefulness?
7   How do laws most directly impact on your life? Which theory best explains their effects? Do you think the answer will be different for people from other social positions?
8   Write a scenario, short story or vignette that exemplifies: (a) a symbolic interactionist approach to law and criminal justice; (b) a Durkheimian analysis of the role of law.
9   Identify a legal issue reported in the newspaper. Explain what is going on from three different perspectives identified in the chapter.

Glossary of Key Terms

anomie – Associated with Durkheim, this refers to a situation in which social norms have broken down, leading to increasing rates of deviance such as crime, divorce and suicide.

base/superstructure model – The Marxist vision of the social order, with the economic base determining what goes on in other spheres of social life.

biopower – Foucault's term for forms of power that are concerned with populations, reproduction, desire and sexuality.

boundary maintenance – The process through which a society retains a sense of identity by marking insiders from outsiders and the good from the bad.

carceral city – The urban form associated with the *carceral continuum* and a disciplinary society. It consists of institutions of social control.

carceral continuum – A term developed by Foucault and referring to the chain of institutions in society concerned with regulating and controlling populations – courts, schools, reformatories, asylums, prisons, etc.

chivalry effect – A theory holding that women are advantaged in the criminal justice system because of beliefs about female weakness and vulnerability.

collective conscience – Associated with Durkheim, this refers to the shared moral codes and sense of belonging that people have in society.

conflict theory – Models of society that emphasize power, struggle and inequality.

consensus theory – Models of society that emphasize cooperation among people and institutions and their shared values and goals.

criminalization – The process through which certain acts are made illegal.

difference – For postmodernists, difference means more than dissimilarity. It recognizes that groups are defined against each other and that categories are related in a hierarchical fashion (some are seen as more valuable than others). Through the creation and application of these orders, the experiences and world-views of lesser categories are silenced, invalidated or denied any existence at all.

disciplinary power – An idea developed by Foucault, this refers to forms of power that are rational and focus on the control and routinization of bodies.

discourse – According to Foucault, a system of ideas that constitutes human subjects, institutions and power relations.

docile body – According to Foucault, this pliant and conforming body is the outcome of disciplinary power.

dominant class – According to Marxism, this consists of the owners of property and is the ruling group in modern society.

economic determinism – The view, exemplified by Marxism, holding that economic aspects of social life determine others, such as politics and culture.

feminist empiricism – The viewpoint that more data and social scientific research are needed to document the oppression of women and develop strategies for confronting this.

functionalism – A social theory that argues that society consists of institutions, roles and norms that work together to maintain a beneficial social stability.

ideology – A system of ideas and beliefs that supports the interests of a dominant group.

labelling theory – An approach looking at the ways in which specific actions and actors are socially defined as deviant and in need of social control.

left realism – An approach to crime and criminal justice that marries neo-Marxism with a pragmatic understanding of the realities of crime and criminal justice policy.

liberal feminism – A form of feminism focusing on the need for equal rights and greater equality within existing institutional arrangements.

master status – The dominant social identity of an individual, e.g., 'deviant' or 'criminal'.

mechanical solidarity – Durkheim's term for the organization of pre-industrial society. There is an emphasis on similarity and little tolerance for deviance with repressive punishments common.

microphysics of power – A term developed by Foucault calling for an exploration of the detailed ways in which power works on the body and self.

moral entrepreneur – A person or group who seeks to have particular acts criminalized or otherwise regulated by law or the criminal justice system.

moral panic – A disproportionate societal response to an episode of crime and deviance.

negative sanctions – Punishments directed against behaviour that breaks social rules.

organic solidarity – Durkheim's term for the organization of modern societies. An advanced division of labour creates tolerance for difference and sees restorative punishments fall into place.

panopticon – An architectural device allowing for centralized surveillance. This is associated with *disciplinary power.*

patriarchy – A term used by feminists to describe a social order organized around the rule of women by men.

postmodern feminism – The understanding that we need to study the ties between discourse, representation and power in order to understand the oppression of women, and indeed to interrogate and deconstruct the category of 'woman' itself.

positive sanctions – Social rewards given to those who conform.

postmodernism – An academic perspective that seeks to move beyond modernism. It involves an attack on ideas of truth, reason, science and universalism and seeks to investigate ambivalence, irony and cultural representations. Postmodernists deny we can locate any 'truth' but rather should treat any such claims with scepticism.

poststructuralism – An academic perspective advocating the importance of *discourses* and giving primacy to the fusion of culture and power in social life.

problem of social order – This refers to the fact that all known societies have to ensure some level of conformity and stability if they are to survive.

radical criminology – A branch of criminological theory inspired by Marxism.

radical feminism – A form of feminism arguing for major cultural and structural changes towards a more woman-centred reality, not just the reform of existing institutions.

rite of passage – A ritual associated with status transition, for example, from free citizen to prisoner.

social contract – The idea that people allow the state to regulate social life in exchange for freedom and the rule of law.

socialist feminism – A branch of feminism which has strong influences from Marxism and focuses on issues of economic inequality.

socialization – The process of learning to be a competent member of a society. This means acquiring skills, values and beliefs.

sovereign power – The form of power in pre-modern monarchical social systems. According to Foucault, this works on the body, is ritualistic and symbolic.

standpoint feminism – The view that we need to privilege women's personal experiences of oppression and reject scientific norms as problematic.

structuralism – The analysis of culture as a system of signs. Usually depicts this as independent of human agency.

subordinate class – The workers, according to Marxism, the dominated group in modern society.

total institution – A social institution that is cut off from the outside world, has a routinized social order and hierarchical roles. Prisons, asylums and juvenile halls are examples of this in the criminal justice system.

Suggested Further Reading

David Garland's (1991) book *Punishment and Modern Society* overviews much of the material covered here on neo-Marxism, Durkheim, Elias and Foucault in more depth. It is a thoughtful book that can provide an important next step for readers interested in theory. Many of the empirical texts reviewed in this chapter are accessible including those by Cohen, Erikson and Goffman. Foucault's (1975) *Discipline and Punish* is essential reading for all theoretical criminologists and is less difficult than many of his earlier texts. The first few chapters of Naffine (1997) offer an outstanding introduction to the ways in which diverse feminist theories and epistemologies have influenced criminological research. Mainstream criminology journals tend to be dominated by routine quantitative work and deliberations on topical issues in justice administration wherein the kinds of historical and theoretical themes we have reviewed here do not take centre stage. However, good articles on social theory, law and criminal justice can still be found from time to time in locations such as *Criminology*, *The British Journal of Criminology*, etc. Yet it is often the case that the most theoretically interesting work is published in journals with a stronger sociological flavour such as *Theory and Society*, *Sociology* or *Gender and Society*. The CD-ROM Sociological Abstracts is the most useful search tool for these.

Suggested Websites

Although we document many websites in later chapters, they are mostly of use because they contain data or research reports. There are comparatively few good sites dedicated to theoretical issues as these impact upon criminal justice.

http://www.theorycards.org.uk   This slightly irreverent site contains small amounts of amusing and informative material on major social theorists, but only some of this will be relevant to the material covered in this book.

http://www.pscw.uva.nl/sociosite/TOPICS/Sociologists.html   This is 'Sociosite' – a more serious online resource maintained by the University of Amsterdam. Although not focused on criminal justice issues, this is very useful. It contains links through which you can follow up on many of the key theorists considered here, such as Durkheim, Elias, Foucault and Marx. As the Internet address is rather lengthy, we suspect it may change in future, but you should be able to find it using a search engine.

http://www.digeratiweb.com/sociorealm   'Sociorealm' is not quite as useful as 'Sociosite' (above) for exploring pure theory, but still has good links to texts by and about key social theorists. The criminology links here are also worthwhile.

2　The Law

Introduction

In our day-to-day lives, the meanings that we attach to law are relatively straight-forward. 'Law' is often presumed to be a discrete set of rules, developed by the state and the courts, and if we get caught breaking them, we might end up in trouble. Usually, this seems pretty fair. But from a sociological perspective, law is sprawling and messy. State law is supplemented and sometimes supplanted by other rules governing social behaviour; our common-sense assumptions about the existence of justice or fairness are often more hopeful than empirically correct. This chapter presents the social scientific perspective on what we mean when we talk about 'law' in Western, liberal tradition. To begin, we briefly describe some of the fundamental structures and ideals of the system. We then backtrack to trace its history and consider the contemporary social context. Following this, key jurisprudential models of law are presented. From a social scientific perspective, these are not particularly useful as descriptions of how law is actually interpreted and applied in societies that are marked by systematic power discrepancies and differences. This is evident when we consider the promise and failure of objectivity and equality, and the usefulness of the public/private dichotomy. We then turn to the role and relevance of rights, a concept that has gained increasing prominence in our day-to-day discourse and as a basis for claims within the formal legal system. It becomes evident that the promise of these concepts remains largely unfulfilled, as jurisprudential ideals compete with social realities.

Legal Systems

In England, the USA and Australia, 'law' usually means the decisions of courts and legislation. These form the basis of the **common law system**. This was developed in Britain and exported to its colonies, including the USA and Australia. Common law is predicated on stability and its development is piecemeal. Precedents are set by earlier case law, and each judgment is rooted in the legal principles of those in the past. When it occurs, change is slow because any disagreement with similar prior decisions must be justified on the basis of distinct and legally relevant differences. In the common law tradition, law has traditionally been seen as practical – a craft rather than a systematic body of theory – and so judges and lawyers, rather than jurists, have played the pre-eminent role in its development (Lloyd, 1973: 223).

While the common law is most strongly associated with case law in both popular imagination and legal discussion, Cotterrell (1984) has noted that contemporary societies are more directly regulated by an extensive system of legislation developed by governments. Legislation does not need the courts' approval to be valid, although judges continue to clarify and apply the legal principles involved, and in some instances can significantly alter the relevance of an Act, its scope and the ways in which it can be implemented. Nonetheless, as foreshadowed in the previous chapter, it is important to recognize the centrality of the state in the development of law. Cotterrell (1984) suggests that this brings into focus questions of the relationship of law and social transition. The details of legislation can be constructed so as to organize social relations directly; Cotterrell (ibid.: 48) has defined it as 'a precision instrument of wide-scale social and economic planning'. In contrast, court cases are reactive and their role as a driving force of change is far less certain. The extent to which laws can effect change is an empirical question, one that is difficult to measure and beyond the scope of this book. However, it is important to keep in mind that while our cultural imagination would suggest that the courts are pre-eminent sites of law making, many have argued that their role is more symbolic than substantial.

The contemporary significance of legislation leads us to a brief consideration of the **separation of powers**. Under this doctrine, judicial, executive and legislative powers must be invested in separate people or bodies. The people who interpret laws (the judiciary) are different from the people who make laws (the legislature), and those who enforce them (the executive). In effect, the system divides up power through a series of checks and balances and in so doing, undermines the possibilities of absolutism and abuse. In reality, the degree to which this occurs varies across countries and historical periods, and some overlap invariably exists in terms of the structure of the government and its practice.

Debate over **judicial activism** provides some evidence of tensions in the doctrine. Commentators periodically express concern over judges who are perceived to be aggressively making new law, undermining legislative power. As we shall see, such debate is premised on an asocial conceptualization of the process of judging. We might also claim, perhaps a little cynically, that the charge is usually levelled against those decisions that do not further the interests of the parties concerned. The presence of such controversies serves to remind us that the legal and political systems that order power are constructed via cultural and ideological claims as well as processes that exist in empirical reality.

The **independence of the judiciary** is a key means of bolstering the separation of powers. It is presumed that judges will make the legally correct decisions when they are removed from the influence of the legislature and executive. To ensure this, judges need to be protected from punishment when they hand down politically or socially unpopular decisions. There are a number of ways of ensuring this. First, the appointment of judges should not occur through political patronage or popular election. Obviously, many countries do not act according to this ideal. Selection processes are informed by political agendas and in the USA, for example, the community may elect new members of the bench. This can marginalize considerations of prospective judges' legal rigour and understanding, in favour of their political ideologies and law and order agendas. Once on the bench, judges cannot be removed when they hand down a contentious judgment. This is usually assured by granting life tenure or providing for a compulsory retiring age. Additionally, a relatively 'flat' status and pay hierarchy limits the need to produce politically savvy decisions in pursuit of promotion. Ideally, these protections create the context in which the law can be applied in an objective and equal manner, in accordance with the rule of law.

In the Anglo-American systems, the judges preside over **adversarial proceedings**. The adversarial system incorporates a conflict or competition between opposing parties in the courtroom, as each argues the validity of their version of the truth. The result is often interpreted in terms of winners and losers, less often as a triumph of justice and truth. More specifically, adversarial systems are characterized by the following:

- *The role of adjudicator*. The judge cannot actively seek and test evidence. Their involvement is restricted to decision-making at the end of the contest. These limits are imposed on the presumption that any earlier participation might encourage a commitment to one version of the facts without measured consideration of the opposing side's story. This also creates the appearance of fairness, increasing society's trust in the process.
- *Discovery and presentation of evidence by the parties or their representatives*. This requirement is linked with the need for the adjudicator's passivity in the proceedings.
- *Defined procedural rules*. These order the parties' conduct before, during and after the trial, and the evidence they present. This creates a dyadic contest over specific issues within a defined period. The regulations shape counsel's behaviour and undermine judicial prejudice by defining what evidence can and must be considered (Landsman, 1983: 715–17).

In other jurisdictions, notably those in Europe, an **inquisitorial system** places different responsibilities on the shoulders of the judges. They have broader powers in terms of questioning the parties to the proceedings, and investigating the case. This is associated with the **civil law system** in which laws are systematically codified into a more coherent whole than is found in common law. However, there is less judicial discretion in the construction and interpretation of law. Civil law is more directly linked to Roman law and canon (church) law, both of which were listed and organized by jurists. The system more obviously reflects the rationalizing of the law with the state legislating its meaning.

Court systems vary according to country and jurisdictions within countries. The following provides a very brief discussion of how courts are generally ordered. Courts are hierarchical. In their original jurisdiction, higher courts address more 'serious' crimes, often those with harsher penalties. They also have an appellate function. This means that parties can appeal to have the decisions reached in the lower courts reviewed, altered or overturned. This only occurs in limited circumstances, and appeals are based on a matter of law, not a question of fact. The division of labour is also affected by different jurisdictions. These may be geographical, in that crimes committed in one area are tried by the court associated with that place. Courts also hear different types of offences. In the USA and Australia, some offences are defined by Federal law, and others are created through state legislation. The courts have general jurisdiction, in that they hear a range of offences. Other courts are responsible for hearing only very specific issues. Juvenile courts are perhaps the most obvious example in the criminal justice system. They hear cases involving perpetrators under a certain age on the basis that young people are impressionable and vulnerable and in need of protection and reformation (Wundersitz, 2000: 103). In more recent times, law and order advocates have argued for a return of particular categories of young offenders into the mainstream court system, to be dealt with as adults. Military tribunals, drug courts, boards and appeals tribunals are other examples of forums that hear particular types of crime.

Liberal Legal Philosophy

The standard texts tell us that the principles and workings of contemporary Western democratic legal systems are informed by **liberal political philosophy**. Stephen Bottomley and Stephen Parker (1994) list a number of elements. They are as follows:

- **Liberty**. Liberalism recognizes all individuals as fundamentally free, in that they are not bound by obligations to others unless they have expressly entered into an agreement. The nature of liberty, however, is subject to debate. Negative liberty refers to freedom *from*, usually freedom from state intervention. Positive liberty, on the other hand, is freedom *to*, which requires the state to actively promote social conditions that allow people to pursue benefits, rights or interests. In the broad sweep of history, political ideology has moved from an emphasis on negative liberty to positive liberty.
- **Individualism**. Society is a collection of individuals; it does not exist as an entity that is more than the sum of its parts. Liberalism seeks to protect the individual, rather than society as a whole.
- **Equality**. Each individual is equal before the law but the definition of equality is contested. Debate focuses on formal and substantive equality; we consider the difference later in the chapter.
- **Justice**. Like equality, justice has conflicting meanings. Formal justice demands that legal procedure be followed. For example, as long as police and court procedure and the rules of evidence are followed, an outcome will be just. Substantive

justice focuses on the details of the decision, rather than the process leading to that point.

- **Rights**. Rights have become a dominant discourse in contemporary Western society. They are discussed in greater detail from p. 72.
- **Utilitarianism**. As with some of the above concepts, the details of utilitarianism alter according to the flavour of liberal philosophy. But at its most basic level, utilitarianism concerns itself with the pleasures and pains of the individual, demanding that the actions and laws of the state be judged with reference to the outcomes. The philosopher, Jeremy Bentham provided the original and most succinct definition of this principle, arguing for the greatest happiness among the greatest number of people.
- An assumption that people are **rational actors**. Liberalism presumes that people behave in a logical and reasoned manner in order to achieve particular goals.

The roots of these ideals can be traced to the **Enlightenment**, when the significance of the Church and religious law, precepts and explanations receded. In their place philosophers emphasized the value of human reason as the basis for knowledge. This belief developed alongside a commitment to scientific methods, the mastery of the natural world for the benefit of humankind (or more accurately, mankind), and a belief in the possibility of progress. Rationality and objectivity were accordingly incorporated into jurisprudence, and the emerging concept of the **Rule of Law**. Whereas the rule of men has the potential to be changeable, arbitrary and discriminatory, the Rule of Law demands that the law can and must be certain, accurate and value-free. It is applied to everyone, including those who formulate it. This approach recognizes that we are all entitled to equality before the law. This in turn necessitates objectivity and impartiality on the part of the judge or legislator. The ideal is symbolized by the figure of Themis, the Greek goddess who balances the scales of justice, blindfolded, outside many of our court buildings. It is a striking image, but as we shall see, it does not always reflect the workings of the legal system.

Law and Norms

The courts may preoccupy popular imagination, liberal philosophy may set the terms of abstract debate, and legislation may indicate the dominance of the state but other social rules also order our behaviours. These may be formally recognized, in the articles of association of a company, the by-laws of a voluntary organization or the rules of a school. They can also take the form of **norms**. Social norms define some acts and omissions as deviant. This means that our behaviour breaches social expectations but has not necessarily broken any laws in doing so. Conversely, illegal acts are not necessarily deemed to be unacceptable by other members of society. These interpretations may alter according to the circumstances. For example, speeding 15 kilometres over the limit might be fine on an open highway, but is unacceptable near a school; in both instances, the act is formally against the law. The distinction between deviance and illegality is taken for granted by sociologists, but it is nonetheless useful as a reminder of the multiple rules that order our lives.

Eugen Erlich (1936), a law professor writing early last century, developed one of the first sustained sociological critiques of the claimed dominance of state law. He noted lawyers' preoccupation with state law, its implementation and problems does not necessarily reflect people's day-to-day practices and expectations. Our interactions with others are not usually undertaken with reference to specific legal principles or laws, which are rarely invoked and usually only relevant in extreme circumstances. Typically, we are guided by 'living law', incorporating cultural practices and norms of conduct that have little to do with the legal precepts that will inform a judge's ruling on any particular case. Living law steers people away from the courts and state institutions. To exemplify his argument Erlich pointed out that if you asked a traveller about the organization of social life in a foreign place, they would not point to how a court case proceeded. They would describe a series of customs and norms that are more visible because they have more relevance in daily life.

Erlich's deceptively simple point remains pertinent in contemporary, multicultural or diverse societies. At a prosaic level we might note that subcultural norms may have more direct relevance in guiding people's behaviours than legislation or court decisions. In the USA, the religious law that legitimates polygamy among Mormons conflicts with mainstream legislation. In multicultural countries, religious dictates or cultural customs might conflict with dominant law. Given that the non-dominant cultures are often explicitly defined as oppressively patriarchal by feminists or backward, illiberal and undemocratic by legislators and armchair philosophers, the questions that such cases raise are often addressed by pointing to the deficiencies of the culture in question, rather than the more challenging issue of the extent to which a mono-cultural law can produce or reflect equality in multicultural societies.

The system of rules that preoccupies lawyers and sociologists is one form among many. In this, our present society reflects the multiplicity of laws and jurisdictions that were evident for much of the past millennium. Rationalization and centralization are more of an on-going process – and an imperfect one at that – than an end state at which we have arrived. The reach of state law and power is incomplete. Nonetheless, as we shall see in the later sections, the plurality of norms, rules and legal concepts is ignored in the majority of traditional jurisprudential approaches to law and liberal philosophy.

Past Processes: The Emergence of Law

Our contemporary practices and systems have not simply emerged by chance. Tracing the history of the English legal system (from which many others draw their basic structure and practices and fundamental premises) reveals a process of rationalization and centralization of law and the developing power and authority of the state. We have already touched upon this in the previous chapter where we discussed the work of Parsons, Weber, Giddens and Foucault. This process was fluid and did not occur in a neat progression of events: legal history is a sprawling subject and its details are beyond the scope of this text. The following discussion is a very brief and simple overview of some of the key events and processes that contributed to the development into the current adversarial and (relatively) centralized system.

Originally law grew out of the folk law and mores of early societies. There was a close fit between what was demanded of people and what they considered to be right and legitimate expectations. There is no easy way of identifying an era when law became codified. However, the Ten Commandments, the priestly rules of Deuteronomy and the codes of Babylon all represent attempts to collect a series of precepts and customs that ordered those societies. These processes were not necessarily examples of codification, that is, they did not amount to a systematically collated and exhaustive set of a series of laws that it was deemed necessary for the public to know (Lloyd, 1973: 240). Nonetheless, by the time of the Roman Empire, the civilizations of antiquity had developed relatively stable and complex formal legal systems.

Jumping forward several centuries in Europe, the forms of law altered after the disintegration of the Roman Empire. Many places returned to customary law, supplemented by lingering fragments of Roman law, imposed by lords in their local, feudal courts, beyond the centralized control of a single ruler (Lloyd, 1973; Berman and Reid, 1994). Law did not exist as a series of separate and easily identifiable institutions – it was part of the general social, political and religious order (Berman and Reid, 1994). This type of law was flexible, a necessity in the context of rapidly changing social relations and conditions.

After time localized laws were again evolving into written codes. This began on the watch of feudal lords and then more quickly when the rise of cities and trade demanded a set of legal precepts that could be recognized and applied beyond the immediate geographical or administrative context. The relatively coherent set of civil laws of the late Roman Empire were rediscovered and formally studied and refined, gradually being incorporated into the emerging secular law. At this time, canon or papal law, which was also derived partially from Roman law, was developed into a set of extensive and sophisticated written rules, enforced by an emergent Catholic bureaucracy. The laws themselves addressed issues that today would be considered to lie far beyond the scope of legitimate Church authority: criminal and civil laws and procedures, family law, and inheritance law were covered, as well as liturgical law (Berman and Reid, 1994). The general arc of these developments was from diversity to an increasingly coherent system.

In England the origins of common law are often linked to the Norman conquest. As part of the process of consolidating power, the early kings began to centralize and rationalize the courts (although differentiated jurisdictions continued into the nineteenth century) (Berman and Reid, 1996). This in turn hastened the development of a coherent set of laws. Customs that were peculiar to local areas were superseded by 'the common custom of the realm'. This was primarily developed through judicial decision-making and supported through a professional lawyer class (see pp. 142–144). In these early centuries judges were not bound by the precedent that is now understood as one of the fundamental features of common law. Past cases were used to illustrate legal principles but were not themselves a source of law (ibid.). The recording of case law, at first through the efforts of law students' 'Year Books' (journals in which they kept an account of hearings attended) and then later in the form of the commentaries by distinguished lawyers and judges, notably the Reports of Sir Edward Coke, provided the means of tracing court custom, or precedent. However, it was not until the nineteenth century that courts were doctrinally bound by particular, earlier decisions, rather than being guided by a customary approach (ibid.).

How can we reflect on this process sociologically? Max Weber has provided the dominant sociological account of changes in the form and application of law in the West. Weber positioned legal changes within the broader social processes and structures of technically advanced societies. Through rationalization the mystical and seemingly *ad hoc* elements of the law were streamlined, categorized and rendered 'scientific' and logical. Weber created a typology of the ideal types of law, based on their formal and substantive rationality. He identified the following:

- Formal irrationality, in which the law is applied in ways that may not make logical sense.
- Substantive irrationality, in which each case is determined with reference to its internal characteristics, rather than any external and generalized norms.
- Formal rationality, in which rules are determined and applied with reference to a system of principles, rather than with a simple recourse to consideration of the facts of the immediate case.
- Substantive rationality, where decisions are based upon ethical rules or values. These may be applied without reference to the expectations of due process.

According to Weber, these categories are ideal types. This means they are not necessarily so clearly identifiable in empirical reality, and elements of each might exist in some systems of law. However the march of history saw a shift from one form toward another.

Weber contextualizes these categories within a series of transformations in the sources of law and authority:

- charismatic 'law prophets' (such as oracles or priests who presided over trials by ordeal) revealing law;
- 'legal notables' (permanent functionaries);
- secular and religious powers creating law through legislation;
- professional legal administrators.

Again, these are ideal types and are not necessarily sequential in empirical reality, although Weber's discussion does suggest some evolution rather than simple change.

Changes in authority were associated with broader social developments, particularly the emergence of capitalism. Weber does not posit a direct relationship between capitalism and the rationalization of the law, and he skirts questions as to the extent to which economic and legal processes are linked. He focuses more closely on the role of the legal profession and the political context in England, and argues that both these forces were key in the development of the common law and its procedures.

In Weber's analysis, profession and politics were associated with class. As we have noted, the common law is an amalgamation of rules and procedures from a number of sources – not quite as streamlined as in other European jurisdictions. Weber explained this with reference to the 'practical' orientation of the English legal profession, which emphasized skill and technique, and generated a 'pragmatic jurisprudence' rather than a scholarly one (Roach Anleu, 2000: 27). The judiciary was drawn from the bar, and they were a conservative force. So too were their decisions, which given the incremental nature of change under the common law, did little to alter existing power arrangements. The necessity of lawyers and their high fees prevented those from the lower classes accessing the legal system. In these ways, the law supported the interests of capital. Although some rationalization did occur, the relevant actors and principles created barriers to the greater rationalization of law evident on the continent, which might have worked against the dominance of the legal system and the interests they served.

While Weber's analysis is one of the classics of the sociology of law, it is of course not above criticism from other sociologists. It is argued that Weber failed to fully describe the relationship between the rationalization of law and economic structures. He argues that the two are complementary but neither structures the other, which falls short of a full causal explanation. Further, he states that his long discussion of law and capitalism in England is not generalizable beyond the particular circumstances of that time and place, which marginalizes the analytical relevance of the work. Others have noted that truly formal rationality is impossible. As Roach Anleu (ibid.: 30) points out, it is difficult to imagine a law or legal system that is not to some extent informed by religious, social or political values. Finally, Weber does not approach the different types of law in an objective manner. Rather, he is explicit in his characterization of rational law as more advanced than irrational law.

Current Questions: Law, Postmodernity and Globalization

Weber's focus was on changes that have already occurred. However, new social processes are altering the structure and significance of law. We have already discussed postmodern critiques of law but it is useful to remember that 'the postmodern' refers not only to an intellectual position; postmodernity is a historical epoch. In this age, life is fragmented and pluralistic (Schanck, 1992). It is marked by the absence of 'grand narratives' (Lyotard, 1984) that promised the reliability of knowledge and the certainty of progress (Lipkin, 1994). In the absence of previous certainties and in light of rapidly unfolding social, economic, structural and cultural changes we come to distrust the institutions whose authority was once taken for granted (Schanck, 1992). For example, where it was presumed that law limited the abuse of power and reflected the truth of the matter, people may now be rather more suspicious of its functions (Lindgren-Alves, 2000: 488). However, empirical evidence to support these presumptions is difficult to generate.

Globalization is part of the postmodern landscape. Countries have always been involved in a web of relations but in contemporary society the nature and implications of these links have altered. In a classic definition, Robertson (1992: 217) describes globalization as 'the increasing acceleration in both concrete global interdependence and consciousness of the global whole of the twentieth [and now twenty-first] century'. Things that happen on the other side of the world have a far more direct impact on people's day-to-day lives. Banking, communications, trade, criminal activities, cultural practices and artefacts, and institutions of governance cross state boundaries (Roach Anleu, 2000: 216).

The implications of globalization differ from country to country. States and other institutions do not hold equal economic, military and cultural power and influence. Thus, some are more easily able to impose their agendas upon international law and affairs. Conversely, others are susceptible to the demands of organizations like the World Bank or the International Monetary Fund. For example, these organizations are able to tie financial aid to state reform, effecting political and social change and reinforcing Western liberal ideals upon 'recalcitrant' states (Roach Anleu, 2000: 220; Alvarez, 2002). These processes have impacted upon international law.

The end of World War II marked the emergence of a new, coherent (though imperfectly recognized and enforced) international order. This initially occurred under the authority of the United Nations; more recently, we have seen the emergence of the European Community. These bodies have been associated with a number of legal developments and by some accounts, the marginalization of the nation–state. For example, we see an increased number and broader scope of multilateral treaties. These are created with the involvement of not only countries, but international law scholars, and civil servants, NGOs, interest groups, and expert international commissions (Alvarez, 2002). Changes associated with globalization have called sovereignty into question. States are increasingly called to account for their actions to other members of the international order. International law is also emphasizing the rights and duties of individuals, in contrast to the previous focus that rested upon relationships between states. This is most obviously evident in the systematic enumeration of human rights (see pp. 73–74) and the prosecution of those who participate in, for example, crimes against humanity or genocide. These can combine to produce a tension between the principle of non-intervention in domestic affairs versus the need to protect the human rights of citizens (Roach Anleu, 2000: 219).

Globalization is also tied to colonialism and the uneasy relationship between law and custom within nations. In former colonial societies, liberal legal philosophies were imposed at the expense of the pre-existing, complex systems of indigenous law. For example, indigenous Australians developed a system of punishment that is referenced to kinship obligations, and can include corporal punishment. These practices continue among some traditionally oriented groups but under the Anglo-Australian criminal law, may themselves be crimes. Further difficulties arise when we acknowledge that many of the pillars of liberal legal philosophy are not recognized among Aboriginal societies. With the exception of a few instances of *ad hoc* incorporation of traditional punishment as a consideration in sentencing, or as an alternative to jail, Australian courts have not systematically acknowledged indigenous law or its principles and they rarely apply it beyond instances involving traditionally oriented Aborigines. When it is recognized, the structure of law and power in Australia remains unchanged – Aboriginal law will be incorporated only in so far as it does not breach the dominant system and non-indigenous interests, and to the extent that it can be rewritten to conform to pre-existing legal concepts.

Weber's approach to the rationalization of law, questions of postmodernity and globalization all indicate the need to locate law in its social, historical and cultural context. However, as the following overview of jurisprudential texts shows, the role of the social is not universally recognized. A jurisprudential approach to law is concerned with its nature and the relations between law and justice. These are often abstract philosophical questions based upon what the law *should be*. Empirical questions as to what the law *is* and how it works in our societies are marginalized. Despite their sometimes loose relationship with reality, these jurisprudential principles frame legal decisions, debate and practice. For this reason, we discuss them in the following pages.

Jurisprudential Approaches to the Law

Legal formalism/positivism

Legal formalism or **legal positivism** is associated with the Enlightenment and the rise of Western 'science', which produced a desire to develop a rational and objective means of measuring and valuing laws (Cotterrell, 1989: 123). Within this approach, law is a self-contained system of rules and concepts, the validity of which is determined with reference to the legitimacy and coherency of the system itself, rather than the justness or morality of any particular law or judicial decision. Social justice, reform or policy considerations are not relevant. Borrowing from John Austin, one of the key theorists associated with this school, we might say that the approach seeks to describe how the law is, not how it ought to be.

Decisions in individual cases and the validity of particular laws are judged through recourse to rules that create an internally logical system. For example, Hans Kelsen attempts to set out a 'pure theory of law', a science of law. He conceives of society's many laws as constituting a system, with each rule deriving its legitimacy from those higher order laws governing it. All of these are ultimately measured against the *Grundnorm*, the original norm. Kelsen's approach provides an example of the reasoning process through which the legitimacy of any law lies in its creation, not in its substance or the implications of its application. Another positivist, Ronald Dworkin, defines the law as a 'seamless web'. Even in instances where there is no directly applicable legal principle, there remains a right way of considering the issues. Ultimately, then, decisions cannot originate in individual creativity or discretion. In some slight contrast, H. L. A. Hart (1961) identifies primary rules, which are rules of obligation, and secondary rules, those concerned with questions of procedure, recognition and adjudication. Unlike Dworkin, he recognizes that in some rare circumstances there are no clear, settled rules, which creates a 'penumbra of uncertainty', and only in these cases will judges have some discretion (Hart, 1980: 55). All of the above theorists share in common the belief that a system of law is not judged with reference to its extra-legal implications.

This is not to say that morality is irrelevant. Rather, legal positivism requires us to approach the nature of law as an issue separate from that of morality. Austin (1982: 184, in Cotterrell, 1989) states that, 'The existence of law is one thing; its merit or demerit is another. Whether it be or be not is one enquiry; whether it be or be not conformable to an assumed standard, is a different enquiry.' For Bentham and Austin, early scholars associated with legal formalism, incorporating ethical judgements into the law is dangerous because it undermines the legitimate authority of the state. It does this by providing a basis upon which people can second guess what the state legislated for. Further, its basis is morality, a slippery and relative notion (Cotterrell, 1989: 119).

From a sociological perspective, a fundamental problem with legal positivism lies in its failure to adequately engage with the actual processes of the legal system and its actors. To some extent, this is not a fair criticism, as the approach does not set out to do so. However, arguments about the discovery of law completely fail to recognize the human agency that is bound up with the creation and application of laws, and the practical need to interpret law and fact in order to properly apply them. Recognizing this opens a series of questions on objectivity and equality, for example; these are described in more detail later in this chapter, and again in Chapter 5.

Natural law

In contrast to legal positivists, proponents of **natural law** assume the existence of fundamental principles that define the standards of justice and morality, and the validity of laws. These principles exist in nature; they are discovered but not created by human reason (Cotterrell, 1989: 123). If laws deviate from these absolute standards, they are neither legitimate nor legally binding. Within this approach there are two types of law. One rests on divine or natural authority and one is created by people. In the event of a conflict, the first has precedence over the latter (Lloyd, 1973: 70). The legitimacy of law goes beyond the proper promulgation of rules and looks instead to the ways in which laws operate, how they play out, whom they affect, and how.

The idea of natural law has ancient origins. Plato was not directly a proponent of natural law but his discussion of idealist philosophy – the perfect form of law of which actual laws are a shadow – in *The Republic* gives some indication of the process of divination. Plato believed that men could perceive the ideal through a thorough and proper education in (his) philosophy, as applied by philosopher kings (Lloyd, 1973: 74). Early Christian jurists argued that natural law, conceptualized as God's divine laws, was to be discovered in part through reason and in part through divine inspiration (ibid.: 79). In this tradition, Thomas Aquinas is a significant source for natural law theorizing, although he hedged his bets. He, like many other jurists who argue for natural law principles, recognized the authority of the state to legislate and argued that laws on morally neutral issues conform with natural law so long as they contribute to the common good (Cotterrell, 1989: 126). When this standard is broken, one should obey God's law but if the law is simply unfair, unjust, or against individual conscience, it can be better to obey it. To do so avoids the greater evils of disorder and social breakdown (see Cotterrell, 1984: 127).

Natural law has played a large role in buttressing the right and ways to rule. For example, it was significant in guiding early interpretation of the US Constitution, where judges looked to moral precepts as a means of filling in the blanks of the written document (Cotterrell 1989: 122). In England the approach was used in the form of the divine right of kings to bolster the monarch's privilege and limit the powers of the parliament. After the establishment of parliamentary sovereignty, it became less important, and, gradually, legal positivism, with its emphasis on the appropriate enactment of laws, took over as the key paradigm (ibid.: 121). Natural law regained significance in the context of international condemnation and judgement of Nazi Germany after World War II (see Box 2.1). Many of the actions now commonly defined as atrocities were strictly legal within a positivist framework. Natural law was useful because it allowed prosecutors to argue that the formal requirements of what constitutes a law cannot be separated from its substance (Roach Anleu, 2000: 9). Regardless of human legislation or interpretation, there are fundamental rights and wrongs in society.

Box 2.1   Positivism versus Natural Law: the Case of Nazi Germany

How should the actions of Nazi Germany be judged? This question was played out in a debate between H. L. A. Hart (1958) and Lon Fuller (1958) an American natural lawyer.

Hart argued that the questions facing positivists are limited. Whether or not a particular law should be obeyed on moral grounds is beyond the scope of consideration; it is outside the parameters of the particular intellectual exercise of legal positivism.

In this case, the legality of the actions in Nazi Germany must be judged with reference to their 'fit' with properly constituted laws. Although morally repugnant, systematic discrimination, assault and even mass murder may be allowed under properly constituted laws. The creation and application of law are the proper focus within a positivist framework.

Fuller countered Hart, arguing that positivism is dangerous because it creates a false dichotomy between a legal obligation to obey and a moral obligation to disobey in unjust or oppressive regimes. For Fuller, a more pertinent question is: how do systems maintain 'fidelity to law'? A legal system can cease to have a claim on citizens' obedience when it no longer incorporates minimum moral qualities. According to Fuller, the necessary morality is procedural. Hart might assume that within the positivist paradigm the difference between Nazi and English law was the ends to which they were put, but Fuller argues that much Nazi law was enacted and applied in improper ways, through strategies that breached procedural regularity and justice. These breaches included:

- retroactive statuses;
- secret laws that denied citizens any knowledge of the basis upon which authorities were acting;
- perverse interpretations that allowed laws to be applied or ignored according to ideological and political needs; and
- regularised informal laws (Fuller, 1958: 650–2).

These practices were problematic because they breached the 'moral understanding' between rulers and subjects. In this understanding citizens accept laws as right and good and the state ensures that they are indeed so (ibid.: 642). The Nazi regime failed this contract and so its legal system ceased to exist; it cannot be recognized by later courts. Cotterrell makes the fine point that 'Fuller's claim are symptomatic of an impatience with legal positivism's *silences* – with what it refuses to say about the law, rather than with its explicit tenets' (1989: 134, emphasis in the original). Ultimately, Fuller's arguments are perhaps less a critique of positivism's logic and analysis, and more a harsh comment on the social or political marginality of its narrow aims and focus.

Which approach do you think is more useful in judging (or interpreting) the role of law in Nazi Germany?
Do the weaknesses of positivism lie mainly in its social or political marginality?
Does the above example suggest any problems in the formulation and application of a natural law approach?

From a sociological perspective, the natural law paradigm raises a series of problems. It is difficult to claim the existence of fundamental rules given that their content varies so much. A common contention is that Western nations impose their own understandings of what is just upon countries that have lesser economic and political power. This links into a more basic question, and one that can also be applied to formalist approaches to the law: how do we 'discover' pre-existing rules? Sociologists are commonly wary of claims that it is possible to uncover, without bias, through scientific or philosophical methods, some truth that is not dependent upon legal processes or people for its existence. Additionally, the approach cannot adequately address the increasing complexity and technical focus of law, and the ways it shapes (and not simply reflects) social order. If the law can change quickly in response to social needs and circumstances, it cannot at the same time be rooted in and reflective of some fundamental and unchangeable order (Cotterrell, 1989: 124). According to Cotterrell (ibid.: 124) the problem is not so much that people cannot discover or agree upon a set of 'natural order' principles, but that even if they do exist, they do not offer a sound and convincing guide for the complexity and technical specificity of modern law.

Legal Realism and Critical Legal Studies

Legal realists respond to the myth of positivism. They recognize that there can be no way of disassociating decision-making from the value judgments that are bound up in the interpretation of facts. Outcomes of particular cases are not derived from the disinterested application of the correct legal formula, and rules are not simply discovered. Legal realism emphasizes the humanity of the judge, a person with biases and values, and not a mechanistic, law applying robot (Roach Anleu, 2000: 7). Decisions are made and then justified through the authority of the law, rather than arising solely from within the law. Legal realists conclude that the law cannot exist as a separate entity from the legal officers who apply it.

From a sociological perspective, **legal realism** is useful in locating law within a social context. But it can be criticized for not going far enough. Judges are not simply individuals who happen to make pronouncements that are followed by others. It is important to consider the bases for law's legitimacy, and why people respect and follow judicial decisions. Given that law is more than a series of unconnected pronouncements and decisions, legal realists are too narrow in their focus on individuals. Law is a structure that is entrenched in our society and supported through interconnected institutions and ideologies. It enables judicial power but also limits it through rules, statutes, checks and balances, precedents and informal norms (ibid.: 9). In short, realists fail to systematically trace the social, cultural and structural context in which laws are created and decision-making occurs.

More recently, the Critical Legal Studies movement has reiterated and refined some of the arguments of legal realists. This group of scholars do not claim to be developing a coherent theory; they are a movement sharing a common set of orientations and concerns. Many of these concerns echo those of legal realists. In particular, they critique the existence of the rule of law and do not accept that a coherent series of legal rules is waiting to be discovered and applied to individual cases. Judicial decision-making draws upon legal principles to justify the processes and outcomes of judging; it is not determined by them. Those who are judged are often fitted into a framework that transforms them into a series of legally relevant actions and characteristics. This creates the image of objectivity and marginalizes broader questions of social justice. This conclusion reflects Marxist critiques of the ways in which law legitimizes and naturalizes inequalities (see pp. 19–24). It has also informed an extensive critique of human rights (discussed in more detail below).

The past pages have provided a brief overview and critique of the dominant jurisprudential perspectives. Each approach fails to fully acknowledge the effects of the social on the identification, articulation and application of law. In the following discussion we extend this criticism through an interrogation of some of the fundamental pillars of the Western legal system – equality, objectivity and the law's relationship to the public and private realms. There are of course others, notably the full complement of concepts suggested by Bottomley and Parker (1994), listed on pp. 50–1. Nonetheless, these three have been subject to extensive sociological critique and as such, provide an insight into sociological approaches to the nature of law and the criminal justice system.

Equality

The **equality** of all men (the term is used advisedly) is a fundamental pillar of liberal political and legal philosophy. If each individual is equally valuable, and equally a citizen, it follows that each has a legitimate claim to be judged by the law in the same way. This is the principle of *formal equality*. Traditionally, formal equality has been the primary aim within liberal democratic legal systems. It is purely concerned with the treatment of individuals. As we shall see, this is a narrow focus that ignores questions of social justice and the possibility of systematic or structural discrimination. This has led many sociologists and scholars to conclude that although equality is fundamental to the rule of law, its promise is not always fulfilled.

In contrast, *substantive equality* addresses the context in which the law is applied, and the consequences of its application. This is a concept that has more recently been acknowledged as a legitimate legal principle, perhaps most controversially through equal opportunity legislation and/or 'quotas'. The approach argues that formal equality presumes a pre-existing sameness among citizens, but sociologists have long recognized socio-economic characteristics such as income, educational level, gender, sexuality or ethnicity as important in structuring social life. Institutions and interactions are shot through with relations of power, inequality and difference. This raises the question: How can the law treat people equally when they are not in fact the same?

Within classical jurisprudence, differences are irrelevant to the processes of judging and legislating. People can be treated equally through the process of **abstraction**, an intellectual exercise that strips individuals of their social characteristics, experiences, and histories in so far as they are deemed to have no bearing on the issues at hand.

Their actions are relocated from a social to a legal context (Naffine, 1990). As a result, those who come before the law are conceived of as abstract individuals, who are ascribed the characteristics of the legal being of Western liberal philosophy. People are rendered alike, and so they can be treated alike for the purposes of the law. They have no race, gender or class in so far as they are formal legal subjects.

Formally, the legal subject is a free and autonomous agent. This is implicit in the construct of the rational actor who is a fundamental element of liberal legal philosophy, and the presumption of individualism. In contrast to the claims of classical liberal jurisprudence, critical legal scholars and feminists have argued that the abstract individual of the law is in fact a very particular being, not a universal one. Ngaire Naffine (1990: 53), for instance, argues that the being is one who is suited to flourish in modern, capitalist societies: *he* is 'able bodied, autonomous, rational, educated, monied, competitive and essentially self-interested'. Other theorists emphasize the unspoken assumptions about the ethnicity of the legal individual. In effect, the presumed characteristics of the legal individual are those of the group of people who are privileged in the daily workings of the social world, even if this is not recognized in the abstract realm.

Critics argue the law and its subjects have been constructed in terms that best fit the experiences of one, already privileged group in society. This has implications for formal and substantive justice. In terms of formal justice, we are forced to consider the extent to which particular legal principles can be universally applied in the 'real' world. In terms of substantive justice, those who do not conform to the ideal are unlikely to enjoy outcomes as favourable as those upon whom the law is patterned. More fundamentally, as Naffine (1990: 53) bluntly comments: 'it is a nonsense to abstract people from their social contexts, because we are all so much a part of them'. We can consider this comment in more detail by focusing on feminist debates on gender equality. These issues have become one of the defining features of the contemporary socio-legal landscape.

Feminist debate has emphasized three approaches to equal treatment. The first is formal equality, leading to strictly identical treatment. We have already described this with reference to the liberal ideal of equality, which does not recognize any systematic and meaningful differences between social categories. It claims that people are fundamentally alike and should be treated as such. Any differences that do exist are considered to be legally irrelevant. This approach has been historically useful in arguing for suffrage for women, or formal equality for indigenous people in Australia, or African Americans in the USA. If all people are legally identical, there can be no argument for denying citizenship rights or legal benefits to particular groups of people.

Regardless of its usefulness, there are a number of problems with formal equality. Most obviously, as we have already briefly noted, this approach fails to recognize the existence of entrenched social and economic differences between people. There are systematic inequalities between men and women, classes, and ethnic groups, to name but a few categories. These are not biological, nor are they necessarily ubiquitous, nor unchangeable, but they are often based on ideologies and institutional practices that are not easily ignored or denied, and their outcomes are real. Extending formal equality to groups who have been systematically discriminated against may reinforce social and legal inequalities because it fails to address the context that structures their choices and actions and others' responses to them.

Additionally, the approach does not interrogate the implications of treating people 'alike'. When we talk about similarity, similarity to whom? In fact, the particular experiences of the liberal subject remain the yardstick against which others are measured. This in turn raises a problem of comparison: treating men and women alike becomes practically impossible when the groups have different experiences that may be legally relevant. How can women be treated like men when men cannot experience menstruation, pregnancy, childbirth and lactation? Because men's experiences are the norm against which others are measured, strict equality requires the law to ignore important facets of many women's lives. Similarly, how does the law begin to compare the institutionalized racism faced by African Americans in education, employment, and in governance? How is it possible to compare the Indigenous Australian history of invasion, colonization, and under some definitions, genocide, with the manifestly bloodless and anonymous, but implicitly privileged legal subject? History and contemporary reality can be fundamentally unalike and it is arguably little more than an intellectual game to deny the significance of this.

In recognition of the above difficulties, an alternative approach to equality has been formulated: people are treated identically to the extent of their similarity, but are treated differently to the extent of their dissimilarity. This is the Aristotelian model of justice. It can recognize men and women's differences in terms of, for example, reproductive capabilities, but limits the extent of disparate treatment, and the basis upon which this discrimination occurs. Within this approach women and men's immutable biological differences have led to different social and economic positions and needs, and these must be addressed when the outcome is systematic discrimination or disadvantage.

There are a number of problems with the Aristotelian model. First, it can be difficult to foresee the outcomes of different treatment. What will benefit pregnant women, for example, and what will further disadvantage them? Second, how do we define disadvantage? Consider the actions of the American company, Bunker Hill, or the Australian Mt Isa Mines (see Graycar and Morgan, 1990). Both introduced a policy that excluded fertile female employees from any jobs that involved exposure to lead. The decision was made to protect foetuses from harm, and (perhaps more pertinently) save the company from legal claims arising out of damage to the foetus. Does such an action disadvantage women? On the one hand women's physical well-being – or at least their precious and fragile reproductive organs – and the health of their future children have been safeguarded. But, on the other hand, we might also argue that in limiting their access to employment, women's economic position has been undermined. Third, the boundaries of advantage also need to be considered. Reconsidering the example of protective guidelines, we can ask whether, regardless of the immediate outcomes for any one woman or group of women, it is in women's long-term interests to be defined, protected or differentiated on the basis of their reproductive capacities. Historically, women's claims to equality have often been countered with 'scientific' arguments that transformed presumed biological imperatives into social inequalities. Fourth, it is also important to note that the approach can stereotype women or other groups and universalize a very specific experience. The differential treatment in the above examples was imposed on the basis of women's potential to get pregnant, not their actual impending motherhood. Not all women are pregnant and not all will have children, regardless of their fertility.

Conceptually, treating 'unalikes, unalike' raises some of the same issues as formal equality. Regardless of which differences the court focuses upon, men are the standard from which others deviate. Catherine MacKinnon (1987: 37) makes this point clear:

> Why should you have to be the same as a man to get what a man gets simply because he is one? Why does maleness provide an original entitlement, not questioned on the basis of *its gender*, so that it is women – women who want to make a case of unequal treatment in a world men have made in their image (this is really the part that Aristotle missed) – who have to show in effect that they are men in every relevant respect, unfortunately mistaken for women on the basis of an accident of birth?

Thus, we turn to the final approach, one that moves beyond the concept of difference and instead reframes the issues as one of subordination and domination. Catherine MacKinnon, the first theorist to describe this approach in detail, argues that men and women are not only dissimilar; women are subordinated to men on the basis of their dissimilarity. She argues, 'difference is abstract and falsely symmetrical. [A] discourse of gender difference serves as ideology to neutralize, rationalize, and cover disparities of power, even as it appears to criticize them. Difference is the velvet glove on the iron fist of domination' (MacKinnon, 1989: 219) (see Box 2.2). Our earlier questions on which differences count for legal purposes, or which are disadvantageous, are no longer so significant in light of a new question: do current practices oppress women and advantage men?

Box 2.2   Catherine MacKinnon

MacKinnon has become one of the foremost feminist legal theorists. She has consistently focused on the structures of gendered domination and subordination that shape the interactions between men and women, and the construction and application of laws. She argues that the law is itself a structure of masculine domination, and women will not find relief from inequality through recourse to the law. In a somewhat contradictory move, she has been heavily involved in legislative attempts to ban pornography, a move that placed her in cahoots with far-right Christian fundamentalists – a paradoxical and somewhat confusing relationship in the eyes of many feminists.

MacKinnon has been very influential in theorizing the masculine nature of the law, but she has also been the subject of sustained criticism, largely on the grounds of her gender essentialism. MacKinnon's work has emphasized gender oppression at the expense of a focus upon other hierarchies. In particular, those working on racial disadvantages have pointed out that African-American women, or Indigenous Australian women, are not oppressed solely on the basis of their gender. Their ethnicity is also a fundamental component of their experience: it matters that they are African-American women, for example. This creates a context in which alternative relations of power play out, and in which structural disadvantages are imposed in ways that differ from the experiences of white women.

Catherine MacKinnon's approach demands change to social structures and laws. It reframes these claims in ways that move beyond an implied deficiency of women, or the assumption that any dissimilarity is little more than an *ad hoc* deviation from the norm. Her approach does not naturalize difference, nor does it flatten out the hierarchy in which difference is located. Women need not be either drawn into or marginalized from an already existent, patriarchal society. While percipient, MacKinnon's arguments are difficult to apply in practice. It is perhaps a little hopeful to assume that law-makers will be able to identify the power structures in which particular laws are located, and the extent to which they subordinate women.

Objectivity

The significance of a male benchmark in questions of equality is also pertinent in interrogating law's claims to **objectivity**. Carol Smart (1989) argues that this objectivity is what supports claims to law's status as 'truth'. It is the basis for law's universality and legitimacy. It buttresses the definition of reality that is presented by the courts. Legal positivism and the rule of law assume that the law and its agents are value-free. Decisions are based on disinterested and logical reasoning, with only the relevant issues taken into account. We have already noted this presumes that knowledge can be neutral, a series of facts and principles to be discovered by a decision-maker, rather than constructed within their own hermeneutic frame.

Various critiques have defined objectivity as a 'smokescreen' (Naffine, 1990: 44) that disguises the social and political nature of law and its application. People's social characteristics do play a role in the decision-making process, from the framing of legislation, through police discretion and into the courts. This is not necessarily manifest in deliberate prejudice. It may be a function of the socio-economic position and experiences that create the frame in which we view the world. To some extent this has been recognized, but subjectivity tends to be seen as a failing within the liberal legal ideal, rather than the prosaic reality of the criminal justice system.

When a failure of objectivity is recognized, concern is directed towards those people who are defined as 'different'. Women and African Americans in particular, have had their neutrality and objectivity questioned. Omatsu (1997) lists a number of instances where female adjudicators have been challenged on the basis of their feminist backgrounds. In 1993 a Canadian human rights adjudicator was removed from her post, with some suggestion that her experience in sex discrimination law, as well as her role in bringing a sex discrimination complaint against a university, contributed to a reasonable apprehension of bias. In an extreme example, in 1989 an Australian solicitor challenged the inclusion of a pregnant woman on a planning tribunal, presenting evidence from a well-regarded doctor that pregnant women 'no longer have the clarity of mind and precision of thought' as when not carrying a child. Complaints have also been directed towards male African American judges in the US legal system. That women and African American decision-makers are the focus of such complaints highlights the implicit content of 'neutrality', and its presumed relationship to objectivity.

The white heterosexual, middle-class, able-bodied men who constitute the majority of the bench are largely shielded from such claims. When they are sanctioned, it most often occurs in extreme instances. For example, in Australia in the early 1990s, Justice Bollen, when handing down his judgment on a case of marital rape, commented that it was acceptable for husbands to use 'rougher than usual handling' in order to 'persuade' their wives to agree to sex. In a rape case, Judge Bland, when directing the jury, claimed that 'no often subsequently means yes'. These decisions appalled feminists, and the widespread media attention created outrage among the general public. It might be argued that such outraged responses support claims that male judges are held accountable for their partiality or bias. But an alternative reading suggests that such examples reinforce the presumption that objectivity and impartiality are possible, by punishing those who breach this expectation, but only those who do so blatantly. MacKinnon notes that such individual instances of censure do not address the structural bias that creates an objectivity that is in fact gendered.

Box 2.3   Battered Woman Syndrome: An Example of the Male Standard of the Law

Questions of neutrality are relevant beyond the conclusions of individual decision-makers. The male point of view is systematically incorporated into legal principles. This is exemplified in the strategic use of Battered Woman Syndrome as evidence to support an argument of self-defence or provocation in circumstances where a woman has been charged with the murder of her abusive spouse. Typically, she kills her partner after long-term physical abuse, but not necessarily in a context of more immediate violence. Her husband might be sleeping when he is attacked, or sitting on the couch. This has made it difficult for women to claim they have acted in self-defence, which has as its basis a requirement that an attack be imminent, and that the force is proportionate to the threat. Provocation has demanded a direct relationship between some act and the loss of control that has led to the killing. The difficulties arise through the origins of these laws, and the ways in which they have been interpreted.

Both self-defence and provocation developed from male experiences. The classic self-defence scenarios involve a sudden and unexpected attack or a fight between two people of equal strength. Provocation often occurs as an insult of a personal nature. These have run the gamut from jibes about height, to impotency, to family honour. Neither instance has been developed to address the circumstances in which an abused woman might find herself: the subject of long-term abuse, having developed an intimate knowledge of her attacker's moods and patterns of violence, but weaker than her attacker, and often lacking the social, economic or personal resources necessary to leave the relationship. Additionally, the legal system has a history of minimizing the seriousness of domestic abuse, only reluctantly responding to complaints, prosecuting perpetrators, and often re-defining violence as marital discord. Thus, women find it difficult to present their experiences in ways that conform to the existing legal framework. The killing of an abusive spouse in the circumstances listed above has been interpreted as a revenge killing, an over-reaction to 'domestic problems', or vigilantism. In part, this is an example of individual judges' assumptions, but it also reflects a failure of the legal categories that have been developed through the common law.

Courts have now started to accept evidence that a woman suffered from Battered Woman Syndrome to support defences to murder. Battered Woman Syndrome is a psychological condition where, in a state of learned helplessness, women no longer feel that they have control over their lives or circumstances, and can no longer conceive of the possibility of leaving their abusive spouses. Its use has sparked a debate stretching over two decades, with many commentators concerned that it medicalizes and individualizes a social problem. It also implicitly defines the woman's actions as irrational when in fact they are an understandable response to her abuse. This critique points to the systematic gendering of legal concepts, and the ways in which the objectivity of the law in fact reflects the male experiences of violence, regardless of the benign intentions of individual judges.

How do these issues impact upon claims of the neutrality of the law and equality before it?
Do the problems associated with the use of BWS outweigh its usefulness?
Are the problems with the law structural, or might they be overcome by educating judges?

Public/Private Dichotomy

Liberal philosophy is concerned to minimize state power through limiting its intrusion into individual lives. Particular social spheres and relationships are defined as 'zones of exclusion' (Berns et al., 1996: 169), beyond the legitimate reach of state regulation. The distinction between the public and the private spheres is the cornerstone of circumscribing state power. The difference is not simply descriptive; it is also normative in its definitions of appropriate boundaries of control and power. But as we shall see, there is no objective content to the **public/private dichotomy**. The doctrine assumes that the private sphere is what MacKinnon (1989: 190) terms 'hermetic ... it is not part of or conditioned by anything systematic outside of it. It is personal, intimate, autonomous, particular, individual ... gender neutral.' Because it is seen to be separate from the state, acts that occur within it are understood to be unrelated to its policies and laws.

The distinction between the public and private spheres originates in the *laissez-faire* economic principles that demanded freedom from state intervention in business. Originally the divide was drawn between government/state and commerce/capitalist activities, with the latter defined as an inappropriate focus for government regulation. A distinction is also drawn on a different axis, between the civil sphere (including commercial and political activities) and the private, or domestic sphere, notably the family and sexuality (Berns, 1992). This second divide has enjoyed more systematic attention from social scientists working on the law and criminal justice system.

Sandra Berns (ibid.: 183) locates the origins of the family as a private sphere in classical liberal thought, which emphasized the autonomy of the head of the household. She argues:

> What was autonomous was not the family as such, but the authority of the male head of household. Because his dependents were not, strictly speaking, legal persons, the family itself was thought of as autonomous. The earlier political autonomy of feudal lords, their authority over those bound to them by vows of fealty, was re-instituted in vestigial form in a conception of paternal authority over the family as a unit, an authority that depended on his roles as breadwinner.

Yet despite its origins in patriarchal authority, many jurists and political theorists have avoided the question of power and justice within the family. Earlier theorists such as Rousseau and Hume explicitly excluded the family as a site of justice, defining the concept as solely a concern of the public realm, relevant only to the relations between men. The family was ordered on the basis of love, or, as Hume terms it, 'enlarged affections'. Thus, according to Rousseau 'in order to act right [a husband] has only to consult his heart'. However, it seems that too often, talks between a man and his heart break down.

Claims that the law has no place in the private sphere are empirically unsupportable and conceptually muddled. Legally there is no formal and universal zone of privacy (O'Donovan, 1985). Legislation and case law order people's lives, including their relationships and home lives, on a daily basis. The regulation is ambiguous and not rationally ordered with reference to explicitly stated overarching principles. But Berns (1992: 157–8) argues that in the day-to-day lives of its members, in the 'actual incidents of such relations, as opposed to the legal characterisation of appropriate incidents', the state maintains its distance, so long as behaviour conforms to the dominant social norms.

The absence of laws that directly order the private sphere does not equate to a lack of regulation. This is evident when we recognize marriage and families. These are defined by law, which thus draws the boundaries and identifies the parameters of the private sphere. In England, marriage was a church concern until the passage of Lord Harwick's Act in 1753. Today, marriage is regulated by the State, with the Church functioning in a largely symbolic role. The definition of marriage precludes the recognition of any relationship other than that between a man and a woman. Even those jurisdictions which extend the legal definition to gay and lesbian relationships still define the private sphere, albeit in slightly broader terms.

Abortion law has been held up as the pre-eminent example of the falsity of the public/private dichotomy. In the USA, the Supreme Court in *Roe v. Wade* established women's right to access abortions on the basis of a right to privacy. This right was implied in the fourteenth amendment to the US Constitution, which extends the right of personal liberty. Justice Douglas stated that 'a woman is free to make the basic decision whether to bear an unwanted child', on the basis that liberty included 'freedom of choice in the basic decisions of one's life respecting marriage, divorce, procreation, contraception, and the education and upbringing of children' (cited in Graycar and Morgan, 1990: 202).

The inspirational rhetoric on these 'basic decisions' has been undermined through subsequent failures to recognize the connections between the public and private spheres. Cases following *Roe v. Wade* held that a woman's right to privacy is a separate matter to the State's responsibility to protect or fund that right. The bench in *Harris v. McRae* accepted the argument that the US Federal Government was not required to fund abortions. Nine years later in *Webster v. Reproductive Health Services*, the US Supreme Court upheld a Missouri statute prohibiting the use of State resources in abortion procedures, save in instances when the woman's life is at stake. The legal principles upon which these are based are not applicable to other legal jurisdictions but the issues surrounding *Roe v. Wade* and the subsequent decisions have a conceptual relevance to our understanding of the existence and usefulness of any private/public distinction.

More significantly, claiming a right to privacy cannot address the structural issues associated with reproductive choices and privacy generally. Tribe (1985: 243) argues that 'a right to end pregnancy might be seen more plausibly as a matter of resisting sexual and economic domination than as a matter of shielding from public control "private" transactions between physicians and patients'. Similarly, calls to 'keep your laws off our bodies' frame the question as one of women excluding the State from a personal and private realm (Kingdom, 1985: 153). It might be more useful to consider the structural and ideological issues that define women as primarily mothers, the welfare system that provides inadequate income and other forms of support to women and poor families, the social disapproval of single motherhood, and the failure to provide useful sex education. Fundamentally, framing the issues in terms of privacy separates the interconnected private and public spheres.

There are other social dimensions beside gender that affect the ideas of public and private. For example, Jacques Donzelot (1979) describes the way in which the day-to-day lives of working-class families were policed through the medical profession and public heath programs that controlled how working-class families ordered their domestic routines. As poverty came to be seen as a moral fault, the state had a legitimate interest in regulating those families who struggled socially and financially. It did so indirectly, through encouraging a philanthropy that guided and assisted working-class families in conforming to the dominant, middle-class ideals of family life. The same movements, with their philanthropic overtones, legitimated middle-class women's movement from their families into the policing of working-class families.

Feminists have been concerned at the conceptual basis of the public/private dichotomy, and its results, in part because the law can refuse to intervene on the basis of liberal philosophical ideals, as much as it decides on other occasions to enter into bedrooms. The demarcation of the public and the private has been posited as a way to protect citizens from an intrusive state, but 'citizens' commonly means males. In the instances where the private sphere has been unregulated, women, not men, have suffered. In the criminal justice context this is evident in domestic violence:

- Domestic violence is often framed as a disagreement between two people (usually a man and a woman), and not a matter for the police. These attitudes have been held by the victims and perpetrators of such violence, the police and society at large.
- Until recently criminal charges against men who beat their wives were instigated by their victims, thus suggesting a civil matter, rather than a crime.
- In England the victims could not be compelled, and in other jurisdictions prosecutors and police were reluctant to compel, a battered wife to give evidence (Edwards, 1996: 191).
- Some indigenous writers argue that domestic violence among colonized people must be contextualized within the dispossession and racism suffered by all members. Colonial relations, rather than patriarchal relations, are the primary source of violence in the home. This adds another dimension to linkages between public and private, and highlights the ambiguous value of drawing the law further into relationships that have already suffered under the institutions of the dominant, white group.

As this discussion has highlighted, the usefulness of the public/private dichotomy is limited. Empirically, it is unsustainable, as the state has a long history of involvement in 'private lives'. Analytically, the fluid boundaries make it difficult to apply.

As Frances Olsen (1985) points out, if public and private are defined with reference to intervention and non-intervention, the issue becomes more unclear, as definitions are partially reliant on where each person stands. Additionally, the approach cannot take account of the varying experiences of 'privacy'. The reasons for and extent of intervention into family life are informed by class status and ethnicity. Further, as MacKinnon has argued, the dichotomy falsely presents each sphere as unrelated, when in fact the decisions, structures and practices in the public realm have significant consequences for the relationships and opportunities of family members.

Rights

In light of the on-going significance of globalization, it is useful to consider the concept of 'rights'. The language of rights permeates our everyday speech. When we argue that we have a 'right' to something, we are often using the phrase as short-hand, a way of claiming that our desires or needs are legitimate. 'Right' also has a formal legal meaning, one that is narrower than its colloquial invocation. This following section describes the nature of legal rights – their sources, aims and practical and jurisprudential significance – and the social scientific and jurisprudential critiques of the concept and its application. Once again, we will see that themes of culture and power need to be considered if the law is to be placed in context as a social artefact reflecting the nature of our contemporary society.

Citizenship rights and human rights

In the first instance we must distinguish between citizenship rights and human rights. Although published over half a century ago, T. H. Marshall's (1950) essay, 'Citizenship and Social Class' continues to provide the touchstone for descriptions of citizenship rights. In it, he presents three elements of citizenship. The first is civil rights, necessary for individual freedoms. The next is political rights, which allow people to involve themselves in the political processes of the state. Third, social rights ensure a basic standard of living. Marshall argues that these emerged over time, developing under particular philosophies. Over time the rights become cumulative. This is significant when we consider the seemingly paradoxical situation where citizenship rights do not dismantle social inequalities. Marshall argues that it was not until the twentieth century and the implementation of social rights that inequality could be systematically (though imperfectly) addressed through claims to citizenship rights.

Marshall's approach and discussion have been criticized on a number of grounds. Roach Anleu (2000: 204–8) lists the following:

• Inconsistent definitions of 'citizenship'.
• The theory is weakened in light of the roll-back of the welfare state.

- There is a failure to look beyond class to systematically consider ethnicity, sexuality and gender as dimensions of inequality.
- He neglects to test his theory beyond the English context.
- Marshall never critically and properly considers the extent to which nation–states deny rather than extend citizenship rights.

As Bryan Turner (1997) notes, citizenship rights are limited. Citizenship can be withheld, an effective means of denying people these rights. Further, the types of rights available are prescribed by the State through law and policy. Finally, the State may grant different rights to groups, thus creating 'second-class citizens'. Human rights, in contrast, attach to people simply by virtue of their human-ness. Thus, they have greater potential to offer protection from abuse, even if this is often unrealized.

Human rights, as we know them, arose within the logic of modernity, in that modernity is 'the attempt to find absolute grounds for knowledge, to discover abstract, transcendent principles that would be the basis for all philosophical questioning' (Davies, 1994: 221). They are understood as the children of reason, evidence of the moral, social and economic evolution of human kind (Gaete, 1991). The source of rights varies according to one's philosophical position. In their early incarnation in the seventeenth and eighteenth centuries, particular rights were understood to exist independently of human will or state decree, thus reflecting natural law principles (see pp. 58–61). Bottomley and Parker (1994: 30) argue that this conception gradually waned and with the rise of legal positivism and utilitarianism, rights were recognized as limited to and dependent upon law and legislation. Today (with some exceptions) people can claim rights only if their country is a signatory to the instrument that enumerates them (Aceves, 2000: 130).

The question of the sources of rights regained immediacy following World War II. The atrocities committed by the Nazis and the prosecutorial needs at the Nuremberg trials shocked people and contributed to a formal recognition of a series of claims and interests that deserved supervision and protection, across state boundaries and across time. These were first incorporated within the Universal Declaration of Human Rights (UDHR), in 1948. This was the first document that attempted to systematically and exhaustively list human rights. The UDHR echoes the precepts of natural law. The enumerated rights are described as universal truths. Their existence is independent of state law; they are omnipresent, valuable and worthy of international supervision and protection (Otto, 1998: 17). This is evident when we consider the first clause of the preamble to the Universal Declaration of Human Rights. The declaration begins, 'Whereas recognition of the inherent dignity and of the equal and inalienable rights of all members of the human family is the foundation of freedom, justice and peace in the world'. Rolando Gaete (1991: 149) notes that the first clause is 'not a legal statement but an ethical truth and a political programme', recognizing the pre-existence of rights, and presenting them as a 'natural truth, which is not for humans to change because it predates them'.

The original and relatively well-established set of rights has since been termed the first generation of rights. They are the civil and political rights. The second generation of rights are social, cultural and economic. Since these initial formulations, a compendium of other claims has been established. Collective rights, attaching to groups of people, rather than individuals, are categorized as third generation. These are advanced by developing nations, and include the collective rights to independence and development, the right to peace and the right to economic sustainability. The fourth generation, argued by indigenous people, include the right to self-determination. Today international law is cluttered with resolutions and conventions – many of them toothless.

The rights documents frame their provisions in terms that imply a natural law basis. But in the practice of international law these are not binding on states until they become signatories to the instruments and implement domestic legislation to recognize and enforce them. Thus, the natural law stands in tension to the positivist approach informing the State's direct role in creating rights that can be claimed. But then again, breaches of fundamental rights, as occurred in the genocides in Rwanda or Bosnia-Herzegovina can be prosecuted (on the individual level) regardless of state commitment to human rights ideals … if there is the political will to do so.

Rights are well entrenched in international law but their theoretical or jurisprudential basis and practical legitimacy are contested. Questions as to the universal, inalienable and indivisible characteristics of rights lie at the root of these critiques. Much of this questioning of universalism has been framed in terms of **cultural relativism** – the idea that all values are arbitrary and none can be privileged as a source of truth to judge others. However, this approach is itself being reconsidered. It implicitly constructs culture as a coherent, integrated and unchanging set of beliefs and processes, yet in reality, the components of any culture are contested and reinterpreted, and they change with the passage of time and a variety of social processes (Preis, 1996). Local cultures are not isolated from the broader world but exist in tension and dialogue with it. Thus, the system of international human rights can be used as a resource and strategy for resistance – it is not only a site of Western domination (Merry, 1997).

Post-structuralist and Postmodernist Critiques

Post-structuralists and postmodernists argue that human rights are not universal, 'true' or unquestionable but are entrenched in and constitutive of relations of power. This approach rejects any claim that law – or any other discourse – exists independently of human construction. Thus, it is not possible to identify or discover foundational concepts. Given their source, it is not possible that any right or concept can be universally applicable. Nor is knowledge rationally ordered in ways that legitimate the privileging of first generation rights (Otto, 1998).

The presence of states that contested even the first generation of rights suggests that rights are not in fact universal. Saudi Arabia, for example, rejected the Declaration on the basis that it could not reflect the Islamic tradition. There was also opposition from Communist states, which interpreted civil and political rights as promoting a primacy of the individual over social obligation (ibid.: 19). Other legal scholars have also pointed out that pre-eminent rights reflect only Western democratic ideals and do not acknowledge the religious, cultural, and political contexts of different countries (Merry, 1997: 248).

Disparities are not a simple question of difference – they are used to discursively construct the identity and worth of other states. When countries do not extend the rights and freedoms imposed by the relevant declarations, they are characterized as oppressive or backward regimes; different priorities or culturally informed expectations of the state and citizens are redefined as failures of civilization. Law and power are entwined in their role in the definition and imposition of rights (Otto, 1998). This is evident in the ways in which rights are used to justify attempts to dictate policy to non-Western and some Western countries. They have provided the basis for military, economic and cultural incursions into less powerful states.

Further, rights cannot address systematic inequalities in the global system. We have already noted that the first generation rights – civil and political rights – are privileged in international law. These reflect the state ideals of developed countries. The focus upon the individual renders the rights of groups – whether in the form of countries or indigenous groups or other interest groups – marginal. And yet many argue that these are the basis for any attempts to alter inequitable global power relations.

Issues about the universality of rights, and the power relations in which they are implicated in turn raise questions as to the efficacy and appropriateness of rights as a strategy for change. A recourse to the language of rights has often been used to legitimize the oppression of particular groups or individuals. This concern has been particularly evident in the critiques of critical legal theorists, to which we now turn.

Further Critiques of Rights

Critical legal studies scholars have developed a broad-ranging and sustained critique of the concept of rights. Significant causes for concern include the following:

- Rights are not abstract, universal and enduring. They are incoherent and unstable. They are developed in and by particular societies and are dependent upon material social, political, economic and cultural structures (Pritchard, 1995; Tushnet, 1984).
- The language of rights masks the need for social and political change. They hide the institutional and structural sources of inequality (Miller, 1998: 54).
- Recourse to rights keeps people dependent upon the State for change.
- Rights often reinforce the privileges of dominant groups in society, at the expense of those who are socially, economically, culturally or politically marginalized (Tushnet, 1984).

- Rights separate out the individual from the obligations and relationships that bind them to their community.
- The articulation of rights is associated with technical indeterminacy. This means that real, embodied and emotional experiences are translated into vague and universal concepts. The process is necessary in order to render them recognizable by law but in so doing, experiences become universalized and trivialized. They are not valued for their own sake, and are not protected or pursued unless they can be measured in a utilitarian equation (Miller, 1998: 58; Tushnet, 1984: 1377).

Not surprisingly, feminists have also critiqued the language and application of rights. There are instruments that specifically recognize the interests and needs of women (Declaration on the Elimination of Violence against Women; Convention on the Elimination of All Forms of Discrimination Against Women; Convention on the Political Rights of Women), but they do so in an incomplete way. First, there is concern that the recognition and enforcement of rights continue to occur within patriarchal legal institutions. Further, the content of rights and the framework of the development continue the presumptions of the gender neutrality of the law (Charlesworth et al., 1991). But as Catherine MacKinnon (1989: 248) points out, rights 'authorize male experience'. Additionally, human rights have been constructed on the presumption of common humanity, and this fails to recognize the ways gender structures experience (Rowland, 1995). Thus, women's needs and interests have not been fully and systematically incorporated in international instruments. For example, the insistence on third generation and fourth generation rights has not specifically incorporated the claims of indigenous women, or those in developing countries (Wright, 1992). Also, the rights framework accepts the division of society into public and private spheres. Typical injuries sustained by women are perpetrated in the domestic sphere but human rights discourses are linked to state and public action/inaction (Byrnes, 1992).

The Use of Rights Discourse

To counter the above critiques, others have argued that rights are one of the few legitimate and politically effective means of gaining advances for under-privileged groups. Otto (1998: 17–18) has noted the importance of the discourse as

> a grass roots language, as well as a formal legal framework, which supported decolonisation, mobilisation around sexual and racial discrimination, the dismantling of apartheid in South Africa, movements against authoritarian regimes, and the rights of a multitude of other exploited and subordinated groups including indigenous peoples, workers, children, lesbians and gay men, the elderly, ethnic minorities and people with disabilities.

Rights are a means of legitimately calling upon the state to recognize the needs of minorities, and demand that it acts. Rights promote the idea that – formally – all people are equal, a helpful proposition for those who are otherwise categorized as society's 'other' and denied the benefits of citizenship (Williams, 1991: 148). Patricia Williams (ibid.: 53) passionately argues 'For the historically disempowered the conferring of rights is symbolic of all the denied aspects of their humanity: rights imply a respect that places one in the referential range of self and others, that elevates one's status from human body to social being.' Williams (1988: 61) forcefully notes that 'This country's worst historical moments have not been attributable to rights-*assertion*, but to a failure of rights-*commitment*' (emphasis in the original).

Further, as Carol Smart (1989: 1) notes, framing claims within a rights discourse suggests a degree of autonomy and assertiveness. In contrast, framing claims in terms of need linguistically reproduces the inequitable power inequities, demanding as it does that men and women are reliant on the beneficence of the state. Damien Miller (1998: 50–1) has offered a similar argument with reference to the interests and needs of indigenous people. Rights constitute an empowering frame within which to claim justice. In particular, they are an alternative to 'welfarism', which has also been used to pursue the interests of indigenous groups, but which is often informed by paternalism. Third, rights oblige states to meet minimum standards; people are not dependent upon their good will. These arguments suggest that as much as rights are discursively, symbolically or theoretically suspect, they are also a practical and useful strategy, available to those who have traditionally been denied that basis for arguing for equality.

Sociological Critiques and Interpretations

The concept of rights was familiar to the early sociologists; claims existed before they were collected and formalized in international law. Early sociologists rejected any natural law interpretation of rights. They recognized their social basis, and in different ways expressed their reservations of them as strategies for change, and as useful sociological concepts. In *Professional Ethics and Civic Morals*, for example, Durkheim (1992) evaluates law from a positivist framework. He was consistent in arguing that social facts (in this case, moral facts that were external, constraining and collective), not philosophy, were the appropriate focus for scientific sociological attention. Marx was also unenthusiastic about the concept. In *On the Jewish Question* he critiques and ultimately rejects rights on the basis of their individualism. Any reliance on rights papered over the real and competitive relationships between people, and could not create the basis for true freedom from social and economic oppression. Weber approaches the question from a different perspective. Within the rationalization of law Weber recognized a continuing role for claims to substantive rather than formal law (i.e., justice, rather than procedure) and saw rights as a basis for these claims. They were very useful for the lower and working classes, and stood in opposition to the dominant classes' reliance on formal theories of law, which were used to control other social groups. These approaches, although divergent in terms of their conclusions, laid the foundation for contemporary sociologists' difficulties in engaging with the notions of rights.

Contemporary sociologists remain wary of the source and usefulness of rights (Connell, 1995: 25). Malcolm Waters (1996), for example, has argued from a social constructionist perspective that the development of any regime of rights is the outcome of political negotiation and conflict and all rights are contingent, varying across time and culture (see also Connell, 1995). R. W. Connell (ibid.: 35) notes that four sets of interests have been served by the politics of human rights:

- the countries victorious in World War II, who used rights to undermine their enemies;
- 'cold warriors', who sought to undermine their opponents;
- superpowers, who use rights to legitimate their intervention in other countries;
- oppressed groups, for whom rights are a means of change.

Bryan Turner (1993, 1997) has attempted to create a new sociological theory of rights that moves beyond critique and description. He ties his argument to the one thing all humans have in common – our bodies are fragile. This 'foundationalist approach' defines human rights as a means of protecting our corporeality, necessary in light of the precariousness of State protection. Their institutionalization results from powerful groups' recognition that they may be subject to physical attack and damage. They thus institute a regime to protect themselves and in so doing, cannot help but protect others. Turner's approach is useful as a means of extending sociological critique so that it forms the basis of an alternative. However, protecting our corporeality will not necessarily safeguard other civil and political expectations.

To sum up, rights are a slippery concept. Our immediate reaction is often positive – it is counter-intuitive to mount a sustained attack on human rights, or citizenship rights for that matter, because we are so used to seeing them as a protection. But the critiques presented in this section are not simply academic word games. They sensitize us to the role of law in creating and sustaining power disparities and a particularized representation of the world.

Conclusion

This chapter has covered a lot of different issues in order to familiarize you with some of the significant debates that arise when we consider the sources and meaning of law from within a sociological framework. It should be clear to you that 'law' is more a social artefact than a set of pre-existing concepts and rules. Our legal system, and what is valued within it, emerge through the ebb and flow of social and cultural forces. The idealized vision of law generally and liberal legal theory in particular becomes increasingly problematic in the following chapters as we describe the ideologies and practices that constitute the key criminal justice institutions, and the divergent impacts on social groups.

Study Questions

1 Consider the difference between law and norms. Which do you think plays a greater role in shaping your actions? Make a list of actions that (a) are illegal; (b) breach social norms; and (c) do both. Discuss these with others in the group. Did all members of the group agree about the norms you have identified? Why/why not?
2 How important are processes of globalization in shaping the legal system?
3 Review the principles of legal positivism and natural law. Then familiarize yourself with a morally loaded legal issue and apply the different approaches. Which do you personally prefer? Which is more useful as a foundation for applying law? Why?
4 Research an example of social inequality. Is it best addressed through formal or substantive equality? How would Catherine MacKinnon's understanding of dominance and subordination fit into the picture?
5 To what extent are rights useful as a tool to promote people's well-being? Do they do more harm than good?

Glossary of Key Terms

abstraction – A process of reasoning through which a real person is transformed into the legal subject, retaining only those individual characteristics that are deemed to be legally relevant.

adversarial proceedings – Cases are conducted through the contest of two parties who present opposing arguments. A neutral arbiter (jury or judge) determines the outcome.

citizenship rights – A series of social, civil and welfare entitlements that attach to membership within a state.

civil law system – A legal system characterized by codified laws that have been collected and interpreted by jurists. Most obviously associated with European jurisdictions.

common law system – A body of law developed in England and exported to its colonies. Created through the gradual and *ad hoc* determination of cases.

critical legal studies – A group of legal scholars who critique dominant legal ideals on the basis that they reify law and mystify its political nature. They explicitly seek to facilitate a more just society.

cultural relativism – The view that all values and beliefs are culturally embedded and there is no universal 'truth' that stands outside of this.

Enlightenment – An era that heralded the rise of liberal philosophy and the modern era. Marked by a presumption that knowledge is rational, truth exists and can be discovered and progress is possible and inevitable.

equality – Includes formal equality, which demands that all people are treated in the same way, and substantive equality, recognizing and acting upon significant differences between people or groups in order to achieve a particular outcome.

human rights – A series of entitlements that are not dependent upon membership of a state. They attach to people because they are human. Human rights have been systematically defined through the United Nations.

independence of the judiciary – Buttresses the separation of powers and promotes the rule of law by ensuring that judges are not appointed for political reasons and are not punished for their legal decisions.

individualism – Individuals and not society are the important unit for the focus and activities of the law. Law aims to protect and order individual people, not society as a whole.

inquisitorial system – The judge plays an active role in the investigation of charges and conduct of the court case.

judicial activism – A charge levelled at judges who are seen to deviate from precedent without legal or factual grounds. Judicial activists create rather than discover law, which breaches the principles of legal positivism.

justice – In common language, the 'rightness' of an outcome. Justice includes formal and substantive justice. Formal justice emphasizes the process of applying the law. Substantive justice emphasizes the nature of the outcome.

legal formalism/positivism – A pre-eminent jurisprudential school that has defined the proper framework within which legal decision-making occurs. Laws and judicial decisions emerge through rigorous legal reasoning; their validity is determined upon this basis, not the moral worth of their content.

legal realism – A precursor of critical legal studies. It rejected positivist/formalist claims and emphasized the human and therefore biased nature of legal decision-making.

liberal political philosophy – Structures legal practice and ideals in Western democracies. Its manifestations vary, but they have in common an acceptance of the Rule of Law, and the pre-eminence of individuals and their liberty.

liberty – Freedom. This includes freedom from (negative liberty) and freedom to (positive liberty).

natural law – A jurisprudential school that argues the legitimacy of man-made law is determined with reference to its fit to pre-existing, divine or non-constructed legal principles.

norms – Informal rules and expectations about behaviour.

objectivity – The ideal and presumption that decisions are made and laws created without bias, through a disinterested consideration of the issues at stake and application of the relevant legal principles.

public/private dichotomy – Conceives of two arenas of social life, unrelated to each other. The public sphere has traditionally been a 'man's world', guided by the precepts of liberal philosophy and ordered by State law. The private sphere is the domestic sphere, which is often defined as beyond the legitimate reach of the State.

rational actors – The liberal legal subject is presumed to behave instrumentally so that the ends of actions are obviously and reasonably facilitated by the means available.

rule of law – Law must be value-free, predictable, and applicable to those who create it.

separation of powers – A system of checks and balances in which decision-making, law creation and law enforcement are allocated to different organs of government to prevent a monopoly of power.

utilitarianism – Judges the value of action/inaction by measuring the good achieved. Something is justified when it results in the greatest good for the greatest number of people.

Suggested Further Reading

Those who are interested in more details on legal history might try *Law and Revolution* by Harold Berman (1983), although it is not particularly sociological; for this, read the relevant parts of Weber's (1978) classic, *Economy and Society*. Stephen Bottomley and Stephen Parker (1994) and Roger Cotterrell (1992) offer excellent overviews and critiques of the theoretical underpinnings of Western legal systems. Ngaire Naffine's (1990) *Law and the Sexes* canvasses many of the feminist critiques of liberal philosophy; Catherine MacKinnon's (1987, 1989) work is challenging but worth reading in the original. Discussions of the theoretical and empirical and practical implications of human rights can be found in the journal *Human Rights Quarterly*.

Suggested Websites

http://www.alrc.gov.au/ In 1994 The Australian Law Reform Commission published a comprehensive review of gendered legal issues. *Equality Before the Law: Women's Equality* provides a very useful summary of key theoretical and practical issues.

http://jurist.law.pitt.edu/ Occasionally you can find useful resources on *Jurist: The Legal Education Network*. Click on the working paper links under scholarship to access work by American law professors and jurists. Most of the work is not socio-legal or sociological, and much of it is highly conceptual, but there are some useful discussions and working papers.

http://mishpat.net/ Mishpat.net is a legal information site. Click on the Jurisprudence link to search for commentaries, lectures and original materials.

http://www.un.org Students can search for the declarations and covenants described in this chapter through searching the UN website. The site also provides detailed information on topical issues and the structures of the UN.

http://www.echr.coe.int/ The European Court of Human Rights Website offers features similar to those listed above.

http://www1.umn.edu/humanrts/ The University of Minnesota Human Rights Library is an excellent gateway site.

3 The Police

Introduction

We can begin this chapter by thinking about the role and function of the police within the criminal justice system. This will serve to introduce the themes covered later in this chapter. Following Barlow (1996), we highlight a number of reasons why the study of the police should be central to the study of criminal justice.

The police have the job of identifying and arresting offenders, discovering breaches of the law and maintaining public order. In effect, they have primary responsibility for enforcing the law. This means that they are the point of entry into the criminal justice system and the place where words on the statutes are converted into activity that maintains social order. Because of this we can think of the police as gatekeepers of the criminal justice system – people who decide which individuals or groups are investigated or arrested, given a fine or ticket, told to move on, pulled over or otherwise policed. Hence the police play a major role in determining who is officially defined or labelled as a 'criminal' and will be processed for action by the courts and prisons. Consequently, police discretion has emerged as a central theme in research. This concerns the decision of the individual officer whether to make an arrest and, thereby, start the formal criminal justice process in motion, or to take no action. The police also have considerable freedom in choosing which kinds of offences are targeted. Because police resources are finite, strategic priorities have to be made in enforcing the law. Along with discretion, this pattern of working hard at some issues and neglecting others means that the police have a significant impact in determining what the law means in practice. Such decisions are invariably influenced by input from the community, the political world, the media and legal codes as these collide with entrenched or innovative policing cultures and strategies. Paradoxically, the fact that the police make priorities also influences crime patterns by opening up or closing down criminal opportunities. Criminal activity will often flourish in fields of illegal endeavour where the police are unwilling or unable to expend resources. Likewise, a displacement effect will often see crime move from neighbourhoods that are heavily targeted to those nearby.

The police are also important as a symbol of the law. For many people the only contact they will have with the criminal justice system is with the police – perhaps through a traffic violation or in reporting a crime. These experiences can have a major impact upon subsequent perceptions of the law as a whole. Images of the police are also prevalent in the media. Television series on the police far outnumber those on other components of the criminal justice system. To obtain some idea of the cultural significance of policing, simply flick through a weekly television guide and count the number of shows. Although these media portrayals and direct personal experiences are plentiful, it is equally important to acknowledge that they are diverse. We can think of the police variously as a symbol of authority and social responsibility, as glamorous and exciting or as racist and oppressive. Which of these we choose might well depend on our social location, life experiences and outlook on life.

Finally, we need to think of the police as a political and economic force. The police are a vast bureaucracy that soaks up a large proportion of the total budget for the criminal justice system. They are important as a large employer (London's Metropolitan Police, for example, has around 30,000 officers) and as a purchaser of goods and services. In most nations doctrines about the separation of powers suggest the police should be outside politics. Yet reality repeatedly shows them to be major players. The police will often lobby the government for resources or for changes to the law. In many cases the police have supported authoritarian and conservative regimes, especially when 'get tough on crime' policies promise more money and high-level support. In the United States there are exceptionally strong ties between police forces and the political parties in big cities, with the post of Police Chief almost as politicized as that of Mayor. The police are also political in a less obvious way as an ideological symbol. In other words, their political importance is tied up with their cultural meaning. For example, from 1850 to around 1950 the British police were generally seen in positive terms as bearers of legitimate authority. To most, if not all people, the 'Bobby' symbolized honesty, decency and the conservative possibilities of a society built upon peaceful coexistence. In the subsequent 50 years PC Plod became a 'pig'. Scandals and corruption became widely reported, the policing of riots, strikes and racial minorities was seen as controversial, and the police were seen as a bureaucracy of outsiders (Reiner, 1985). In this new image, the police were a token of a divided society, with their policy and reputation taking on a manifest rather than latent political significance. In other words, the police were no longer seen as 'above politics', but were increasingly seen as a fundamental part of it.

To sum up, we should study the police because of the following:

- They determine what the law means in practice through enforcement activity, discretion and priorities.
- They are a key cultural symbol.
- They have political and economic importance.

The History of Policing

Tracing the evolution of the contemporary police force provides a classic illustration of some of the major themes of social theory. Most notably we can see at work

differentiation into a specialized role and a linked process of **professionalization**. The emergence of the police is commonly seen as a response to the social change in the West as an agrarian society shifted towards industrial modernity. During the Middle Ages policing was a largely voluntary and honorific activity. Within the feudal system members of the nobility and leaders in the community were responsible not only for maintaining peace, but also for collecting taxes. The titles of High Constable and Sheriff were often bestowed upon the aristocracy in recognition of this status. Hence in Robin Hood mythology the Sheriff of Nottingham is an overlord who tries to bring to heel a bunch of brigands objecting to his tax-collecting policies! Petty Constables were members of the community appointed for a period of a year and were charged with ensuring good behaviour at the parish level. These men were of variable quality, largely untrained and often subject to the authority of aldermen and justices of the peace (Emsley, 1996). Law and order were also maintained by watchmen, especially in towns. Their most important job was to patrol the streets at night and look out for trouble. Responsibility for detecting, apprehending and investigating offenders belonged to a haphazard mix of these watchmen, along with magistrates, aldermen and the victims of crime themselves. The result was a system that was community driven, but also amateurish, often ineffective, prone to abuses and lacking in a healthy separation of powers.

By the eighteenth century such a system was in crisis. Cities were growing rapidly thanks to the rise of manufacturing during the Industrial Revolution. These urban settings lacked the customary social ties that had restrained crime in small-scale agrarian settings. Migration and poverty exacerbated the problems arising from anomie and anonymity. Elites came to believe there was a rapidly growing 'criminal class' that was in need of regulation and control – a problem evidenced by mobs and riots. Fear of crime was on the rise, with urban disorder, whether real or potential, understood as a major social problem (for a review, see Brogden, 1987: 5–9; Emsley, 1996). This was particularly the case in London, where in a publication of 1796 the reform advocate Patrick Colquhoun approximated 115,000 people (about 10 percent of the population) were profiting from crime. Big cities were seen as magnets for vice as malefactors flocked to them from outlying areas. Hence Colquhoun considered London to be 'the general receptacle for the idle and depraved of almost every country, and certainly from every quarter of the dominions of the Crown' (quoted in Emsley, 1996: 18).

In the United Kingdom citizens were reluctant to use the army to solve the crime problem. Bringing in the army would be like using the sledge-hammer of force to crack the nut of disorder. There was also fear that this practice might lead to anti-democratic outcomes such as martial law. A solution was found in the Metropolitan Police Act of 1829. This provided for a full-time, salaried, uniformed professional police force that was under the control of government. Originally intended as a solution for London alone, the Metropolitan Police Act became a template for subsequent police forces. Thanks to support from the Home Secretary, Sir Robert Peel, an unintended consequence of the Act was the emergence of 'Bobby' and 'Peeler' as nicknames for police in the UK. Less trivially, the Act clearly separated the police from the army and led to the formation of the doctrine of **policing by consent**. This is the notion that the police are a substantially unarmed body who rely upon community support and goodwill, rather than force, in the conduct of their duty. As such, the Metropolitan Police have become an important model for other settings, especially in the English-speaking world. In Boston, in 1837, for example, the first modern police force in the United States was established following the Metropolitan Police pattern.

From the perspective of social theory we should understand the origins of the police not only as a historically specific response to urbanization and disorder, but also as part of wider shifts tied to the emergence of modernity. They denote a move from a society where agricultural elites controlled criminal justice to one where the urban bourgeoisie were responsible (O'Malley, 1983). They are also an indicator of the growing power of the state as it mopped up the unruly fringes of society in the transition to modernity. As discussed earlier, Max Weber defined the modern state as an organization that held a monopoly on the legitimate use of force (see pp. 36–37). Because powers related to the administration of criminal justice and the use of force were taken away from the aristocracy, citizens and civil society we can understand the rise of a professional police force as strongly consistent with this model of centralizing political control. The Weberian perspective also stresses the strongly bureaucratic and rational organization of the modern world and the way that this replaced *ad hoc* systems of traditional government. These are qualities we find in policing organizations with their developed hierarchies, elaborate structures of power and written rules of procedure. Such attributes contrast markedly with the informal community administration of policing functions in pre-modern times. The rise of the Metropolitan Police model also shows changing understandings of the nature of social life. Egon Bittner (1990) argues that policing reflected the ethos that old ways of controlling disorder were no longer suitable. During the nineteenth century the belief was that the haphazard, repressive and violent control of dissent was no longer acceptable. Forms of social control should be peaceable or in some way 'civilized' and the police were a step towards this aim of a permanently peaceable society (note how this position is consistent with that of Elias, see pp. 37–39). As part of this social contract the police were given a monopoly over the use of force and the ability to compel people to obey. Many, including Bittner himself, have claimed this monopoly on force to be the defining feature of policing.

Although we have mapped out a core story in the paragraphs above, it is also important to remember that debate exists concerning how to most accurately narrate the rise of the police (Reiner, 1985). The traditional liberal perspective emphasizes shared problems caused by urbanization and focuses on the democratic and consensual origins of the police. During the 1970s, however, critical theories provided another narrative of the ties between modernity and the birth of the police. These saw the police as an instrument through which the ruling class controlled the dissent of a growing working class in the nineteenth-century city. The police imposed for the first time a routinized apparatus of bureaucratic surveillance over marginal populations in the interests of this dominant class, not the interests of the community as a whole. Ties have also been noted between policing and colonialism in the nineteenth century. The claim has been made that dominant histories of policing tend to be Eurocentric and ethnocentric. They neglect the fact that the evolution of early policing was linked with the maintenance of order in colonial settings (Brogden, 1987). The Royal Irish Constabulary, for example, pre-dated the Metropolitan Police and had some of the qualities of an army of occupation. Operations were supervised from Dublin Castle, officers lived barracks and conducted paramilitary policing activities aimed at the suppression of political dissent among the Irish and the maintenance of British rule (Tobias, 1972).

We have explored some of the ways that the emergence of the police can be tied to the transition to modernity. Some scholars argue that we are now moving beyond modernity towards a state known variously as postmodernity or late-modernity in which policing itself is undergoing change (e.g., de Lint, 1999; Reiner, 1992). We can briefly itemize themes in such arguments as follows:

- *Globalization.* This refers to the way that the world is becoming more and more interconnected. Processes of economic, political and cultural globalization have shifted much policing activity into the transnational arena. Efforts to control drugs, organized crime and corporate crime often fit into this category. Just as crime no longer fits into a national container and crosses borders, neither does policing.
- *Risk.* Some commentators argue that we are moving towards a 'risk society' (Beck, 1992), in which the analysis of risk situations and control of uncertainty has become more central to social life. According to this understanding the police are becoming risk managers. They are involved in collecting information about risks, identifying populations and types of individuals who are 'at risk' and implementing risk containment strategies. For example, the police might have to evaluate possible dangers to public safety associated with major sporting events, new drug policies or an ageing population.
- *Multiculturalism.* Ideas of the liberal subject that informed the rise of policing in modernity have come under attack as individualistic and Eurocentric (see pp. 62–66). A shift in political ideology towards multiculturalism has been coupled with the increasing heterogeneity of populations due to international migration. The result has been a move in policing activity towards an engagement with difference. Strategies such as community policing (discussed below) are often tied to this broader societal change.
- *Retreat of the state.* Squeezed by globalization, the roll-back of welfare ideology and the rise of corporate power, it has been argued that the modernist state is retreating from policing activity just as it is from many traditional areas of state activity (e.g., health, education). The rise of private policing over recent decades can be seen as one response to this changing reality. We discuss this in more detail later in this chapter (see pp. 112–115).

- *The rise of the media and public relations.* Policing today is increasingly concerned with image and 'spin' (see pp. 115–117). Policing policy and activity are shaped in part by the need for positive publicity and positive community relations, in a sense, then, it is scripted. Such trends are consistent with arguments (such as those made by Jean Baudrillard (1983)) that reality and its representations are being blurred under postmodernity, with the 'real world' following cultural templates and the media constructing rather than reporting on reality.

Police Culture

So much for the history of policing. What are the police like today? Over the years sociological research has built up a picture of policing mentalities, world-views and cultures. Early ethnographic studies, many of them informed by symbolic inter-actionist perspectives (see pp. 26–28), showed 'a layer of informal occupational norms and values operating under the apparently rigid hierarchical structure of police organisations' (Chan 1997: 43). Studies from around the world are remark-ably consistent in their findings of just what these are. They suggest that there are strong ties between the characteristics of the job and the ways that this is translated into individual personalities, collective beliefs and routine activities. Research has also pointed to processes of socialization in the police academy and on the beat. This ensures the reproduction of established ways of doing and thinking when new police officers are taught the ropes by old hands. In combination, such a mix of ideas and activities is called **police culture**.

Jerome Skolnick's (1975) writings on police culture developed the distinctive con-cept of the 'working personality'. This arose from occupational involvement in situations of danger and the need to present an image of authority to the public. More recent approaches have tended to argue that police culture inheres less in individual psychology and more in collective patterns of beliefs and values as these influence behaviours in everyday policing situations. Peter Manning (1989: 360), for example, speaks of 'core skills, cognitions and affect' and 'accepted practices, rules and princi-ples of conduct that are situationally applied, and generalized rationales and beliefs'. Simon Holdaway (1983: 2) locates police culture in 'a residual core of beliefs and values, of associated strategies and tactics relevant to policing … a principal guide for the day-to-day work of the rank-and-file officer'. Robert Reiner (1985) speaks of a 'cop-culture' that 'has developed as a patterned set of understandings which help to cope with and adjust to the pressures and tensions which confront the police'. Regardless of these definitional differences, there is not only strong agreement about the themes that are in hand, but also a broad consensus that police culture is a bad thing. Indeed, discussions of police culture are as full of negatives as a charge sheet. The following paragraphs review and synthesize the key attributes of police culture as described in the literature, with the main themes indicated in *italics*.

The Police World-view and Behaviour

The police see themselves as having a *mission* to protect decent people and maintain a decent society. In this mythology they are the thin blue line between order and anarchy. This heroic self-image does not preclude a deep *cynicism* about the social world, and their ability to control wrong-doing with limited resources, political interference and public indifference. Within this global vision police learn early on to be *suspicious* and *defensive*. Suspicion comes from viewing the public as potential or actual wrongdoers. The public themselves contribute to this mentality. In the course of their routine activities the police continually encounter individuals who lie or try to cover up crimes and misdemeanours. Having a day full of negative interactions leads to the belief that people are rarely honest or law-abiding and seldom tell the truth. Suspicion also arises from the inherent dangers of police work. The police need to be constantly on guard against the possibility of violence. A defensive mentality comes from the accountability of police work. Unlike most other occupations, the police are continually at risk of reprimands from superiors. Legal suits are also possible – some perhaps legitimate, but many simply vexatious. The police know that their work could be subject to intense scrutiny during cross-examination in a court of law and so justifications are always close to hand. The *suppression of emotion* is considered essential to good police work. The police are expected by the public and the law to be rational and objective – failure to present an appropriate mental state might look bad in court or on the street. Moreover, showing emotion or becoming too close to the public is seen as sign of weakness within police culture. The officer who cries or who shows fear is considered to be a liability to their colleagues and an embarrassment to the force. Because the police are an authoritarian and quasi-military organization characterized by bureaucracy, *deference to authority* frequently marks police work. Officers learn to follow orders rather than question them. A tendency towards hierarchy separates not only police ranks but also perspectives on diverse policing activities. Uniformed general duties (e.g. patrol) are seen as the lowest form of policing. Those in management positions tend to look down on those who have to interact with the public. Similarly, detectives see themselves as superior to the regular police officer. Hence being returned to uniform branch is often seen as a form of punishment within the service. Just like another hierarchical organization concerned with force, the army, the overall culture of the police is also marked by *masculinity*. Value is placed upon physical and mental toughness, the ability to perform well in a fight or drive fast. Police culture can also be quite *racist*, and shot through with assumptions about the criminal tendencies of certain groups or the competency of fellow officers from minority backgrounds. This situation leads to problems within the police force as well as in dealing with the public. Women and police from minorities report feelings of isolation and marginality alongside physical or verbal harassment. In terms of numbers, women are very under-represented. This problem is compounded at senior levels, where glass-ceiling effects have a dramatic impact upon gender ratios. Issues specifically confronting women include the following (Brown, 1998):

- Selection and promotion panels tend to be stacked with older men who are unsympathetic to female candidates, and tests can be gender-biased.
- Women are employed in policing activities that are less valued (e.g. social work roles, mediation) and this interferes with their career prospects.
- Little concession is made for child care and other familial responsibilities.
- Sexual harassment in the workplace.

From the traditional masculine perspective, women are a liability in dangerous situations, where they are allegedly unable to look after themselves. Policing research, by contrast, suggests that women are often better officers. They are able to defuse situations that might lead to violence, and tend to be more sensitive and supporting. These skills are particularly important given that – as we will see – a considerable proportion of policing is all about social work activities.

As with women, racial minorities tend to be under-represented – especially at senior ranks. This can be a major problem given the centrality of racial issues to much contemporary policing activity. In many communities the police are seen as a hostile and alien force. It is often suggested that increasing the proportion of minority police will help change perceptions and lead to more sensitive policing in multicultural settings. However, the situation is quite complex with minority officers experiencing hostile reactions from some members of their communities. They might be seen as traitors. The situation can be very stressful as officers are torn between their loyalty to their workmates and to their community, with the former pushing them to assimilate to the dominant police culture.

Box 3.1   Police Culture

Janet Chan (1997: 43–4) provides perhaps the most succinct summary of police culture:

> Features of police culture are said to include: a sense of mission about police work, an orientation towards action, a cynical or pessimistic perspective regarding the social environment, an attitude of constant suspicion, an isolated social life coupled with a strong code of solidarity with other police officers, political conservatism, racial prejudice, sexism, and a clear categorisation of the public between the rough and the respectable. Among these characteristics the so-called 'siege mentality' and 'code of silence' have often been linked with the concealment and proliferation of police misconduct.

Why are the above characteristics commonly argued to be cultural rather than examples of individual psychology?

Detail how the above characteristics might contribute to police misconduct. Are there any potentially positive outcomes that might arise from this type of police culture?

Researchers are in broad agreement that the aspects of police culture and police mentality discussed so far have a number of negative implications. Suspicion, defensiveness and hyper-masculinity make it difficult for the police to establish bonds with the wider community. The result can be a style of policing that does little to encourage good communication or trust and generates a 'them-and-us' world-view. This is compounded by public attitudes. The police have to enforce laws that may be unpopular even if necessary. Who likes to receive a speeding ticket? As the community wants little to do with the police, the police turn inwards and socialize with each other (Skolnick, 1975). The result is high levels of *in-group solidarity* and a tendency to erect barriers against outsiders. The suppression of emotion can lead to mental health problems arising from the stress levels of the job and the need to bottle up problems rather than seek formal or informal help. Deference to authority can undermine creative and critical thinking. Such qualities are reproduced over time by the fact that police officers self-select into a police career. Those who do not fit or who carry different values will often find themselves motivated (or pushed) to leave.

Routine Policing

Watching television provides the impression that policing is all about detecting and apprehending villains. This truth is rather more prosaic. Conklin (1992) cites data showing that only 45 percent of police on duty at any given moment are on patrol and that only 15 percent of police time is spent on crime-related activities. This is compounded by the so-called 'rule of ten'. For every police officer actually on the beat there are ten others who are not. These inactive police might be off duty, undergoing training, on vacation or sick leave, in court or providing administrative and back-up duty at headquarters. In short, the fixed costs behind the small amount of time that some police officers spend dealing with crime are simply staggering. Research overwhelmingly shows that much police work simply has little to do with criminal justice. Egon Bittner (1990: 355) suggests that the police are best understood as an organization whose members deal with events where 'something-is-happening-that-ought-not-to-be-happening-and-about-which-somebody-had-better-do-something-now'. In other words, they are the people who we want to fix things when the wheels fall off ordinary life. This model indicates that the police are concerned with a vast array of situations in addition to crimes. They might be called to road accidents, regulate crowds at demonstrations, take control in emergencies, be asked to look for missing persons or to sort out neighbourhood disputes. These are all situations in which order is threatened, business as usual cannot go on and the capacity to use force might have to be invoked to regain normality or to allow the repair of the fabric of everyday life. Several scholars have indicated that 'social work' or 'social service' activity seems more important than catching criminals. This might include helping a missing child find their family, checking up on the welfare of an elderly person who has not collected their mail, assisting motorists who have broken down, providing informal counselling to victims of crime, running a police youth club, providing a taxi service for people in trouble, advising people on crime-related issues, and so on. The police can also be required to provide protection to others as they go about their jobs. For example, they might escort a social worker as they make a dangerous house call. In addition, there are vast amounts of administration to be done back at the station, as well as training activities and briefings. The upshot of all this activity is that only a small percentage of police time is spent preventing crime or chasing criminals.

In thinking about what the police actually do, we should also remember that they are a large bureaucracy. Large numbers of trained police are also involved in routine tasks such as one might find in any such organization: as typists, archivists, computer systems operators, radio operators and accountants. This is increasingly seen as a waste of training and resources and many police forces are boosting the number of civilian employees (Bayley, 1994). Be this as it may, such people seem to replace sworn officers only in non-management positions. There is still the belief that only those who have worked in routine policing at some stage in their career are fit to be police managers.

The study of police culture spills over into the exploration of policing activity when we look at routine beat policing. The formal role of the police is to uphold the law. In practice, however, legal codes exert only a limited influence on what the police do. Ethnographic studies have long shown that officers tend to be less concerned with following the letter of the law than with *maintaining public order* – in a sense, keeping a lid on things. The police will often ignore or selectively enforce the law if such action makes the task of maintaining order too difficult. Research also suggests that the police deal in the **stereotypes** that form a core part of police culture. They generally work from appearances and assumptions. Drawing on their practical, day-to-day experience they view certain places and classes of people as dangerous or as law-breaking rather than law-abiding. Usually these are poor neighbourhoods and minority populations. They might also focus on those who appear 'deviant' thanks to long hair, tattoos or unorthodox clothing. These characteristics lead such persons to be subject to 'the stop' – stopped and questioned, perhaps searched. Through such routine activity a feedback loop is established. Stops lead to the discovery of crime (e.g. drug possession) and subsequent arrest. Hence police/civilian encounters tend to confirm stereotypes. Conversely more affluent and privileged groups tend to escape police surveillance. Thus, we have very little idea, for example, about the deviant activities of Mercedes and Rolls Royce drivers.

Central to the process of stereotyping is the tendency of the police to divide the world into those who are law-abiding and those who are likely cause trouble and who make the job of policing more difficult. Jerome Skolnick (1966) identified the 'symbolic assailant' – a person who the police think might be violent on the basis of cues such as appearance or the use of bad language. Other policing scholarship has subsequently expanded on this theme. Albert Reiss (1973) suggested that those who challenge police authority and who behave without respect are likely to be subject to hostile policing. He mentions drug addicts, alcoholics and juveniles as examples of this. Likewise, John van Maanen (1978) speaks of the 'asshole' – a person who answers back, refuses to answer questions and insults or provokes the police. Hence those who challenge police status and behave inappropriately (even if not illegally) are likely to be the targets of punitive policing activity. It has been argued that it is through stereotyping that the police become moral guardians of the social order and enforce mainstream standards of appropriate behaviour. The kinds of moral judgement that inform police stereotyping are clearly spelled out in the example given in Box 3.2.

Box 3.2   Robert Reiner: Stereotypes in the British Police

Drawing on several sources as well as his own work, leading British police researcher Robert Reiner (1985) has provided a detailed inventory of the stereotypical classifications held by the British police officer. These offer an insight into the conceptual universe and patterns of thinking of police culture. Many are tied to a distinction between those who 'accept the middle-class values of decency which most police revere' and those who challenge these values. Some go beyond simple offender stereotypes to look at other categories of person with whom the police come into regular contact.

Good class villains are worth dealing with. These are experienced and professional criminals who are worthy adversaries. Arresting them will bring prestige.

Police property are the refuse of society – drunks, drug addicts, prostitutes, vagrants, the poor and underclass. The police consider that the rest of society has dumped these people on them and their job is to keep them under control. Dealing with these people is usually frustrating and unpleasant and involves discretion rather than the rigid application of the law. According to Reiner, the police have to be careful not to mistakenly treat a member of a middle-class group as police property.

Rubbish are undeserving people who ask for service – typically members of 'police property' who feel they have been a victim. The police see little reason to help such people and tend to give them the brush off.

Challengers are a potential threat to police autonomy and information control. These are outsiders who get to see how policing works. Examples are doctors, journalists and social workers. The police need to engage in diverse strategies to ensure their version of reality is not challenged by the perspective of an educated outsider.

Disarmers are trouble. They are members of vulnerable groups (e.g. children, women) whose complaints against the police are likely to be taken seriously. The police need to be sure to do things by the book when dealing with them.

Do-gooders are usually critical of the police and are seen as unrealistic, bleeding heart liberals. They might talk about issues such as civil liberties, prisoners' rights and police brutality. Sociologists and critical journalists might fall into this category. *Politicians* are possibly worse! According to the police they are idealistic, corrupt and weak.

How do the above stereotypes reflect a broader police culture?
How might these stereotypes shape police practice?

The reason that stereotyping can play such a key role in policing is **police discretion**. This refers to the fact that the police work with very little direct supervision once they are in the field and often have to make choices about which course of action (if any) is to be pursued. The police have considerable powers whether to arrest, caution or ignore problems. They can deal with them formally, informally or not at all (Goldstein, 1960). Critics suggest that this freedom permits police officers to be selective and unaccountable in their routine activity. Discretion, of course, exists at other levels of the criminal justice system – for example in sentencing or plea bargaining – and it has been criticized here too (Davis, 1969). However, it is arguably more important with the police thanks to their gatekeeper role. Some suggest, however, that discretion is a good thing in that it allows the police to be flexible and exercise autonomous judgement. Researching police discretion is difficult because it involves looking at negative cases – episodes where something did not happen. Information on these does not exist in official records and paper trails. Existing studies suggest the police can decide not to invoke the law act for a number of reasons:

* Limitations of time and resources, for example, lack of holding cells in the police station or a surfeit of paperwork.
* A belief that the particular offence is trivial or takes too much trouble to enforce.
* Victims who are unwilling to press charges, making a conviction unlikely and an arrest 'pointless' (this can happen, for example, in the case of domestic violence).
* Local community beliefs about which laws deserve priority or which are unpopular (e.g. laws about keeping dogs on leads might not be enforced).
* Possible harm to the offender outweighing harm to the community, for example, a young person accused of shoplifting.

In the literature issues of discretion almost invariably lead to discussions of racism and the ways this influences policing activity. Tensions between the police and racial minorities have been perhaps the major challenge for the legitimacy of policing over the past few decades. The argument has repeatedly been made that racial minorities are disadvantaged by police discretion. We return to this theme later in the chapter (see pp. 104–106). Conversely, those who appear respectable or polite according to prevailing norms often benefit from police discretion (Piliavin and Briar, 1964).

Police culture sustains the activity cycle of routine patrolling, and consequently this is the most common form of police contact with the community. When not responding to calls from the public, this policing strategy is heavily concerned with monitoring public spaces such as shopping malls and streets. A good deal of recent policing research has explored what goes on during this kind of routine patrolling. It has been argued that with this activity the police reinforce dominant standards and moralities and or that they operate in the interests of capitalist stakeholders (e.g. shopkeepers). Robert Reiner (1994) refers to this as the 'moral street sweeping' component of policing – the fact that the public expects the police to keep public spaces orderly and allow respectable people to feel safe when using them. There is now a substantial body of literature on such policing activity exploring relations between the police and young people (James and Polk, 1996; White and Alder, 1994) – two groups who are inevitably brought into contact by moral street sweeping activities. Tensions will often arise as the police invoke stereotypes of deviant youth to identify potential problems in public spaces. A typical scenario involves a group of youths hanging out in a shopping mall whose management are pressing the police to do something about this 'problem'. The police then use move on powers. This is likely to be seen as harassment by the young people – especially if they have broken no law – or if laws against skateboarding and similar activities seem to single them out for persecution. Mutually negative perceptions eventuate and with them an escalation of confrontational behaviours. Young males, especially those from minority backgrounds, are also the group most likely to have negative and violent interactions with the police. They are more likely to be stopped and searched and subjected to verbal or physical abuse. When repeated time and time again police community relations become damaged and policing takes on a rather military feel. Information from the community dries up and stop-and-search activity increases (Kinsey et al., 1986).

Styles of Policing

Studies of police culture usually emphasize commonality rather than difference. Notwithstanding this, scholarship has identified diverse styles of policing. An important early study in this genre is James Q. Wilson's *Varieties of Police Behavior* which was published in the late 1960s. Wilson (1968) looked at police departments in various US cities and noticed subtle differences in approach. 'Watchman'-style departments were characterized by lazy policing. Officers on the beat were not particularly concerned with minor crimes and tended to turn a blind eye to activities such as prostitution, petty drug dealing and illegal gambling. They would intervene only in the case of serious incidents. Corruption is widespread in such departments thanks to ties with vice industries, and there is often a cosy relationship between the police and the authorities in City Hall. Wilson suggests that such a style of policing is common in cities with large minority populations and is a throwback to the early days of urban policing when the priority was to keep a lid on things. 'Legalistic' policing is obsessed with accountability, impartiality, procedure and professionalism. It is often found where reformers have tried to clean up a watchman-style organization. There is a strong emphasis on doing things by the book and having a spotless public image. 'Service'-style departments give priority to advice-giving, counselling and referral. They are often found in affluent areas without much street crime and where the police think of the public as law abiding. The priority here is to help the public and to maintain very positive community relations. We can think about the differences between these in terms of responses to a routine traffic violation – perhaps driving with a broken tail light. The officer in the watchman department would ignore the offence or ask for a small bribe to forget about it. In the legalistic department a ticket would be written. With service-oriented policing, the driver might be given a lecture on the dangers of driving with a defective vehicle. They might be asked to show up at the police station the next day with a receipt showing the problem had been fixed by the repair shop.

We can also identify styles of policing at the level of the individual. John Broderick (1973), for example, speaks of the 'enforcer' prepared to use violence and bend the rules; the 'idealist' who wants policing to be a profession; the 'realist' who has a cynical attitude; and the 'optimist' who likes helping people. Other typologies share patterns of this nature. Thus, Michael Brown (1981) identifies 'old style crime fighter', 'professional' and 'service' orientations in officers. Such labels may over-simplify a complex reality, but in so doing they provide a starting point for thinking about the diversity of approaches to policing at organizational and individual levels and offer leverage for a comparative social inquiry into the causes and consequences of these.

Reactive Policing and its Critique

Much contemporary research on policing looks at strategies for managing policing activities and attempts to evaluate their effectiveness. Policing approaches are diverse and each brings with it a particular set of problems. In the literature policing innovations are usually contrasted to a traditional model of reactive policing – an approach we follow here.

The dominant form of policing in western nations is **reactive policing**, sometimes also known as 'fire brigade policing' or 'incident driven policing'. This involves following up on civilian calls notifying problems. Central to this police strategy is routine patrolling – an activity form that we have already discussed in part. In effect, this means being on the move and ready to respond to calls for help when they come in. Such an activity is supported by a technology-intensive (communications, motor vehicles) and hierarchical infrastructure. Currently around 50 percent of police are deployed to motorized patrol work. The public give strong support to this kind of policing. They like to see the police come around if there is a problem and provide a visible presence, and to know that if they encounter trouble the police can be there quickly. Interestingly, however, only a minority of calls relate to criminal matters. Bayley (1994) suggests the figure is around 15–20 percent. This confirms the point we made earlier that policing is mostly about resolving diverse problems and providing social services rather than dealing with crime.

Reactive policing activity is not without its critics (Brereton, 2000). Claims have been made that because it is 'reactive', it can do little to prevent crime, and is essentially about mopping up after an offence has taken place. It has also been said to damage community relations thanks to the use of technology. Motorized patrols in particular are considered to cut the police off from face-to-face contact with the public, and consequently information from them. The police spend more time talking to each other in the car, or to other police via the radio, than they do to the people around them on the streets. Motorized patrols make the police seem distant and authoritarian. Critics also charge that reactive policing is essentially lazy. Policing managers have to do little other than to ensure that routines are maintained and calls are responded to with some efficiency. Hence police reports will document the average response time to calls or the number of patrols mounted as evidence of good policing. The organizational hierarchies and budget constraints tied to this form of policing are believed to make flexibility and innovation difficult to implement. Reactive policing has also been criticized as unable to deal with non-reported crimes such as white-collar crime or 'victimless crimes' such as drug dealing and prostitution. Hence advocates of alternatives to reactive policing suggest their models can be more strategic, flexible, community-supported and will do a better job at crime prevention. Calls for new policing strategies have been supported by policing policy-makers who realize that simply throwing more and more money to the police will do little to reduce crime. Something else is needed, it is argued, and the police should give more time to crime prevention or develop alternative forms of policing activity. Such concerns have been given credibility by urban riots that have occurred periodically in the United States and Britain since the 1960s in cities such as Los Angeles, London, Liverpool and Chicago. Reports emerging after such events have almost universally suggested that existing police/community relations are in poor shape and that radical reforms are needed. However, changing policing can be difficult, with new models running up against the following:

- entrenched bureaucracies and practices;
- ideas about good policing in police culture;
- public expectations about police visibility and a rapid response to problems;
- the desire of the police to preserve their lead agency status in dealing with crime-related issues.

For these reasons efforts at improving existing reactive policing have been sought out, especially when they mesh with the current bureaucratic and cultural climate of policing activity. It has been argued that the use of computer technology and geographical information systems (GIS) software to map 'hot spots' will allow the police to identify areas for extra patrolling and response priority. Closely allied with this process is the idea of **problem-oriented policing** – identifying a repeated problem and then setting out to devise a solution. This can involve traditional reactive techniques, but may also require innovative and cross-institutional work or be tied to community policing initiatives (see below). Pivotal to problem-oriented policing is the fact that a small number of spatial locations provide a large proportion of reported crime. Consequently, the police target such zones, tackling the causes or facilitators of crime as much as on arresting offenders. For example, by helping the authorities to improve lighting or the built environment the police might be able to reduce levels of assault in a particular neighbourhood. Ideas about 'partnership' are often tied to this strategy. The term is rather nebulous, but involves the police working with community and local government organizations to negotiate and innovate crime prevention programs. Efforts at partnership often falter due to the difficulty of coordinating diverse institutions and chains of command as well as budgets.

A further initiative that is gathering momentum is **evidence-based policing**. This means trying seriously to evaluate policing activity and perhaps using properly designed trials to see 'what works' to reduce crime or respond to community needs. Proponents suggest that evidence-based policing can see existing practices and routines subject to scrutiny, better resource accountability and change enabled. Until the 1980s there was resistance to such evaluations among policing authorities. They were sceptical that any studies could bring benefits and believed that scrutiny by outsiders would bring only criticism and negative press. This climate has now changed, with police administrators keen to demonstrate their efficiency and performance. This is a curious development because the available evidence suggests that a good deal of policing activity is futile. The Kansas City Preventive Patrol Experiment spectacularly questioned the validity of routine patrol activity (see Box 3.3). Clear-up rates for many reported crimes are also very low. This is especially the case for burglary, criminal damage and auto theft. The conventional image of policing is that of systematic and methodical investigation leading to detection. However, an analysis of cases suggests that it is the presence of a witness at the scene of a crime that is the vital factor for solving many offenses, not police work. If there are no members of the public present to provide an immediate description of the perpetrator, then the chances of success are limited (Reiner, 1985: 119–22). Other crimes are often cleared when an offender asks that they be 'taken into consideration' when admitting to another offence under questioning or sentencing. It should be noted that failure to provide closure in many cases arises not so much from faulty police methods as resource limitations. These lead the police to concentrate on crimes that are either very serious or very solvable. Even if it is important to the victim, a low value burglary without witnesses is most likely not worth their time of day. So if your DVD player is stolen from your house you can probably kiss it goodbye.

Box 3.3   The Kansas City Preventive Patrol Experiment

This is one of the most celebrated tests of tried and trusted policing methods. The police have long believed that patrolling (i.e. driving around in cars) acts as a deterrent to crime. In 1973 George Kelling and his team (Kelling et al., 1974) divided Kansas City, Missouri, into 15 beats. These were then further subdivided into groups that were matched in terms of population characteristics and policing demand. Areas were then assigned to one of three policing strategies: no patrolling (responses to calls only), normal patrolling, and abnormally high levels of patrolling. In effect, then, Kelling was using an experimental research design to test the effectiveness of patrolling.

During the course of the one-year experiment citizens were interviewed and crime rates monitored. The study found no significant differences in terms of citizen perceptions of safety, reported crime rates or satisfaction with the police. Incredibly, then, the study suggested that the police could stop routine patrolling for a whole year and nobody would notice!

How does this study undermine common-sense presumptions about the role and usefulness of police in contemporary society?
Can the results of the experiment be validly used to argue for the more widespread implementation of other policing styles?

Community Policing

For a long time now **community policing** has been advocated with enthusiasm by its aficionados, especially as it is consistent with ideas of 'policing by consent' that have been central to the ideology of Western policing systems. Academic discourse on community policing revolves around two issues:

- Question: What is it? Answer: It means different things to different people, but whatever it is, it's not reactive policing.
- Question: Does it work? Answer: We don't really know, and anyway, it depends what you mean by 'work'.

Let us turn to the first of these issues. The community policing approach was identified or labelled in the United States in the 1960s and has been touted as an alternative to reactive policing ever since. Understandings of exactly what 'community policing' means seem to vary, but we can detect a number of core themes to this approach (see Fielding, 1995; Sarre, 1996: 30).

- Substituting foot or cycle patrols for motorized patrols.
- Improving contact with the community and hence information flows. This can extend as far as community service activity.

- Liaison work with organizations such as the church, youth clubs and ethnic associations.
- Building trust through sustained face-to-face interactions.
- A focus on crime prevention and problem-solving.

Pivotal to the idea of community policing is the idea of looking to the community for direction and accountability rather than to policing hierarchies. Under this model the community indicates problems that they wish to be solved and the police then provide expertise, resources and labour to address the issue.

The term 'community policing' has a strong ideological appeal – everyone loves the idea of 'community' and the warm and fuzzy feelings it conjures up. Notwithstanding this, community policing is faced with a number of problems. Not the least of these is deciding who is the community. Typically the most marginal populations (e.g. street kids) are not included in consultations and negotiations unlike, say, religious leaders, school principals, shopkeepers and social workers. Another issue is that problematic conflicts of interest can arise when one group wants action taken against another. Retail interests may ask the police to clamp down on youths playing around in the mall. This might clash with another community policing initiative, for example, a task force working to build better links with young people. Moreover, a line has to be drawn somewhere between community involvement, the promotion of special interests and vigilanteism. Real problems can exist when members of the public are privy to police information or feel they have been encouraged to enforce the law themselves. Vigilante action can result, with possibly serious consequences.

Community policing also gives a great deal of discretion to officers on the street – perhaps leading to possibilities for abuse of power or corruption. It is also difficult to evaluate with little consensus existing over how this can be done. Perhaps traditional means such as crime statistics are inappropriate. Supporters of community policing often argue that reducing fear of crime or improving trust in the police should be the major goals. There is considerable resistance to, and stigmatization of community policing from within the force. Some argue that it is not real policing or that it is 'soft'. A further cultural barrier arises from the police self-image within policing culture. Many police officers like to see themselves as tough and as enforcers of the law. Community policing requires social work skills, communication skills and sensitivity. These attributes are not encouraged by the existing police culture and require the officer to enter into a role that they may be uncomfortable performing. Another source of internal difficulty lies in the fact that lines of accountability and command are blurred. This can lead to resistance from officers more used to hierarchical ways of doing things, particularly middle management. One implication of this is that it is unclear how promotions criteria and career development paths can accommodate community policing skills, given that these have been established in a context of hierarchical control lines within the reactive policing paradigm.

Problems with existing policing culture are also demonstrated in the ways that the police can feel uncomfortable taking direction from the community. As a fundamentally hierarchical organization the police are not well equipped to take on board bottom-up initiatives. Indeed, some have argued that the police seem to decide which initiatives will be implemented and that community representatives have consultative rather than executive powers. Consequently cynics have argued that community policing is more about public relations and getting police messages across than substantive changes to police practice. For example, a study of police–community liaison committees in the UK and Australia found they served as window dressing (Bull and Strata, 1994). Similar concerns have been raised about Neighbourhood Watch schemes. These enlist residents to keep an eye out for suspicious activity. There is little evidence that they reduce crime, but they do serve as a visible reminder of police/community ties thanks to all those window stickers and street signs. Finally, it should be acknowledged that the implementation of community policing might not lead to progressive outcomes, as is often assumed. If this is indeed the case, then better policing might arise with less community input! Community perspectives on crime are often more stereotyped and less factually informed than those of the police – especially the expert policy-makers working for the force. For example, one of the authors of this book once worked on a high level committee with the Police Minister, Police Commissioner, etc. that was involved in setting up 'partnerships' to control crime. The idea was to implement innovative crime prevention programs making use of community resources and ideas. Surveys were conducted asking the public what they thought was a problem in their area. The results of this 'community consultation process' were astoundingly unimaginative. The number one problem was seen to be young people hanging out in public spaces in groups ('gangs') and 'making trouble'. There was a clear tension between the liberal opinions and hopes of the experts, including in this case the police officers on project, and the priorities of the members of the public.

Zero-Tolerance Policing

The hot topic in policing circles during the 1990s was **zero tolerance policing**. According to its supporters, this was a major new policing strategy that would provide a proactive alternative to traditional reactive policing but had more bite than community policing. The origins of the policy lie in the theory of **'broken windows'** expounded by James Q. Wilson and George Kelling (1982). They suggest that a great deal of crime is simply a response to visible signs of disorder. Broken windows in a building that do not get fixed are a statement that nobody cares and are, in effect, an invitation to vandals to simply break the rest. By analogy graffiti, drug needles, squeegee bandits and street corner drug dealers send out the signal that a particular neighbourhood is a place where crime can take place with impunity.

Implemented in New York with the support of Mayor Rudolph Giuliani, zero tolerance policing is in effect a strategy that aims to clean up hot spots by relentlessly targeting those minor offences that give an impression of disorder. The police will saturate a given locale and ticket skateboarders, people that drop litter, loiterers, and so on. They will also pressure drug dealers and pimps, making business difficult for them. After a few weeks of treatment the area will start to look respectable and give off a different set of signals. 'Law-abiding citizens' will use the streets again and criminals will move on once they realize that people care. This work on the beat is supported by information technology and managerialism used in the kinds of ways that are consistent with problem-oriented policing (see above, p. 98). Hot spots are identified by using crime report data and GIS mapping. At coordination meetings objectives are set, benchmarks established for future work and successes and failures with respect to previous targets are reviewed.

Giuliani and the New York Police Department have pointed to crime statistics and claimed that zero tolerance policing is a major success story. One reason for this is that people brought in as a result of zero tolerance policy are often found to have outstanding warrants or can be tied to more serious crimes. As a result, criminals are taken off the streets and put into jails. Supporters can also document considerable public support for the initiative, which is seen as being tough on crime. Finally, the strategy has endorsement from working police officers as it is consistent with their own world-view. There is an ideological mesh with both police culture (e.g. stereotyping) and the reactive policing model. Such positives have brought policing experts from around the world to New York to learn about the system. Nevertheless it has not been widely adopted elsewhere. Problems with the approach (see Greene, 1999) include the following:

- It tends to disproportionately target racial and ethnic minorities. These are often the people who are on the streets in poor areas. Consequently, community ties can suffer. Abuses against minorities have been attributed to the policy. Some claim that it implicitly endorses heavy-handed police tactics rather than sensitive policing.
- Police discretion is eliminated. This means that minor offenders are dragged into the net of the criminal justice system. Perhaps this is not in the long-term interests of the offenders or the community.
- Paperwork increases exponentially as petty offenders are processed by the criminal justice system.
- The approach is resource-intensive in terms of personnel and can lead to higher prison expenditures.
- Claims about the success of zero tolerance have been exaggerated. When we compare New York with other US cities, we find drops in crime regardless of whether or not there is a zero tolerance police strategy. Bowling (1999) indicates that New York murder rates were already dropping before zero tolerance was introduced and suggests that changing crack cocaine markets were a major driver of crime rates in New York, not policing activity.

Policing and Politics

In most countries doctrines about the separation of powers would seem to suggest that the police have little to do with politics. The police are supposed to be above politics, to avoid trading favours and taking sides. Sociological research has questioned this assumption and held it up to be a fiction. Law and order are hugely political issues and, consequently, policing becomes tied up in wider frames of judgement. The police may be pressured by politicians to 'do something' about crime, to improve community relations or to endorse government policy. They may also push politicians, in turn, for tougher laws on gun control or drugs, punishments for crimes against police officers in the line of duty or better pay and resources. The relationship between the police and politicians can rapidly become symbiotic, with both sides trading favours and looking for good publicity. Such a system has become quite institutionalized in the United States, where 'machine politics' in major cities saw elected mayors and police chiefs working hand in glove to ensure each kept their job.

From the viewpoint of much critical theory, this level of analysis is too caught up in the minutiae of specific contexts. We need to step back and consider that as agents of the state the police are always already political – not just sometimes political. They are a limb of the state apparatus that is concerned with social control and which reinforces dominant standards and enforces laws that operate in the interests of powerful social groups (Gatrell, 1996). Given such a perspective, the historical emergence of the police can be understood as follows: they are a tool through which 'better off people disciplined their inferiors' (ibid.: 384); a response to ideological concerns about perceived links between crime and lower classes, and a step towards an authoritarian state that threatens individual liberties. At times of tension and crisis, some argue, this kind of relationship will be heightened. Stuart Hall represents this style of work with his concept of the **law and order society**. Writing from a neo-Marxist perspective, he suggests that during the 1970s Britain entered into a deep economic recession and, at the same time, right-wing, populist discourses fell into place. These argued a need for 'law and order' and discipline, along with free market reforms and a clamp-down on welfare. The state can be understood as enforcing authoritarian social control and reproducing conditions that would allow *laissez-faire* capitalism to continue. In such situations, Hall argues, the police take the side of capital against labour. They are 'not only to be seen policing industrial conflict in a tough manner, but actively involved in formulating official views which are hostile to the rights of workers to strike and picket' (1996: 265–6). The police also become involved in racial conflict caused by poverty and marginality. Their job becomes 'to contain and constrain, in effect to criminalize, parts of the black population in our urban colonies' (ibid.: 266). Third, we see a militarization of the police, with policing by consent replaced by the use of armed and violent force. Hall points here to the notorious Special Patrol Group, a mobile police unit within the Metropolitan Police used to enforce public order. The overall feel of policing in the law and order society is one where repression and control come to dominate over ideas of citizen liberties and rights. Just as importantly, doctrines about the separation of powers are thrown aside. The police come to play a role in designing as well as implementing policy. They form part of the 'law and order bloc' (ibid.: 269), shape public opinion and are consulted by government because of their expertise in issues relating to crime control and public order.

The Policing of Minorities

A major theme in Hall's discussion of policing in the 'law and order society' was the centrality of race issues to contemporary policing, and it is here that contemporary policing has become most obviously a political issue. When we look at studies from around the globe we find a remarkably similar picture. The police not only play a major role in race politics, but also conduct policing activity in ways that can be understood as racist. Janet Chan (1997) identifies several dimensions of racism as this is manifested in everyday policing. Running through these provides an idea of some of the range of issues that can be involved:

- *Insensitivity to language and cultural differences.* Migrants, refugees, indigenous and minority populations often lack confidence or ability in standard English. The police, however, are often unwilling to use interpreters and this can lead to disadvantage during interrogation. Cultural barriers are more nebulous. Minorities may be unfamiliar with mainstream legal norms, concepts and procedures and the police can be insensitive to alternative cultural conventions.
- *Prejudice and stereotyping.* This can involve negative views of minority groups as a whole and the use of racist language. Such views can lead to policing activity that is defined as harassment, producing poor community relations.
- *Over-policing.* Here police time and resources are directed towards particular minority groups. Chan suggests that this has two dimensions, these relating to the degree and nature of police intervention. The question of degree might refer to the number of police officers allocated to areas with minority populations. When looking at the nature of police interventions, we might be looking at the insensitive application of policing procedures such as stop and search, spot-lighting from police cars and move on powers.
- *Abuse of power and excessive use of force.* At stake here are police behaviours which are clearly illegal, such as assault, torture, entry into premises without a warrant and making threats. Complaints and inquiries into such activities often point to infamous squads such as the New South Wales 'Tactical Response Group' and London's 'Special Patrol Group' as pivotal to such activities.
- *Differential application of the law.* Police discretion might see some groups being targeted and others ignored for the same offence. Rules about drinking alcohol in a public park, for example, might be enforced against Aborigines (for whom it may well be a solidaristic custom) but tolerated for a white middle-class couple having a bottle of Chardonnay with their picnic.

Chan points out that minority perceptions of the police are powerfully influenced by the experience of such activities. Fear and suspicion often arise. However, the nature of the police force in a country of origin can also be a factor in relations between the police and migrants and refugees. If the police force in the country of origin has been corrupt or involved in political repression, it is likely there will be less trust of the police in the new host country.

Police racism has been linked not only to political conservatism and stereotyping within police culture but also to wider public attitudes. Repeated psychological studies have shown that police are prejudiced, 'only slightly more so than the community as a whole' (Reiner, 1985), most notably the middle and upper-lower classes. This fact, it has often been pointed out, does not excuse police racism. Nobody would argue that because serial killers can be found in the general public, we should also expect to have a few in the police. Likewise, there is no reason to tolerate racism in the police simply because it can be found more widely. The empirical existence of racism, however, is supported in statistics and studies, mostly from the United States and Britain. These have shown for some time that being young, male and from a minority background increases the probability of arrest, stop-and-search or use of alleged excessive force by the police (ibid.: 127–9). Yet debate remains as to extent to which these policing patterns are due to active discrimination rather than being some form of unintended racism arising from the unreflexive application of routine 'impartial' policing activity. Donald Black (1980), for example, conducted a study in several US cities that involved researchers riding around in police cars on patrol. The results showed that black youths tended to be apprehended for more serious offences than white youths, and that black adults tended to demand strong police action against juveniles more than white adults. These kinds of factors can be complemented by others that might lead to negative outcomes for minorities in the exercise of discretion, such as the existence of a prior record and demeanour.

Confusion over related issues on how to define and demonstrate the existence of racism remains a considerable obstacle not only to policing research, but also to policy formation and improved community relations. Despite resistance from the police to new and more inclusive definitions, there is a general consensus among academics that defining police racism in terms of conscious prejudice at the level of the individual is not very useful. Instead we need to think about policing activity and police culture as the source of racist problems. Routine policing brings officers into contact with marginal and minority populations. Although the police might see themselves as simply enforcing the law in such situations, the communities they are policing look at a different picture – one where racism, harassment and unwanted interference are common. Such themes have been highlighted in recent high-profile controversies.

The Rodney King incident in Los Angeles illustrates the theme of divergent realities. In 1992 the African-American motorist Rodney King was beaten by several white police officers. Unknown to the police officers, the event was captured on videotape. Critics of the police claimed that racism was in play, while the police officers claimed they had used reasonable force to control a dangerous suspect. After the officers were acquitted by a jury, large-scale riots broke out in Los Angeles with African Americans claiming the entire justice system was racist. A subsequent inquiry discovered widespread racism in the Los Angeles Police Department alongside a management structure that informally condoned heavy-handed policing. In the UK, the Scarman Report of 1981 documented remarkably similar problems. Commissioned in the wake of race riots, the report focused on stop-and-search laws and the ways that these had been used against young Afro-Caribbean males. Scarman denied that there was 'institutionalized racism' in the Metropolitan Police, but defined this as deliberate or officially sanctioned racism rather than an insensitive policing culture. Left-wing critics pointed out that the real problem was policing policies which had racist implications on the ground. In other words, institutional racism could be the 'unintended consequence of organisational policies' (Reiner, 1985: 205) as these are played out in day-to-day policing activity.

Many years later the report on the Stephen Lawrence incident raised the question of police racism yet again, but answered in the affirmative. Lawrence, an Afro-Caribbean youth, was murdered in a horrific stabbing in South East London that appeared to have been racially motivated. The police investigation was botched, bungled and half-hearted despite strong evidence pointing to a gang of white perpetrators who were subsequently not convicted in a private prosecution brought by the victim's parents. The MacPherson Report argued that more than incompetence was responsible for the fiasco – it seemed as if the police did not care about Lawrence, had patronized his family and refused to believe the attack to be racially motivated. In sum, there was something wrong with police attitudes that led to his death (and by implication other race crimes) not being taken seriously. According to MacPherson (1999: 6.34), the Lawrence case was indeed evidence of institutional racism defined as:

> The collective failure of an organisation to provide an appropriate and professional service to people because of their colour, culture, or ethnic origin. It can be seen or detected in processes, attitudes and behaviour which amount to discrimination through unwitting prejudice, ignorance, thoughtlessness and racist stereotyping which disadvantage minority ethnic people.

It is notable that the Commissioner of the Metropolitan Police Service disagreed with this definition and finding, suggesting that it would lead to a public perception of the individual police officers in the force as overt racists. This stance indicates the highly politicized nature of the term 'racism' and the fact that struggles over its meaning are becoming increasingly central to policing today. It is also interesting to reflect on the differences between the Scarman Report and the MacPherson Report, paralleling the conceptual shift from radical criminology to left realism (see pp. 21–25). In the era of the Scarman Report the major claim of critics of the police was that they were over-zealous in policing minorities on the streets. Yet the pivotal concerns of the MacPherson Report were those of under-policing and failure to protect minorities.

Police Deviance

Issues of police racism bring us to the more inclusive category of police deviance. We often think of the police as reducing the sum total of deviance in society. Perhaps this is so. However, it is all too easy to ignore the fact that the police are themselves a major source of deviant and criminal activity. Much of this is referred to as corruption. Throughout the world inquiries have uncovered police corruption and malpractice – something that has to be taken very seriously given the position of trust and authority held by the police. Some of the major forms of police corruption include:

- provision of services in return for bribes (e.g. extra patrols);
- taking bribes in return for not enforcing the law;
- police officers actively organizing crime;
- planting or tampering with evidence, obtaining false confessions, lying under oath.

According to police public relations departments, episodes of corruption (such as racism) can be explained as the work of a few bad apples. Such an explanation does not take account of the entrenched quality of corruption and the fact that it surfaces time after time. Sociological investigations often point to the links between corruption and police culture (Punch, 1985). The **code of silence** is a norm which feeds upon in-group solidarity and tells officers not to snitch on their colleagues. This makes investigation of police corruption very difficult. Police culture also encourages the view that the courts, the law and due process make the job of policing too difficult. The police 'know' who is a criminal and who should be put away. Some feel their duty is to do whatever it takes to ensure this end – even if this means bending or breaking the law themselves. The nature of the policing job encourages corruption. The police are paid modest salaries but have to enforce the law against highly profitable, cash-rich enterprises – a situation that can easily lead to temptation. Moreover, officers are subject to only minimal surveillance while working on the beat. Bayley (1994) estimates that a police constable and their sergeant will interact only 15 percent of their working hours. This lack of visibility, particularly for detectives working under operational conditions of secrecy, makes it easy to be dishonest.

Aside from corruption, the other major form of police deviance is the misuse of force – including deadly force. Alleged episodes are difficult to investigate. There are rarely independent and unbiased witnesses to events and accounts are often conflicting as to exactly what happened. Even when an event is caught on tape (such as the Rodney King beating), opinions diverge as to the legitimacy of the violence. In part this is because understandings of what is 'reasonable force' are variable. Although the use of force by the police is shaped by the law and policing guidelines, it is largely driven by interactional dynamics (Phillips and Smith, 2000).

Research by one of the authors of this text, Smith, suggests that the police use force dramaturgically. A good deal of policing is about maintaining symbolic authority and showing that the police are in control of the situation. The use of force can thus become a way of demonstrating power in uncertain situations and maintaining public order. For example, in a multivariate statistical analysis of incidents involving the alleged excessive use of force Timothy Phillips and Philip Smith (2000) found that the level of allegedly excessive force correlates with night time, public spaces, young men and alcohol. This finding is consistent with a picture of the police attempting to dramatize power in an uncertain and hostile environment with an onlooking audience.

Reforming the Police

According to Robert Reiner (1992), the police have been largely unable to deal with the shift towards a 'postmodern society'. He suggests that the qualities of such a society include cultural pluralism and multiculturalism, rapid change, the emergence of vocal subcultures and interest groups and the emergence of an underclass. Although social science studies and critiques from within the criminal justice system such as official inquiries have questioned orthodox police practices and beliefs (we have drawn on many of these in this chapter), change has been slow in coming. The police remain to a greater or lesser degree hierarchical, inflexible, dedicated to routine practices, masculine and racist. The police are also profoundly unreflexive – only recently have they begun to question routinized assumptions and activities, goals, directions and structures. Yet at the same time organizations throughout society are being urged to become flexible, culturally sensitive and open to wider exchanges of skills and ideas. Reflexivity, it has been argued, is the key to success in a postmodern knowledge society. But if the police need to change, how can this be done?

Programs for police reform can be narrowly focused on issues of corruption and law violation or more broadly designed so as to deal with issues of flexibility, accountability and efficiency. Further than this, they can also be directed at intangibles such as making the police more sensitive or responsive to community inputs. A distinction can be made between legislative and rule-tightening changes and those directed at bringing about reform by tackling police culture. Janet Chan (1997) suggests that the former usually sees codes of practice, external legislative change and equity and access policies being announced. Such actions place minority issues on the agenda, sometimes offer benchmarks and make accountability, reporting and monitoring routine. Chan suggests that these efforts are often doomed to failure. This is because, as we have already discussed, in reality, management has limited control over what happens among street-level cops. They have large amounts of discretion and will usually find ways of subverting rule and policy changes. The result can be a scenario in which 'police executives are enthusiastic and optimistic about change, but for patrol officers at the coalface it is business as usual' (ibid.: 55). Similarly, Nigel Fielding (1988) suggests that divergent definitions of 'competent practice' separate reformers from police officers and handicap efforts at change. For police officers, competence is defined in the minutiae of contingent interactions with the public, in quick thinking, in the exercise of discretion, talk and gesture. Within this context of routine police craft, abstract goals and policies make little sense, and efforts to induce change via legislation or managerial initiatives will inevitably misfire.

Sometimes even senior management resist change. An example of this scenario was the Ethnic Affairs Policy Statement, which the state of New South Wales, Australia, implemented in the 1980s. This required all government agencies and departments to prepare audits looking at participation, equality of access, and barriers confronting minorities and to outline strategies that could be designed to deal with these. The New South Wales Police produced its EAPS in 1988. In a survey Chan (1997) found almost no awareness of the document among respondents to a survey she conducted. Many cynical or irrelevant comments were written in response to her question: 'What do you understand to be the NSW Police Service's policy in relation to providing police services to minority ethnic communities?' Chan suggests that the EAPS failed because discretion on the beat meant that most officers could simply ignore it. Many senior management saw it as a pointless and time-consuming bureaucratic exercise that would gather dust on the shelf somewhere. This was especially the case because they were already implementing their own strategy for change based upon community policing. Hence the EAPS was seen as an unnecessary and untimely paper exercise.

Awareness of such problems with legislative change has seen a shift to thinking about ways of changing police culture. This can happen via reforms to recruitment (e.g. hiring more minority officers) and training (e.g. cultural awareness training in the police academy) or by altering police practices (e.g. introducing community policing). For some time now efforts have been made to improve police education. Many years ago, the leading policing scholar, Lawrence Sherman (1978: 19) wrote that: 'Much police education today is intellectually shallow, conceptually narrow, and provided by faculty that are far from scholarly. Rather than helping to change the police, police education appears to support the status quo, teaching what the police do now instead of inquiring what they could do differently.' Responses to this kind of criticism have seen major efforts to attract more intellectually able recruits and reform the curriculum of police colleges, pushing it in a less narrowly vocational direction. The police academy has traditionally stressed the rote learning of procedures, and physical abilities. It has been argued that the curriculum needs to be developed to include discussion of the social contexts of policing, research methodologies and criminological theory. Teaching has to be conducted by non-police academics as well as sworn officers in order to offer diverse perspectives. Sometimes this can involve police recruits undertaking policing studies at universities and other non-police educational institutions. Such reforms are difficult to implement successfully thanks to organizational and financial problems alongside enduring cultural differences between academics and police officers (Bradley, 1996). Moreover, research suggests that training in the academy is soon undone on the beat, where entrenched attitudes remain and cynicism is expressed towards 'politically correct' policy documents. The power of undoing can be seen from that fact that minority recruits often take on the attributes of the dominant police culture. For example, Mike Brogden and Clifford Shearing (1993) found women who entered the police becoming more like their male colleagues in terms of attitudes and behaviour or else being side-lined into service jobs. Likewise, in the United States, Ellis Cashmore (1991) found black recruits taking on the values and personality of white officers.

Evaluating policing practice and building up a reflexive knowledge base would seem to be another way to re-mould policing (Bittner, 1990). However, research conducted by the police themselves is often self-justifying (for example, to demonstrate an expensive new programme 'works') and is policy led (Reiner, 1989). Academic research is more sophisticated but rarely has an impact on concrete policing activity. The police tend to see it as unduly critical, unrealistic, perhaps incomprehensible and without an understanding of the difficulties and constraints that impact upon police work. In response to this situation, collaborative partnerships have been developed between academics and the police, although these are often cumbersome and fraught with tension.

Such negative reflections can lead us to be fatalistic about police services and feel that nothing can be done to bring about long-term change. A study by Jerome Skolnick and David Bayley entitled *The New Blue Line* (1986) suggests that this is not necessarily the case. They looked at a number of US police departments that have been turned around – becoming not only less corrupt but also more responsive to community needs. They saw leadership as fundamental to reform in terms of setting and enforcing new standards and policies and motivating personnel to convert to new ways of doing things. Community support for reform was also vital in providing legitimacy for change. As might be expected, change was made more difficult by the entrenched police bureaucracy and police union, police culture, continuing public support for reactive policing and the administrative and financial costs of innovation.

Other Enforcement Agencies

Although the police are by far the largest body of people involved in detecting breaches of the law, it is very important to remember that there are other investigative bodies at play. These are often forgotten and have been less often the subject of sociological investigation. Although the police are partly in charge of what goes on within a state, they have less responsibility for controlling borders and regulating who or what goes in and out. Customs, immigration and coastguard authorities are generally concerned with securing national boundaries and investigating crimes related to illegal immigration and smuggling. Regulatory bodies are appointed by the state to monitor and control particular spheres such as aviation, pollution and the environment, retail standards, product safety, health care, occupational health and safety, food and drug standards, building codes, and so on. Well-known examples include Her Majesty's Pollution Inspectorate and the Civil Aviation Authority in the UK and the Food and Drug Administration and the Federal Aviation Administration in the USA. These often have levels of authority that are not only more extensive than those of the police, but also are less governed by doctrines about separation of functions and powers. For example, an aviation authority might investigate the cause of an air crash, make a ruling on responsibility and impose a fine or other penalty on the airline concerned.

A major theme in research on such agencies has been to explain the frequent failure of regulation and the rarity of prosecution. In many cases studies have pointed to the cosy relationship between such organizations and their clients and the ways that informal processes shape the effective meanings of the law as it is enforced (Bernstein, 1955). Regulators and those they are regulating often share a common educational background and occupational culture. If this is the case, they may resolve problems cooperatively, looking for a solution that both sides feel is a reasonable interpretation of the law. This is enhanced by the regular movement of staff between the private sector and the government in the course of a career path. Critics suggest that this can lead to complacency and **agency capture**, with regulators seduced into an industry view about the meaning of statutes that demand 'best practice' or 'acceptable risk'. What we are seeing here then is a similar set of issues to those we have already reviewed in the context of police discretion, police culture and everyday policing. In effect, the way the law is played out is determined by informal culture and face-to-face interaction as much as by what is written in black letters in law books.

A contrast is often drawn between the compliance systems and sanctioning systems, with regulatory bodies usually involved in the former (see Manning, 1987: 297–8). In **sanctioning systems** there is a focus on punishment for rule breaking. The system is adversarial, with the state acting against the infractor. Investigations involve collecting evidence and processes of adjudication work with a binary logic (guilty/not guilty). This is the path of criminal law and the court systems as they are conventionally understood. By contrast, **compliance systems** try to minimize possible future harm rather than enforce sanctions against completed past acts. Inspections are used to ensure compliance with rules or norms. Prosecution is rare, and may be avoided because it damages the cooperative relations that are assumed to lead to compliance. Bargaining and negotiation often take the place of binary logic, with agencies and those they are regulating trying to reach a common ground. For example, a compromise may be reached on the trade-off between cost efficiency and pollution outcomes. Within compliance systems the law sits back-stage and is often invoked only in cases of serious breach.

Private Policing

We have already noted that the reform of policing would seem to be moving at the pace of a hobbled horse – not so the privatization of policing which is proceeding at the full gallop of a Derby winner (see Reynolds and Wilson, 1996). This has made it one of the most significant areas of study for police scholars. We can define private policing as activities aimed at maintaining public order and tackling crime that are conducted or financed by for-profit organizations. It is estimated that by 1970 the number of private police already equalled that of public police (Reichman, 1987). The term 'private police' embraces the ways that a number of the tasks traditionally performed by the police have been taken over by profit-making organizations – usually to protect the interests and assets of other profit-making organizations. The precise boundaries of private policing are hard to define. In some cases employees will have had formal training, wear a gun and a uniform and drive a vehicle that looks remarkably like a police car. At the other end of the scale are people like nightclub bouncers and security personnel at rock concerts. Private security firms might offer services to large-scale institutions such as airports, hotels, universities, hospitals, shopping malls and factories as well as 'armed response' and random patrols to affluent homes. They might be involved in crowd control, parking regulation or the monitoring of e-mail and searching for computer fraud within a corporation. Or they might be an old-fashioned private detective agency of the kind immortalized by Hollywood.

Several factors have led to the emergence of private policing (see Reichman, 1987). These include:

- The growing power of corporations in social life. These have a substantial interest in protecting their own financial, intellectual or physical property.
- A general increase in surveillance and the regulation of populations in society. This dynamic has been well captured by Foucault (see pp. 29–30) and increasingly involves non-state actors.
- The emergence of large-scale built forms that are privately owned but involve the circulation of publics. Shopping malls, airports, theme parks and major office buildings are examples of this.
- The growth of white-collar crimes such as fraud, insider dealing, cyber-crime and copyright abuse which have arisen in tandem with the shift to a post-industrial, information-based economy. These are often remarkably complex activities and they generally require specialized resources to be protected and investigated that may be unavailable in the public sector. Because the financial stakes are high, it often makes sense to set up private security systems to protect investments.

There is a close relationship between the rise of private security and changes to mainstream policing. Community expectations about the ability of the police to control and regulate crime have dropped and fear of crime has risen. An awareness has grown that paying for private services is acceptable and sensible for individuals and corporations. Hence private crime control is also driven by a commercial litmus test. It is less concerned with morality and more concerned with the bottom line. It is also less focused on the individual offender and their relationship to the state than the classical justice model (Shearing and Stenning, 1987a). Nancy Reichman for example, looked at special units set up to detect and investigate auto insurance fraud. She suggested that 'in contrast to conventional law enforcers who watch in order to apprehend suspects, the object of surveillance in the insurance context is to minimize insurance losses – to lower insurance settlements or reduce opportunities to engage in fraudulent behaviour' (1987: 251). Discretionary decisions and policies are likely to be informed on the basis of the financial or public relations interests of the employer rather than the public good and the need to uphold the law. For example, the car insurance company might decide not to make a pay-out to a fraudulent claim but at the same time not take the offender to court. The reasoning would be that the cost and time of court proceedings would not make such an action worthwhile. By contrast, for the public police a more serious consideration would be the moral harm of the offence and the normative requirement to see justice done. Other concerns about private policing have centred on themes of abuse of power, relations with the police, and regulation and training (Reynolds and Wilson, 1996). From the perspective of social justice it has also been questioned whether there should be unequal access to protection on the basis of ability to pay.

Probably the leading experts on private policing, Clifford D. Shearing and Philip C. Stenning, suggest that it leads us to rethink the boundaries of public and private within the context of the social contract with the state (see Box 3.4). From the liberal perspective the rise of the police came in tandem with the assumption that the state would take on the job of maintaining public order (see pp. 85–86). In short, public order is a public responsibility. Private policing suggests that at least some of this task has been resumed by the community and is mediated by market forces. Shearing and Stenning assert that the consequences of this can be quite radical. Disputes over the definition of order can arise when private interests differ from those defined by the state – or its agents, the police. They suggest that large corporations have considerable power to define public order, especially when 'more and more public life is nowadays conducted on privately owned and controlled property' (1987a: 15).

Box 3.4   Disney World and Private Social Control

In their work Clifford D. Shearing and Philip C. Stenning (1987c) have pointed to the ways that social control and policing in private arenas are often subtly hidden. They suggest that crowds are regulated through architectural features and that guards are often disguised. Here ensuring voluntary and unreflexive compliance is the name of the game. Their discussion of Disney World illustrates these themes. Disney World 'seems to run like clockwork' because order is a 'designed-in feature that provides ... an exemplar of modern private corporate policing,' (ibid.: 317). Car parking is assisted by smiling young people, a train runs you to the entry, attendants usher you onto a monorail while telling you that you will have fun. Safety instructions (e.g. keep away from the edge) issue from loudspeakers. Flower beds and water features surround pathways and stop you from straying. Shearing and Stenning remark that 'opportunities for disorder are minimized by constant instruction, by physical barriers ... by the surveillance of omnipresent employees who detect and rectify the slightest deviation,' (ibid.: 319). In such a system, control becomes consensual as it is embedded within a context of fun. Much as Foucault (see p. 29) observed, people come to regulate their own behaviour, even if this means waiting in queues for a long time. The result is a place that ensures visitor safety and maximizes Disney profit by minimizing chances for litigation and ensuring the rapid through-flow of thousands of paying customers.

How do the practices of Disney World compare with the policing practices described above?

By contrast to this position, which sees the boundaries of public and private persisting, Gary Marx (1987) suggests a hybridization of private police and state police is taking place. He considers it most fruitful to explore the interweaving of public and private interests in the present era rather than see them as organizations with opposed goals and modus operandi. Marx identifies five areas in which this is taking place:

- *Joint public/private investigations*. An example of this was a sting organized jointly by the FBI and the IBM security division in the 1980s. This involved the sale of trade secrets to an IBM competitor, Hitachi.
- *State delegation of authority to private police*. Large numbers of private security officers work for the state in areas like court houses, airports and public buildings. However, this can also include undercover work – especially in small towns and rural areas where the existing police are known to locals. As in the previous example, a logic that is sometimes at work here is that private individuals can do things that the police cannot. In the United States they have constitutional protections because in conducting their work they are operating as citizens and not as sworn officers. For example, Marx suggests that an improper search conducted by a private party is sometimes admissible in court.
- *Private sector hiring of the police*. An example of this would be a trade association or insurance company contributing funds or other resources to a particular activity. Operation Mod-Sound, for example, saw the recording industry financing an investigation into pirated material to the tune of $100,000.
- *New, hybrid quasi-public and quasi-private organizations*. A curious example of this is the Law Enforcement Intelligence Unit. This is a private organization that the police use to swap information. Because it is private, the police are not

hamstrung by regulations concerning the exchange of information or Freedom of Information Acts. Similarly, the National Auto Theft Bureau collects information from the law enforcement and insurance industries.

- *The circulation of personnel.* Large numbers of state employees have moved into the private sector. Salaries are often better and the private sector offers employment after mandatory retirement ages in the public sector. Strong ties and networks established during a career in law enforcement can be of use to both public and private sectors.

Marx suggests that although such moves can be beneficial, there are a number of potential dangers. Problems of transparency, confidentiality and accountability can arise, along with concerns about checks and balances. Questions about ethics and abuses of power quickly appear once the private sector uses money to buy law enforcement, or the state uses the private sector to sidestep what it sees as troublesome regulations. On the other hand, the relationship can be socially useful. Often the private and state sectors have common goals (e.g. reducing crime) and pooling resources makes good sense. Marx points here to the example of the bail bondsmen who have considerable powers to bring fugitives to court and, unlike the police, are not hampered by jurisdictional boundaries.

Police and the Media

It is difficult to open a newspaper, watch television, visit a bookstore or go to the local multiplex cinema today without coming across something that has do to with the police. From Sherlock Holmes to Dick Tracey and on to Inspector Morse, *Miami Vice*, *N.Y.P.D. Blue*, and so forth, history is full of hugely popular crime and policing narratives that serve as entertainment. Reiner (1985: 14) suggests that, like crime news reporting, such fiction tends to be unrepresentative. Serious crimes predominate, the perpetrators are high status and they engage in rationally calculated criminal acts. White males are over-represented among both villains and heroes. Real crime, in so far as reported crime statistics are a guide, is usually spontaneous, poorly executed, trivial and involves poor people, many of them from minorities. It does not seem too far-fetched to speculate that the kinds of crime found in the media reflect the desires and expectations of mostly white, middle-class audiences and producers.

Fictional accounts of policing are no doubt important in shaping public perceptions, but scholarship to date has concentrated on news and documentary genres. Although the police tend to be conservative and journalists on the left of politics, the relationship between the police and the news media is symbiotic (Putnis, 1996). Stories about social disorder are fundamental to the media; crime-related themes make up a good proportion of this. Studies have suggested that such material makes up about one quarter to one-third of news programming (Graber, 1980). Within this context the police are major providers of stories about crime – they control information and access. It is notable, however, that media reporting of crime and police activity is distorted (Reiner, 1985: 140). There is a focus on violent and sexual crimes, on crimes that are solved and on high status offenders. This kind of reporting generally helps to reproduce a positive image of the police.

The media provide an important avenue through which the police can conduct public relations activities, seek information on crimes from citizens (e.g. increasingly through infotainment programs like *Australia's Most Wanted*) and advise people about crime prevention strategies. The police may also require the media not to leak information that might jeopardize an operation or trial. Consequently, relations between the media and the police are usually cooperative but when the relationship is too close, problems can arise. Because journalists and editors need to be on good terms with the police in order to have access to stories and interviews, this might tempt them to avoid or soft-pedal any criticism of the police in their own reporting.

Critical media scholars have suggested that this cosy relationship has seen the media too often take the side of the police. Scholars such as Stuart Hall (1973) have suggested that photographs of strikes and demonstrations are taken from behind police lines and that political struggles are depicted as crimes that threaten national stability and public order. Notwithstanding such realities, relationships between the police and the media are sometimes strained, with each side feeling used by the other. The police, for example, feel that they are subjected to unfair criticism and scrutiny. A well-known example of this in Australia was the 1991 Australian Broadcasting Corporation documentary *Cop it Sweet* (Putnis, 1996: 205). This followed ordinary uniformed officers around on their daily beat and was intended to provide a realistic picture of policing in a tough inner city area. Although made with the consent of the police (perhaps because they thought it would improve understandings of their difficult job), the documentary was to boomerang on them. Officers seemed oblivious to the fact that they were on camera and were shown pocketing evidence, using racist and sexist language, having contempt for Aborigines and being intimidating towards the public. On the other side of the coin, police media and press units have provided misleading information to the media in an effort to make themselves look better. In the case of fatal shootings by the police, for example, the Police Media Liaison Bureau in Victoria, Australia, tried to draw attention to the links between the victims and previous violent crimes (Putnis, 1996: 207). This deflects questions about the shootings themselves and their legitimacy.

In sum, then, the media and the police have traditionally had a complex relationship of dependency and antagonism. Some claim that in recent years the media is starting to gain more power and that the police are having to respond to this. Under pressure to improve their public image, the police have developed more proactive uses for the media. Although the police still have the whip hand in the area of routine crime reporting, the case can be made that the media is advantaged in wider investigations, and in criticisms and commentaries on policing and police policy. Here they are less dependent and can draw upon a wider pool of sources. The police are also coming to see the media as an adjunct component of investigation and crime control and public image management, not simply as the recipients of press releases. Consequently, media policies and media relations bureau have been established and developed – again suggesting a police perception of the need to proactively control media 'spin' before they themselves are the target of critique.

Such themes of increasing media professionalism within the police are illustrated in a study by Raymond Boyle (1999) of the Strathclyde police force in Scotland. Consisting of over 7,000 officers and covering an area from the Highlands and Islands to the heart of Glasgow, this is one of the largest police forces in the UK. The 1996 Scottish Crime Survey had indicated high levels of fear of crime despite falling crime rates. New policing strategies came into place to deal with this. These were known as the Spotlight Initiative and involved policing hotspots and increasing police visibility. The police realized that they needed to work with the media to combat fear of crime. The media could help reduce crime by suggesting increased levels of police activity. They could also improve the police's image by suggesting they were getting tough on crime and were pushing hard with new and innovative ideas. Boyle points to a number of strategies used by the police to attain this end. These included the use of experts from their own Media and Information Services Department and the cultivation of ties with both national and local press. For example, journalists and photographers were invited to dawn raids. Television adverts and more than 200 billboards were used to highlight falling crime levels. Boyle (ibid.: 246) concludes that 'developing media strategies of the police and the marketing of the range of services it currently offers to the public … are crucial if the police wish to maintain public support in an era of increasing political and financial uncertainty'.

Conclusion

Here we have looked at policing from a number of perspectives. We have explored its ties to extrinsic factors such as modernity and political life, have investigated police culture and styles of police activity and also inquired about some of the changes taking place in policing today. The sociological perspective taken to each of these sets of issues has perhaps dispelled a few myths you may have had about the police. But more important is the general thrust of the chapter. This has asserted that the police will face major challenges in the future. They are essentially a hierarchical, rule-bound modernist organization that is about to enter a postmodern world. We have also stressed that the police are an institution that in many ways confronts injustice but perhaps, in so doing, perpetuates it. In the next chapter we look at another set of modernist institutions, the courts, and find out whether or not we can detect a similarly ironic dynamic.

Study Questions

1   How do new initiatives respond to the perceived failures of reactive policing? Which are the most useful in contemporary society (and how do you define 'useful')?

2   What, in your opinion, are the major challenges facing the police today? How do you suggest these can be overcome?

3   Re-read the description in Box 3.4 of Shearing and Stenning's (1987c) account of social control in Disney World (better yet, read it in the original article). Choose a comparable private space and see if you can identify similar processes.

4   Briefly indicate how the theories of (a) Max Weber and (b) Karl Marx might be used to understand the origins and function of the contemporary police.

5   From the studies presented in this chapter, what do you believe to be the relationship between police culture and police deviance? Describe a research question and methods that might be used to further investigate the relationships. What would be the strengths and weaknesses of your approach? How easy would it be to implement your proposed study?

6   Undertake a series of role-plays showing the likely interactions and their outcomes between the police and the following:

   • a group of teenage boys gathering in a mall
   • a drunk and aggressive businessman
   • a woman who can't find her child in a shopping centre.

7   Research and then conduct a class debate on one of the following propositions:

   • Community policing is the most desirable means of crime prevention.
   • Contemporary policing is about maintaining order not preventing crime.
   • Police culture would be significantly altered through the introduction of more women/minority groups into the service.

Glossary of Key Terms

agency capture – The process in which a regulating body becomes controlled or neutralized by those whom it is supposed to regulate.

code of silence – The informal norm through which police officers refuse to testify against each other. This makes police malpractice difficult to investigate.

community policing – An approach that aims for community input into policing, better relations with the community, a bigger focus on crime prevention and a return to non-motorized forms of patrolling.

compliance systems – Forms of social control involving negotiation and partnership, with the law invoked only as a last resort.

differentiation – The spreading out of roles and functions, usually as part of a long-term historical process.

evidence-based policing – An approach that seeks to improve policing efficiency by formulating policy on the basis of the outcomes of evaluation research.

law and order society – This arises during conservative and pro-capitalist regimes in times of crisis. The police become repressive, racist and partisan, rather than supporting individual liberties.

police culture – An influential system of informal beliefs, values and behaviours that are part of a shared police world-view.

police discretion – This refers to the fact that police officers have considerable latitude in how they respond to a situation. Most importantly, they can decide whether or not to instigate formal action against citizens. Hence they are gatekeepers to the criminal justice system.

policing by consent – A policing model which argues that the police have/should have the support of the community. Usually contrasted with paramilitary policing.

problem-oriented policing – This is a proactive strategy which involves identifying recurrent problems and devising ways they can be addressed.

professionalization – The process of becoming a profession. This involves developing formal training, qualifications and an expert knowledge base.

reactive policing – The dominant policing model, this involves motorized patrols and rapid response to civilians' calls.

sanctioning systems – Forms of social control revolving around the use of the law and punishment.

stereotypes – The images through which police view citizens and potential/actual offenders according to prejudices and rules of thumb. They result in the over-policing of racial minorities, youth, the working class and those whose appearance deviates from white, middle-class norms.

zero tolerance policing – A strategy that involves cleaning up crime-prone areas through saturation policing and arresting or ticketing even minor offenders.

Suggested Further Reading

Once you have finished with this chapter, perhaps try the collected essays in Manning and Van Maanen (1978), *Policing: A View from the Streets*. Like Bittner (1990), these provide a good place to start understanding the police world-view, especially in the United States. Robert Reiner's (1992) text is a little broader in focus and offers a very quick way to get up to speed on a range of themes in the policing literature as it relates to the UK. Books by Holdaway (1983) and Fielding (1995) also give a good account of the British police experience. The collected essays in Shearing and Stenning (1987a) are a little out of date now, but still suggest ways in which private policing is changing the landscape. There are a number of excellent academic journals providing coverage of policing issues. Articles often appear in generalist criminology sources such as *The British Journal of Criminology*, *Criminology* and *Justice Quarterly*. Specific journals dedicated to policing issues include *Policing and Society* and *Police Studies*. Research articles on specific aspects of policing can be located using the Sociological Abstracts CD-ROM.

Suggested Websites

Websites belonging to the police provide an insight not only into the range of policing activity and current operations, but also the extent to which contemporary policing is about public relations. A careful reading will show that much of the material is an effort to present the police in a good light through press releases, statistics and descriptions of innovative new programs. There are few sites containing 'free' material on policing that has an academic slant. Those run by government agencies and research centres tend to be the most useful.

http://www.aic.gov.au/   The Australian Institute of Criminology. You can sometimes access research on police here.

http://www.criminaljusticestudies.com/weblinks   This site belongs to the Institute of Criminal Justice Studies in Texas. They have set up an outstanding series of weblinks to diverse policing related sites.

http://www.homeoffice.gov.uk/rds/   The Research and Development department of the UK Home Office offers some excellent statistics and research reports.

http://www.met.police.uk/   London's Metropolitan Police.

http://www.nyc.gov/html/nypd/home.html   This is the home page of the New York Police.

http://www.ojp.usdoj.gov/   The United States Department of Justice. By clicking about you can usually find material on policing issues.

4 Court Processes and Personnel

Introduction

Courts – and in particular the higher courts – enjoy a privileged position within the social imagination. If we were to take the representations of law dramas as truth, we might assume that an aggressive and emotionally charged trial before a jury, complete with double dealings, slippery ethics and a shock confession, is central to the criminal justice process. In the world of TV drama, each defendant and their victim gets their time in court so that their actions and claims may be interrogated and decried or absolved. The focus of traditional jurisprudence also implies that courts are the most significant element of the Western, adversarial system, a forum in which justice is publicly enacted. Perhaps not so surprisingly, sociologists have consistently argued against either of these positions. This chapter addresses some of the key contemporary issues that attach to the role and functioning of the courts and their personnel. We overview the role of courts, the processes of judging and its outcomes, the declining importance of juries, alternative methods of dispute resolution, and the relationship between the media and the courts. By the time we have reviewed these issues we will have substantially undermined our faith in this pillar of criminal justice system.

The Role of the Courts

From a common-sense perspective, it is often assumed that dispute processing is the primary role of the court. In the instance of the criminal justice system, the dispute arises between the state and the accused. The issues are dealt with in court: each party 'tells their story', and on the basis of the evidence, either the judge or jury determines which version of events is true. But as Roger Cotterrell (1984: 222) points out, processing crimes within an adversarial framework is not the same as resolving a dispute. Resolution is achieved when both parties agree with an outcome, understand its logic, and recognise the norms that are imposed upon them. A process that creates a winner and loser on the basis of often arcane rules is unlikely to generate resolution. Instead, it may contribute to the escalation of disputes. It makes them public, demands careful definition – often over-simplification – extrapolation and de-contextualization of the wrongs that are claimed to have been committed, and removes much of the later experience from the control of the parties most directly involved. Given these processes, Cotterrell (ibid.: 223) concludes that the role of the courts is primarily 'an assertion of normative order, a definition in terms of legal doctrine of the way a particular social situation or relationship is to be understood'. It is not a forum designed to let parties have their say, contributing directly to the outcome.

The importance of resolving disputes is also marginalized because many cases are never heard before the courts. Social scientists have pointed to a process of **rationalization** that detours cases. For example, Lawrence Friedman and Robert Percival (1976) suggest that while the role of courts may once have been adjudication, this has evolved to a contemporary emphasis on processing routine cases as efficiently as possible. This conclusion is supported when we consider the significance of guilty pleas and plea bargaining in contemporary criminal processes. The term 'plea bargaining' covers a diverse range of activities but they share in common the exchange of a guilty plea for the possibility of a lighter sentence or lesser or fewer charges. This may entail explicit negotiations but it may also involve informal expectations, such as an in-court guilty plea made with the expectation of a lighter sentence. Sharyn Roach Anleu (2000) lists a number of manifest motivations for plea bargaining:

- *Strength of the prosecution case.* Plea bargaining can be used when the prosecution believes that they will not obtain a conviction because their evidence is weak, but nonetheless believe that the offender is guilty (Adams, 1983).
- *Substantive justice.* Defence and prosecutors can argue the issues more fully and openly outside of the courtroom because they are unfettered by procedural rules (Mulcahy, 1994). This allows them to reach a fair and logical outcome. However, some argue the interests of the accused are not as important as the needs of long-term players in the system (for example, to free up time for more profitable work, or to reduce courts' backlogs).
- *Administrative pressures.* Plea bargaining may reduce backlogs and contribute to a more efficient management of cases. There is some evidence to suggest that when plea bargaining is unavailable the number of contested cases rises (Church, 1976; Holmes et al., 1992; Padgett, 1990).
- *Organizational relationships.* People working in the criminal justice system know each other and over time create working understandings and relationships. They are concerned with the coordination of a number of interests, organizations, processes and outcomes. The interests of the accused may become a secondary focus to those of bureaucracy, politics and personal convenience.

The above list makes it clear that efficiency, perhaps more so than dispute resolution, matters in contemporary courts. Writing from a critical perspective, Pat O'Malley (1983) points out that when a person pleads guilty in the lower courts, the following occur at little or no expense to the powerful organizations and individuals who would otherwise be part of the trial process:

- *Magistrates* can argue that they fulfil demands that they be 'tough on crime' through generating high conviction rates, and guilty pleas allow them to more easily manage their case load.
- Claims that *courts* are serving justice are substantiated because a guilty plea stands as a marker of contrition.
- The *police prosecutors* more easily manage their high case load, achieve a high conviction rate with little effort and uncertainty, and avoid opening possible illegal police procedure to scrutiny.
- The *defence lawyers* enjoy a high turnover of cases with little preparation time and a minimum of uncertainty.

Although rather old, an early Australian study on the processing of pleas in a magistrate's court in the state of Victoria provides some startling data to support the above conclusions. Lippman (1979: 109) calculated that the average time spent in the determination of guilt was 23.6 seconds per case; 11.1 seconds per charge. Even contested pleas were dealt with shockingly quickly, with an average of a little over 5 minutes per case. These results suggest that the processes of the adversarial system are, to put it mildly, truncated. More time is spent on sentencing than on the determination of guilt (Douglas, 1980; Lippman, 1979; O'Malley, 1983).

It is easy to argue that plea bargaining and the encouragement of guilty pleas are necessary on the common-sense grounds that they begin to counter the problems of lengthy and expensive trials and court backlogs. But from a sociological perspective, this is not 'common sense' so much as an indication that the needs of the court and criminal justice system are defined by the rational and administrative requirements of bureaucratic justice. The judging and processing of defendants are simplified and routinized and in so doing, the uncertainties facing all parties (the length of the trial, the viability of the case, the expected outcomes) are reduced (Blumberg, 1969; O'Malley, 1983: 128). But the edifice of simplicity and efficiency is often built on the presumption that defendants are guilty, not innocent (Blumberg, 1969; O'Malley, 1983). This reverses the central tenet of Western liberal ideals.

Friedman (1978) argues that these often almost automatic guilty pleas are linked to the rise of the police as a professional body (for a review of this historical process, see pp. 84–86). Once investigation was removed from the hands of enthusiastic amateurs and entrusted to experts, it was presumed that an adversarial trial was no longer strictly necessary because police had already identified the relevant issues. Justice became a technical-rational process. Rationalization hides many of the problems of police culture and practice. Pat O'Malley (1983: 135) points out that if charges were more rigorously defended and the evidence presented by the police challenged, mundane policing activities and the routine control of citizens would be vastly more difficult. Any informal and technically illegal components of policing would be systematically uncovered, and the means of gathering previously acceptable evidence would need to become more rigorous. Additionally, the legitimacy of the police would unravel, as their procedures are judged and found wanting. O'Malley also notes that the processes of rationalization are in place before a case goes to trial. Police have almost total control over the pre-trial process, in their discretion to pursue an incident, their interrogation of the suspect, and in the decision as to what charges will be laid (p. 83). O'Malley (ibid.: 136) concludes that as a result, 'the determination of guilt is effectively and systematically transferred to the police in the vast majority of criminal prosecutions'. O'Malley's point highlights that court and policing activities are intimately tied.

The efficient processing of defendants is also linked to the role of the prosecutor. As we have already noted, crimes are committed against the state, even where people suffer the consequences of the criminal act or omission. The state cannot itself prosecute anyone; the prosecutor becomes its representative and in so doing, the representative of citizens. In practice, prosecutorial decision-making, like that of the police, is invisible, and is not usually subject to political or judicial review. Even in the presence of guidelines and policy, prosecutors enjoy a great deal of discretion. According to Davis (1998: 20), this discretion can be used in a random and arbitrary fashion. It can have as much impact on inequalities in the criminal justice system as the decisions of police, juries or judges. The role of the prosecutor includes determining which charges will be pursued in court, what outcomes will be requested, and as we have already noted, whether or not someone goes to trial in the first place.

Ideologically, the role of prosecutor demands that they 'consider whether a conviction is "consistent with the public interest" in conjunction with their personal sense of the defendant's culpability for the crime' (Levenson, 1999: 559). However, this expectation holds within it a series of difficult questions:

- What is the public interest?
- Where does the accused fit within the 'public'?
- Where does a sense of the defendant's culpability come from?

Davis (1998: 51) notes that the public interest is served when trials are fair, a broader definition than a simple expectation that any one accused person is found guilty. This position acknowledges the discrepancies in the application of law, at all levels of the criminal justice system. Theoretically, the interests of the defendant, as a member of society, are important in the trial process. These interests can conflict with those of society, a difficult tension for the prosecutor to reconcile. Davis (ibid.: 52) points out that the prosecutor's duties include both the enforcement of criminal laws and the equitable treatment of victims and offenders in the criminal justice system – a responsibility owed to individuals and to society as a whole. The difficulties emerge 'not in the conceptualisation of these responsibilities but in their implementation' (ibid). In light of what we know about race, class or gender disparities in the criminal justice system, the prosecution of an individual case may include interests at odds with the broader ideals of the justice system. Further, as we have already noted, efficiency in the processing of cases is increasingly valued, and has itself been claimed to be in the public interest.

A sense of the accused's culpability may also be problematic. Presumably, few prosecutors would be guided by explicitly discriminatory attitudes. Rather, inequalities may be the flow-on effects from police practice. We have already noted that police practices may be either latently or manifestly discriminatory, which may in turn affect the available evidence. Other considerations such as prior record or likelihood of conviction are also taken into account, again, with indirectly discriminatory outcomes. Or, the negotiations with the accused's representation may affect perceptions of guilt. These perceptions and the ethical expectations of prosecutors intersect with the organizational drives and imperatives to efficiency to shape the ways in which an accused is moved into the adjudication process. It is clear that the resolution of disputes is not a significant factor in these decisions.

Language and Power

The expectation of dispute resolution and the central tenets of justice are again called into question through elements of the trial process. The relatively small proportion of people who come before the courts face a new set of problems: they cannot simply and easily tell their story. Courtroom interactions are ordered by the logic of the Western adversarial system. This incorporates formal rules of evidence, informal norms of professional conduct, and expectations of how witnesses, defendants and experts should present themselves. John Conley and William O'Barr (1990: 9) sum up the conclusions of many social scientists when they comment, 'Official legal discourse ... is far removed from the language of ordinary people. It tends to transform or simply ignore the discourse of the disputants whose problems are the law's very reason for being.' In the following pages we consider language and communication, and how they reflect the dynamics of power in the courtroom. This has become an increasingly significant area of academic research.

There are different ways to approach the play of language and interaction in the courtroom. Ethnomethodology is one major tradition. It recognises that people's practices and language create the social order; they are not constrained by its preexistence. For example, Harold Garfinkel's (1956) early discussion on criminal trial processes defined them as 'degradation ceremonies'. He argued that interaction in the courtroom is guided by rules of communication and evidence. These are rituals designed to reconstruct the identity of the offender as deviant. To achieve this, actions must be represented and reinterpreted. A set of rules of interaction effectively ensures success in this venture. More commonly, social scientists work outside of ethnomethodology and have been influenced by critical theories such as Marxism, feminism and postmodernism. A focus on courtroom language provides an insight into broader processes and relations of law. Studies have emphasized the ways in which shared or contested realities are constructed through court processes and in particular, examination and cross-examination. Bryna Bogoch (1999a: 244) comments that legal discourse occurs in 'a public rule-governed arena in which such issues as power and privilege, constraints and conflict, and norms and deviance are worked out through a range of discourse strategies including coercion and resistance, persuasion and negotiation, narrative and argument'. For example, witnesses are 'silenced', so that they cannot have their say on their own terms

(Eades, 2000: 162). While studying how Australian Aboriginal witnesses communicated in court, Diana Eades became aware that they said very little. She found that they were rarely given the chance to speak, and their knowledge was almost never sought by either the defence or prosecution. Eades argues that the silencing of Aboriginal witnesses highlights racial relations because it reflects the lack of interest typically extended to Aboriginal perspectives. She concludes that both judges and lawyers are most likely to silence, ignore or stop witnesses when their answers relate to aspects of Aboriginal culture that they do not understand, and of which they cannot appreciate the relevance. Such principles of power are extended to other groups who take the stand (ibid.: 190).

Gregory Matoesian (1993, 1997) describes the 'rhythms of domination' in the William Kennedy Smith rape trial. This involved a claim that Kennedy Smith had sexually assaulted a woman after she willingly accompanied him to his home, a classic 'date rape' scenario. In this instance, Kennedy Smith was found to be not guilty. Through detailed analysis of the interactions between counsel and witnesses, Matoesian highlights the ways in which a charge of rape is pursued and defended through a series of discursive and interactional strategies rooted in dominant cultural understandings of sexual identity. He focuses on the way in which the defence strategies of cross-examination can be used to construct a series of 'logical inconsistencies' which are built upon assumptions about the 'appropriate' way for a woman to act towards men in whom she is/not sexually interested. He also presents the witnesses' ultimately unsuccessful attempts to counter these. Matoesian (1997: 56) argues 'legal realities such as inconsistency emerge not just from some logical, rational, or natural juxtaposition of contradictory issues of evidence but from an interaction between cultural ideologies and linguistic resources in the trial context'. As a result, a particular reality is created and patriarchy is reproduced. His perspective fits within more general feminist concerns over the construction of rape victims, as well as the gendering of the legal subject (see pp. 62–72).

Displays of power are most obvious in the **question–answer format** that is used to elicit information from witnesses on the stand. This reinforces the power discrepancies between the questioner and the witness because questions are actually demands. People must answer the question, and they must answer in response to that particular question, rather than presenting the evidence they believe to be important. Witnesses are not able to introduce new topics or lines of inquiry. As a result, lawyers have the freedom to present their perspective on the evidence so that significant issues might be misrepresented or left unexplored (Harris, 1984; Luchjenbroers, 1997). Asking questions is also a culturally specific way of obtaining information – in some cultures it is considered rude, invasive or threatening.

A number of studies have identified the more specific issue of the intersection of power and syntax (the structure of the phrase) (Danet and Bogoch, 1980; Harris, 1984; Matoesian, 1993). For example, a declaration with a question tagged on at the end, is very manipulative ('You walked into the bar and hit him for no reason, isn't that so?'). Questions demanding a 'simple' yes or no answer are also coercive because they do not allow the witness to develop a coherent story (Matoesian, 1993). 'How', 'what' and 'why' questions allow a little more scope for witnesses' answers (Woodbury, 1984).

These are more likely to be used by the defence counsel in their examination-in-chief to construct a narrative, which sounds more truthful and thus has added weight as evidence (Woodbury, 1984). Similarly, William O'Barr (1982) describes the powerless language of witnesses. He draws upon the work of Robin Lakoff (1975) who describes characteristics of women's speech patterns. These include:

- hedges (sort of, like);
- intensifiers and empty adjectives (very, really);
- hesitations (umm, err);
- direct quotations ('He said ...').

O'Barr (1982: 70) concludes that rather than specifically feminine speech forms, these patterns are characteristic of social powerlessness more generally. This may have material consequences for the outcome of a case. In an experiment, O'Barr found that mock jurors described those who spoke in a more powerful style as more believable, more convincing and more trustworthy (results that held for both male and female witnesses).

Conducting proceedings in English creates further difficulties for witnesses and defendants from a non-English-speaking background. This is exacerbated by the absence of any right to an interpreter. In the US, the lack of an interpreter has been argued to be a breach of the sixth Amendment guarantee of a right to face one's accuser (O'Barr, 1982: 41); more generally it may conflict with the right to a fair trial. In Australia, for example, an interpreter is provided at the discretion of the judge. Michael Cooke (1995: 105) has pointed out that deciding if an interpreter is necessary can be more difficult than it first seems. A person may be able to answer direct and simple questions, but not necessarily follow the colloquialism, nuances, 'legalese' or rapid speech of the court proceedings. Cooke discusses a case involving an Australian Aboriginal witness. The presiding judge decided he did not need a translator on the basis of a series of questions to which the most grammatically complex answer was 'I work for council plumbing'. Further, interpreters are only provided for the time an individual takes the stand. As a result, a defendant may experience almost the whole of his or her trial without actually understanding it, or getting only the 'gist' of what is being said. The limits indicate that the role of an interpreter is often first and foremost that of meeting the court's interests, and not those of the witness – translation is used so that court personnel can extract the information they need, not so that the witness or defendant is cognisant of the complexities and outcomes of interactions.

On a similar theme, O'Barr (1982: 40-1) lists a series of assumptions that are made about the comprehension and language skills of English speakers in the courtroom. These include expectations such as:

- People who speak English can understand the courtroom proceedings and do not require an interpreter. This holds true irrespective cultural or ethnic backgrounds.
- When English speakers do not understand courtroom talk, counsel, and not the court, needs to take action.

- English-speaking jurors understand English-speaking witnesses.
- English-speaking jurors understand the judge's instructions.
- Jurors have heard and understood the evidence presented, unless they explicitly state that they have not.
- Jurors do not need to directly ask questions of the witness.

Presumptions about language in the courts have very real consequences. Consider the comments of an indigenous Australian man:

> As soon as Aboriginal people enter the courtroom, they feel different, they become afraid. I have seen old men (i.e. men who have power and stature in Aboriginal society) shaking with fear. When I ask them: 'What is the matter?', they say: 'I don't know what's going on.'... People who are frightened of the court will often plead guilty, even when they are innocent, so as to get finished and out of court quickly. They can also plead guilty because they don't know what's going on. One old lady from Maryvale Station was picked up on a 'drunk' charge. She doesn't drink at all. She went to the hotel looking for her daughter; she was worried about her. I said: 'Why did you say "guilty"'? She said: 'I didn't understand what was happening, so I said the same as the woman in front of me'. (Lester, cited in Cooke, 1995: 101)

The preceding discussion might give the impression that witnesses have no power to shape the evidence they present. But of course even in rule-governed court contexts, people have some agency to counter the strategies of their examiners with their own. Anita Barry (1993) describes 'narrative cooperativeness', in which the witness and their examiner cooperate in the construction of a coherent narrative. This occurs during examination-in-chief, when the person in the stand and the lawyer are 'on the same side'. In these instances, both parties share an interest in creating a logical account of the issues at hand, and work together to do so. The power discrepancies remain, but their effects are not as dire as in cross-examination, where the parties may be attempting to create alternative narratives. Gregory Mateosian (1997) notes that witnesses are not simple dupes in the examination process and do not respond to questions as though they were a neutral request for information. They recognise the implicit blame, disbelief and accusations of questions and can often identify the narrative counsel attempts to produce. This in turn makes it even more desirable for attorneys to dominate the process. Given this necessity, and in light of the formal rules and practices listed above, the possibilities for a substantial subversion of the processes are always available, but often limited.

Sentencing

As we have already discussed, the traditional legal perspective assumes that judges apply the law in a rational and objective manner (see pp. 66–68). They are guided by the law, supposedly filling in any gaps with rigorous legal reasoning. However, there is surprisingly little direct sociological commentary on the ways in which judges adjudicate the issues that come before them. Traditionally, judges have not explained their decisions to the public or sociologists, beyond formal and legalistic justifications and sentencing statements. Thus, we have little direct access to the mental and social processes of judging.

Concern over the judicial discretion and decision-making is most marked in the extensive collection of studies focusing on the aggregate effects of race and gender on the sentencing of defendants. After being found guilty in a court, the criminal is subject to **sentencing**. This is the process in which a penalty is applied for a given crime. Perhaps not surprisingly, this issue of discretion and imprecision in sentencing has caused considerable controversy (Zdenkowski, 2000). In light of our earlier critique of the law's claims to equality, impartiality and its ethnocentrism (pp. 61–68), we might expect obvious and systematic instances of ethnic and gender discrimination in terms of sentence outcomes. However, the available evidence does not easily support this assumption.

Research shows sentencing to be a haphazard activity where judges have to balance up a number of factors. These include the gravity of the offence, the prior record of the offender, the range of penalties available by law, parity with other recent decisions and harm to the victim. These more factual matters are cross-cut by the various ideologies of punishment discussed in the next chapter: retribution, deterrence, reform. In pulling all these together, the judge may well have to rely on rules of thumb. It is noteworthy in this respect that factors influencing sentencing can contradict each other. An often cited example is the fact that an emphasis on retribution looks backwards to the offence, while one on deterrence might look to the future and focus more on crime reduction. The relative importance of such factors might also vary with swings in policy, ideology or the *Zeitgeist*. In the 1960s and 1970s theories about rehabilitation were dominant, but by the 1980s a conservative backlash saw older ideas about just desserts return to prominence.

Ethnicity

In the USA in particular, sociologists have been involved in an ongoing attempt to see if ethnicity affects how a person is judged. From a common-sense point of view the presumption might easily be that race does make a difference. Cassia Spohn (2000: 433) quotes a series of figures that show that Black and Hispanic offenders are more likely to be sentenced to prison, and on average receive longer sentences. Similar data are associated with ethnic minorities in Britain, and Aborigines in Australia. These numbers are evidence of disparities, but not necessarily discrimination. **Discrimination** occurs when people are treated differently through extra-legal or inappropriate considerations. Thus the question inevitably arises: are ethnic minorities subject to racism or do disparities simply reflect the fact that they might be involved in particular types of crime?

The question of justifiable difference remains pertinent even in light of the sentencing guidelines that were introduced in part to limit judicial discretion and discriminatory outcomes (Tonry, 1996: 164; these issues are discussed further on pp. 136–139). In the Federal US context, there is still scope for judges to discount or add to sentences, according to prescribed circumstances. As we shall see, this leads to discrepancies between ethnic groups. Given that the most systematic consideration of these issues has occurred through studies of the US criminal justice system, the following discussion focuses on this context.

When sentencing guidelines were absent, the evidence of racial discrimination in sentencing seemed relatively straightforward. A series of studies from the 1950s to the 1970s concluded that black people were treated more harshly than white offenders. Unfortunately, these studies used unsophisticated statistical techniques. In particular, they failed to control for the seriousness of the crime committed and prior criminal records (Hagan, 1974). These are relevant, legal issues a judge must consider when sentencing an offender. When these were included in the equations, John Hagan concluded that race and the severity of the sentence can be linked in a statistically significant relationship, but the influence was only minor. His conclusions were supported by the later work of Gary Kleck (1981), who found that many disparities simply disappeared when analyses included a prior criminal record. Both writers argued that claims of racial discrimination were only supported in the South, and only in crimes that attracted the death penalty. They concluded that there is an absence of direct and systematic racial discrimination (cf. Hagan and Bumiller, 1983; Wilbanks, 1987).

In more recent years questions of *direct discrimination* have increasingly given way to studies of subtle and institutionalized racial disadvantage (Zatz, 1987: 70). Offenders from minority groups might suffer *indirect discrimination* (Spohn, 2000). This means that race (the independent variable) and sentencing outcomes (the dependent variable) are linked through a third factor. Differences might result from economic or social disparities that attach to race. For example, better lawyers or the ability to raise the bail money for pre-trial release have been found to contribute to more lenient sentences; Black and Hispanic offenders are more likely to come from a lower socio-economic group, and are less likely to be able to afford these privileges (Steffensmeier and Demuth, 2000, see also Holmes et al., 1996).

Indirect discrimination is also evident in the ways in which organizational priorities interact with racial and cultural differences. Ronald Everett and Barbara Nienstedt (1999) note that when a probation officer prepares a recommendation under the Federal sentencing guidelines, they must consider the extent to which a defendant accepts responsibility for their actions. This is often determined with reference to expressions of remorse. Remorse is also taken as an indicator that the offender is unlikely to offend again (Drass and Spencer, 1987: 281). Defendants might engage in behaviours that do not symbolize remorse or a proper respect for the courts' authority, and be punished for it (Robinson et al., 1994; Steffensmeier and Demuth, 2000). Everett and Nienstedt (1999) also comment that remorse might not be accepted as genuine, and the presiding judge may reject the probation officers' findings, often on the basis of interactions in the courtroom at the time of sentencing. These writers do not go far enough in considering the extent to which ethnic, gender and class differences might affect judges' and probation officers' interpretations of expressions of remorse and responsibility. In light of interactionist studies that describe the cultural differences in courtroom communication, it may be that demeanours that deviate from dominant norms, for example, those of minority youth cultures, may be read as disinterest, disrespect or guilt.

Increasingly, social scientists have been turning to the concept of *contextual discrimination* (Walker et al., 1999: 17) to explain disparities between groups. Contextual discrimination recognises that sometimes offenders are treated equally, but other times they are not. Outcomes may be affected by the intersection of the type of crime and the place of its commission, the age, gender and race of the offender, the race of the victim (Spohn, 2000: 434). This is termed an interaction effect. Recent studies provide support for interaction effects when data do not indicate any direct effects of race. For example, Samuel Walker, Cassia Spohn and Miriam DeLone (1999) report that Blacks as a group do not receive harsher sentences than whites but those without a job and living in Chicago receive longer sentences than their white counterparts, as do unemployed Hispanics. In a different study Darrell Steffensmeier and his colleagues (Steffensmeier et al., 1998) find that young, Black males suffered harsher sentences that any other combination of race, gender and age. Such studies suggest that race is a significant factor in sentencing outcomes, but its effects may be contingent.

Interaction effects remind us that we are not simply raced beings – our social identities are constituted by additional characteristics, which may be relevant when our actions are judged. The findings support a point we make several times in this book. It is less useful to look for 'racism' in the criminal justice system in terms of individual mental prejudice and more useful to appreciate the complex and unintended consequences of policies, procedures and practices as these impact upon diverse populations. This is not to deny that the criminal justice system is closely tied to issues of race politics but rather to suggest such connections need to be systematically theorized in a sustained, sociological way rather than opined away as simply 'prejudice' or 'racism' without a fuller detailed inquiry.

Unfortunately, efforts to consider *why* any disparities exist are not particularly impressive. Some writers argue that the more knowledge a person has, the more confident they feel in their decision. Judges are no different in that they, like everybody else, act with incomplete information. To minimize this and create a sense of consistency and certainty in their sentencing, judges draw upon a set of expectations and stereotypes. Steffensmeier et al. (1998) have developed this perspective in their '**focal concerns theory**'. They argue that sentencing decisions are guided by the offender's culpability, the need to protect the community and the social costs of sentencing decisions. These priorities are pursued with only limited information and so judges work on the basis of racial, age and gender assumptions and stereotypes to 'fill in the blanks'. Steffensmeier et al. describe this as 'perceptual shorthand' for a series of 'objective' reasoning processes. Not surprisingly, they argue that judges are harshest towards those who are assumed to be more deviant, dangerous or likely to re-offend. Their conclusions derive from their findings on the disadvantages faced by young, black male offenders but Spohn (2000) notes that this conclusion may be extended to other groups who are perceived to dangerously deviate from the norm. They suggest that discriminatory decisions are not informed by overt racism, but are justified by a covert racism of which individual judges are possibly not aware.

An alternative, the **'liberation hypothesis'** (Kalven and Zeisel, 1966), argues that racial minorities attract harsher treatment for less serious crimes. When sentencing serious crimes, there is very little discretion available to judges: the law demands long terms of imprisonment. But when it comes to lesser offences, there is more leeway in determining the appropriate sentence. In these circumstances factors such as race or age might be taken into account, with discriminatory outcomes. Crawford, Chiricos and Kleck (1998) report data that provide some evidence of this. Racial differences in sentencing are most marked in less serious crimes, notably property and drug offences, compared to weapons and violent offences. Crawford et al. (ibid.: 506) argue that judicial decision-making is linked to the 'racial threat', which is associated in judicial minds with an 'urban underclass [of] blacks and drugs'.

Other writers have linked racial differences in the sentencing of drug offenders to the effects of moral panics (see p. 17). They locate judicial discretion in the context of the 'war on drugs' that has disproportionately drawn Black and to a lesser extent Hispanic people into the criminal justice system. Further, these groups are more closely linked to drug crimes in media representations and the popular imagination. Sentencing judges, it has been suggested, are not immune to the effects of this discourse (Chiricos and DeLone, 1992; Jenkins, 1994; Tonry, 1995).

Alternatively, Jo Dixon (1995) argues from an **organizational perspective**. We have already noted the desire to ensure the justice process runs as smoothly and efficiently as possible. To do this, offenders are encouraged to plead guilty or cooperate with prosecutors, in exchange for decreased sentences (pp. 122–123). This encouragement is extended to white people, more so than African Americans. The rationality of sentencing is in part based on organizational policy, but the application of this policy is informed by discriminatory practices. Again, race is not a simple input variable. Its effects will alter according to the crime and the organizational context and the meanings attached by the judge (Kautt and Spohn, 2002).

Before we leave this discussion, it is useful to overview the limitations of the body of work as a whole. In the US context the following issues make it difficult to draw any final conclusions:

- *Jurisdictional differences*. Federal and State criminal justice systems have authority over different crimes, and are subject to different sentencing guidelines. Further, the cultures and stresses of the jurisdictions might create divergent sentencing priorities and judicial attitudes. As a result, we must be careful when generalizing results from one context to another.
- *Methodological problems*. Concern over discrimination in sentencing has often outpaced the development of statistical methods that can adequately measure the effects of race. Earlier studies in particular failed to account for all valid factors.

- *Contradictory findings.* The previous discussion makes it abundantly clear that we have not yet developed a set of coherent and complementary findings. It can seem that each finding of discrimination is countered by another study concluding that sentencing decisions are race neutral.
- *Modest effects of race.* Some commentators have argued that any relationship, even if not statistically significant, is nonetheless of concern but others claim that the 'take home message' is an absence of systematic and widespread discrimination.
- *Quantitative methodology.* The methods identify sentencing patterns but they cannot generate information on the *process* of judging. Many studies are in fact only tangentially investigating the reasoning processes that lead to discrimination. We have little information on just how judges interpret characteristics of the offenders.
- *Poor theorization.* We have a great deal of data on what matters and what does not, but this has been generated at the expense of coherent and conceptually sophisticated explanations of why some groups are – or are not – treated more harshly than others.

Overall, the data on this question point to an absence of direct and deliberate discrimination on the part of criminal justice personnel generally and judges, in particular. Those who are disadvantaged in society generally are more likely to become caught up in the criminal justice system and at each step their disadvantage is compounded. These conclusions present a massive challenge to those who wish to address bias and discrimination in the courts. Success cannot come from the appointment of 'better' judges, judicial education or sentencing guidelines. It will be encouraged through the dismantling of entrenched processes and thinking in a more structural and sociological way about the often unintended outcomes of policies when these are played out in the real world.

Gender

Just as there has been a presumption that some ethnic groups are systematically disadvantaged, feminist scholars have also been concerned that judges treat women differently. Some studies have found no statistically significant differences in the treatment of male and female defendants. Contradicting these findings, other researchers have concluded that women are treated more leniently in sentencing. For example John Hagan, Ilene Nagel and Celesta Albonetti (1980) found that gender affects the length of the prison term in white-collar cases, so that women receive shorter imprisonment terms than do men. Simon and Landis cite a 1988 qualitative study where 11 of the 12 judges interviewed acknowledged that they treated female offenders more leniently than male offenders. It has been suggested that women with families received shorter sentences because court officials do not want to punish children by taking their mother away from them (Daly, 1989). Probation officers are more likely to presume that women will be 'scared straight'. Officials believe that the threat of prison is more frightening for women than for men and so criminal women do not need to be penalized in the same way or to the same degree as men (ibid.).

Other researchers have focused on the differences between women. They argue that sentencing decisions are informed by the ways in which women conform to the cultural ideal of womanhood. For example, David Farrington and Allison Morris (1983) reported that marital status makes a difference to the sentences imposed upon women but has no effect on the severity of a man's sentences. Kathleen Daly (1989) concluded that family ties were significant for both men and women, but women were treated even more leniently than familied men. In the same vein, Pat Carlen (1983) found that Scottish authorities assumed that a husband would be likely to keep his wife 'in line', so that imprisonment was unnecessary. Carlen also argued that being a 'good mother' could lead to a non-custodial sentence, on the grounds that children should not suffer by the absence of their mum. Jailing women who do not fit the ideal – those whose houses were untidy, or who are deemed to be insufficiently nurturing towards their children, or whose actions might lead to an unsavoury home life – was not seen by officials to have such negative effects on children. The types of crime might also be significant: Matthew Zingraff and Randall Thomson (1984) discovered that women who assault or abandon their children received harsher sentences than men in the same circumstances.

These studies indicate that gender is important in shaping how judges weigh the effects of their sentencing decisions. They suggest that if an offender can be presented as a 'good woman', she might receive a more lenient sentence. This is sometimes said to be the result of **chivalry**. Ilene Nagel and Barry Johnson (1994) note that this term is not rigorously defined, but basically refers to paternalism and protectiveness towards women. These attitudes are rooted in stereotypes that represent women as weak and in need of care (as opposed to the harsh punishment of prison), and submissive, a characteristic which renders them less responsible for their crimes. But as the studies above highlight, only some women – those who do not deviate from dominant constructions of womanhood – are seen to be in need of protection and guidance, rather than punishment.

We might conclude that chivalry and paternalism are not particularly worrying if they result in more lenient sentences for women who have been marginalized in legal discourse. But Elizabeth Moulds (1980) notes that these attitudes assume a power relationship similar to that of a parent and a child. Women are not children – they are capable of rational decisions, calculating risks, knowing what is right and what is wrong and acting accordingly. To presume otherwise echoes traditional constructions of womanhood that have denied opportunities to women in a number of spheres. Further, it is a little problematic to argue for equality, save in those circumstances in which women benefit from discriminatory attitudes.

Such matters aside, there is a flipside to chivalry. The **Madonna–whore dichotomy** has represented women as either perfect, or sinful and beyond redemption. The duality is rooted in the Judaeo-Christian tradition, with its emphasis on controlling and defining women's sexuality. In the courts it is translated into a secular form. Women are expected to be good, asexual, passive and obedient. Those who are not are whores – evil, sexual, disobedient and aggressive. This reasoning is exemplified in the comments of Cesare Lombroso, an early 'criminologist' who was guided by nineteenth-century scientific pretensions:

> Her normal sister is kept within the paths of virtue by many causes such as maternity, piety and weakness, and when these counter-influences fail, and a woman commits a crime, we may conclude that her wickedness must have been enormous before it could triumph over so many obstacles. (Lombroso and Ferrero, 1895)

These cultural expectations are still evident, but they play out in complex ways. On the one hand, women who commit crime but otherwise conform to the ideals of womanhood, may be treated more leniently than men in the same criminal context. On the other hand, they may be seen to be **doubly deviant**, in that they have (a) broken the law; and (b) breached the norms of femininity. This will be particularly relevant in crimes such as assault or murder/homicide, where the women's destructiveness directly rebuts expectations of nurturance. As a result, women may be punished more harshly than men who commit similar crimes. Prostitution raises the same dangers: the ideals of women's passive sexuality are undone by the explicitly sexual nature of the crime. Traditionally, only women's involvement in sex work was criminalized. Today, clients are also potentially subject to arrest, but are far less likely to actually suffer this indignity. Again, there is a suggestion that women's behaviour is not judged solely with reference to the criminal law – gender ideologies can also be important.

Sometimes, it can be difficult to decide if women are being punished or protected. This is especially evident in **status offences**. The term refers to behaviour that is not illegal for adults but is considered to be inappropriate when undertaken by children. The behaviours are usually defined in terms of 'incorrigibility' or placing children 'at risk'. Juveniles of both sexes can be imprisoned for these types of actions, but studies have shown that a disproportionate number of girls have been charged and found to be guilty, receiving harsher sentences than boys in a similar position. These outcomes stand despite evidence that young males are involved in crime at a far higher rate than young women. Status offences are often used to limit female sexuality and punish 'unfeminine' behaviour (Allen, 1988; Chesney-Lind, 1974; Naffine, 1986). These are not as common as they once were, but they remind us that being a woman in the criminal justice system cannot be simplistically equated to either favourable or negative outcomes.

As well as being 'bad', criminal women have been defined as 'mad'. Their crimes are sometimes represented in psychiatric or psychological terms so that a woman is defined as mentally ill, rather than a rational actor. In so doing, the ideals of femininity are reinforced. Actions that might otherwise undermine our cultural expectations of a passive and safe womanhood are neutralized. The offender is understood to be sick and therefore exceptional; her actions only reflect the problems of an individual. For example:

- Women's menstrual cycle, and in particular severe pre-menstrual syndrome, have been used to support pleas of diminished responsibility to charges of murder (Allen, 1984; Laws, 1983).
- Extreme post-partum depression has been used to explain why women kill their infants. In some jurisdictions, this has been incorporated into criminal law, through a separate charge of infanticide (Wilczynski, 1997).
- Battered Woman Syndrome (BWS) is used as evidence to explain why a woman would kill her abusive partner, rather than leave him or protect herself by less extreme means. The syndrome presents women as suffering a psychological problem that has arisen as the result of her helplessness in long-term domestic violence contexts (see Box 2.3, pp. 67–8).

The first two examples are presumed to be caused by biological processes that in effect unhinge women's minds. In BWS, a woman's actions are located within complex psychological processes. In all cases, it is assumed that women cannot control their actions. Feminist commentators have argued that each decontextualizes an offender's actions by individualizing what are in fact social processes. This is particularly the case in Battered Woman Syndrome, where a woman's choices are influenced by a series of structural constraints that make it difficult for her to leave an abusive situation, and to continue to protect herself and her family. Similarly, explaining violence with reference to post-partum depression fails to acknowledge the sense of desperation that might be occasioned by a lack of emotional, financial and practical support – social, not mental difficulties.

Commentators are concerned that definitions of madness do not necessarily lead to 'easier' sentences. Ania Wilczynski's (1997) study on legal responses to men and women killing infants highlights this. She found that compared to men, women were less likely to be charged with murder or have further action taken against them, and less likely to receive a custodial sentence. A greater proportion of women who were sentenced were required to undergo counselling and psychiatric treatment. But we must guard against assuming that these outcomes are more 'pleasant', 'lenient' or 'easier' than those imposed on male offenders. They have their own difficulties, including consistent surveillance in the case of non-custodial sentences, and emotionally intrusive 'soul training' in the case of psychiatric treatment (see discussion of Foucault, pp. 28–32).

Minimizing Discretion in Sentencing

Particularly in the United States **sentencing guidelines** have been proposed as one solution to inconsistencies caused by discretion. These are currently in use in one form or another in around half the US states. Guidelines might involve allocating points for various factors (most often gravity of offence, prior record, drug-related crime, etc.).

The number of points can then be cross-checked with a table or **sentencing grid** specifying appropriate penalties. Such initiatives are sometimes unpopular with the legal profession even if they find political support. They run up against considerable resistance grounded in the occupational culture of lawyers and judges who interpret them as removing their professional autonomy. For this reason workshops and training programs are often preferred. Another solution has been the suggestion that the legislature should provide a clearer indication of the hierarchy of sentencing aims (rehabilitation, deterrence, etc.) so that judges can allocate priority to particular outcomes.

Issues of discretion do not end with sentencing by the judge. At the back end of a prison sentence the parole board exercises considerable power. Hence a contrast is often drawn between **judicial discretion** in the courtroom and the subsequent **executive discretion** of administrative bodies. Usually a prisoner is eligible to apply for parole after about one-third to two-thirds of their sentence and they rarely know exactly how long they will be inside. A good record of behaviour in prison is vital to attaining parole. There will be an expectation of participation in programs (e.g. sex offender programs, substance abuse programs) and positive assessments from prison staff. The availability of employment and stable family ties outside prison are also important. Typically a raft of experts in fields such as psychiatry and social work are involved in such decisions. Parole boards often make the news when an offender on parole commits a heinous crime (see Box 4.1). Critics on the Right claim such cases make a mockery of the criminal justice system and signal that we do not take crime seriously.

Box 4.1   The Politics of Parole

Sentencing options and discretion are not applied in a vacuum. Politics can also impact dramatically upon the law – and vice versa. The Willie Horton episode provides an example of this. Back in the 1980s Massachusetts Governor Michael Dukakis supported a rehabilitative programme that allowed prisoners temporary stays away from prison. Horton, a convicted murderer, never returned after a short-term release in 1986. He subsequently engaged in torture, assault and rape. The unpopular Prison Furlough Program was removed from the books after grassroots pressure. The episode was to wreck the political aspirations of Dukakis. His rival for the US Presidency in 1988, George Bush, initiated a controversial prime time advertising campaign. This used the Horton case to attack a 'revolving door' prison policy and argue that Dukakis was soft on crime, perhaps even indirectly responsible for events. Critics of the campaign suggested that it preyed on middle-class, white fears of the black criminal. For example, the visuals of the advert showed a black man walking in then out of a revolving door. However, advocates claimed the commercial was not specifically racist, but simply highlighted the need to be serious about jailing dangerous individuals.

The episode reminds us that the decisions of individual judges or administrative bodies can be linked to broader social, political and legal controversies and debates that constrain and encourage particular sentencing options. To reiterate a continuing theme of this text: the law itself is an artefact of the social.

What does this incident suggest about the public's expectations of prison and punishment?

One result of such events has been moves towards the elimination of parole. In the Australian context the idea of '**truth in sentencing**' has come to the fore. This has attempted to remove executive discretion and at the same time is associated with 'tough on crime' perspectives. The idea is to mandate the minimum amount of time a prisoner has to serve before becoming eligible for parole, thus limiting the possibility of early release. Despite public support, there has been resistance to this from within the judicial and correctional professions. They see such legislation as an attack on their expertise and autonomy and as undermining prisoner motivation for good behaviour. Anecdotal evidence suggests that judges have compensated for the legislation in their sentencing activity. In a situation where there is parole, for example, they might give a 12-year sentence, expecting the person to be released after 8. If the parole option is not available, they may well just hand down an 8-year sentence.

Critics on the Right have also advocated **mandatory sentencing**. The idea here is to remove judicial discretion by prescribing in law penalties for certain offences. In many jurisdictions mandatory life sentences have existed for some time. This is especially the case for serious crimes such as murder. More recent initiatives have focused on repeat offenders and on drug-related offences and are informed by doctrines of selective incapacitation (discussed on pp. 174–175). Perhaps the most controversial form of mandatory sentencing takes the form of '**three strikes legislation**', with prison terms of a specified minimum length mandatory for offenders convicted of their third eligible criminal offence. In Western Australia, for example, such legislation was introduced in 1992 to combat stolen vehicle crime, while in the Northern Territory the focus was on property offences.

Critics suggest that by removing judicial discretion, the unique and particular facts of each crime and each offender can no longer be considered relevant. They have pointed to notorious cases in which prison terms have eventuated for minor crimes such as stealing a towel, a bottle of Coke or a pizza. They have also argued that mandatory sentencing policies are often a political stunt designed to garner election support by getting tough on crime. Whatever the merits of such criticism, it is clear that such initiatives have had unintended implications for the administration of criminal justice (see Findlay et al., 1999: 270–1). There is a reduction in the number of guilty pleas, with courts becoming backlogged. In effect, offenders will fight a case all the way because they know they will be sent to prison. There can also be overcrowding of correctional institutions and a strain on finances. This is because putting people in detention is expensive relative to community corrections. Such policies have also shifted discretion from the courts to the police. Knowing that a prison term is inevitable for a minor offence, police decisions on whether or not to proceed with an arrest and charges take on a new significance. The use of mandatory sentencing against juveniles has also caused controversy. The United Nations Convention on the Rights of the Child stipulates that minors should only be detained as a last resort. Critics argue that laws that demand imprisonment without attending to individual needs and specific facts are in violation of this protocol and the 'last resort' quality of the punishment needs to be proven in each individual case. Finally, detractors have argued that such policies lead to the further over-representation of minority groups in the criminal justice system. Those who are economically and socially marginal are more likely to be arrested for the property and drug-related crimes that are often at the centre of mandatory sentencing legislation.

Judging Victims: Rape, Gender Stereotypes and Victims of Crime

A focus on the sentencing of those formally accused of crimes should not disguise the ways in which victims and witnesses can be judged. Women can also be punished for being 'bad' when they are a victim and not a defendant. The characteristics of bad or unfeminine women have mitigated the severity of the crime, at least in the eyes of some judges. This is most obvious in the instance of rape, a crime in which women are overwhelmingly the victims and men are the offenders. Despite this, feminist commentators agree that the development and interpretation of the law reflect a male perspective on women's sexuality. In these cases, the sexual activity of the complainant can become important in light of the expectations of chastity attaching to the Madonna ideal described earlier in the chapter.

Once, a woman's sexual history – and not only her relations with the accused – could be tendered as evidence of her consent. This is now prohibited or severely limited by what are termed 'rape shield laws', but general presumptions about a woman's appropriate sexual behaviour continues to be evident in judges' comments, and presumed in juries' reasoning. This might seem far-fetched, given that pre-marital sex is generally no longer considered to be deviant, but when we deconstruct judicial decisions, these assumptions are rendered transparent (see Box 4.2).

Box 4.2   *R v. Hakopian*

When a woman claims to have been raped, court processes focus as much on her as the accused. The Australian case of *R v. Hakopian* highlights the ways in which a judge's determinations are strongly informed by expectations of female sexuality and definitions of 'good' and 'bad' women.

Upon negotiating to provide sexual services, a female sex worker entered her client's car. After a disagreement, she demanded to leave, but the man kidnapped her and sexually assaulted her while holding a knife to her throat. The offender was found to be guilty, but the judge's sentencing comments caused outrage among feminists and legal scholars. He stated that the nature of her work made her less vulnerable to the distress caused by forced sex with a stranger than a married women would be.

This is a disturbing example of a number of gender stereotypes. Most obvious is the Madonna–whore dichotomy. The housewife is seen as sexually naïve and sheltered, which presumes she has only experienced intercourse with her husband. She is also located in the private sphere, demonstrating her appropriate social role. Yet it is well established that women are at far more risk of attack by their intimates, in their homes, than by a roving rapist (Esteal, 2001). Conversely, the judge seems to believe that a sex worker, through her occupation, is inured to the horror of not only non-consensual intercourse, but physical violence as well. The decision is suggestive of a muddled understanding of consensual and non-consensual sex: prostitution involves a series of contracts with individual men; it is not a general agreement to engage in intercourse with all comers, on any terms. From a feminist perspective, in both instances rape is misunderstood as sex, rather than a violent act of sexualized power.

Why might it be argued that this case is an example of a woman being punished for failing to fulfil gender ideals?

Such reasoning has led Gregory Matoesian (1997: 58) to comment:

Contrary to popular belief, the rape trial … does not determine if there was consent or non-consent, force or lack of force, from an individual woman's or man's point of view … Instead, the rape trial determines if the female consented to arbitrary yet misrecognised male standards of sexuality. If a woman had had sex with the man before, if she was intoxicated, if she kissed him, if she was out till the early morning hours, if she went to his apartment or home, if she had found him attractive or interesting, if he was an acquaintance, date, or friend, then the woman has, to varying degrees, consented to sexual access.

Feminist commentators have pointed out that women's sexuality is presumed to be passive and there for the taking: women are meant to say 'no', even when they mean 'yes' (Esteal, 2001). As a result, the simple rejection of sexual advances has not always been taken as evidence of a lack of consent. This renders accusations of rape without any supporting physical evidence of violence – bruises, scratches and breaks – suspect because if a woman really meant 'no', she would fight for her virtue hard and early. Traditionally, the absence of a struggle signalled consent and today it is still practically necessary in order to obtain a conviction (Edwards, 1996: 337). This expectation fails to recognizse intimidation, women's fear of fighting back, and their socialization which has taught them not to.

The presumptions about women's sexuality are also evident in the informal categorization of **real and not real rape**. Real rape is typified by the predominant cultural image of a violent attack by a stranger, against which the woman fights valiantly but unsuccessfully. Patricia Esteal (2001: 126) quotes from the Justice's comments in an unreported case as an example: 'In my view, this was a serious rape. It involved a breaking into a house, the forcible rape of a woman living in it and an absence of any remorse.' At the other extreme, date rape, marital rape and other assaults by a man known to the victim are defined as not so serious, if they are even categorized as 'rape': 'This is a different sort of case. It is really the simple refusal of a young man to take "no" for an answer at the end of an outing with a girl. There were no threats and no great force.' The second quote echoes the presumptions evident in *R. v. Hakopian* above, and provides an example of the test defined by Matoesian, above. It also provides a worrying picture of what are presumed to be 'normal' heterosexual relations. In fact, the 'simple refusal ... to take no for an answer' is a blunt but legally correct definition of rape, and is by far the more common type of rape committed against women.

Even those women with an unblemished sexual record have not been immune to charges against their personal morality. Until recently, judges were required by law to warn juries against conviction on the uncorroborated evidence of those who belonged to a class of people recognized as unreliable witnesses. Women – and children – are supposedly two such groups. The warnings often took the form of a statement that women have been known to lie and cry rape in order to protect their reputations or to exact revenge upon a man who loses interest in them. No other charge held this requirement. Carol Smart (1989: 34–5) concludes that rape trials are 'Kafkaesque for the woman who has experienced terror and/or humiliation but who is treated like a bystander to the events she apparently willed upon herself and for which she is seen as seeking an unjustified and malevolent revenge.' Even when a woman as an individual is faultless, her very gender renders her claims and behaviours suspect in a way that a man's does not.

This section has reviewed the ways in which women are constructed in the courtroom. As we noted in the earlier discussion on ethnicity and sentencing outcomes, we do not have access to the judges' actual reasoning processes. Rather, we are forced to 'read off' the significance of gender through their comments and formal decisions and the sentencing outcomes. The data we have available suggest that women – as offenders and as victims – are measured with reference to dominant cultural norms of femininity. These are applied at the expense of the legal precepts outlined in Chapter 2 of this book. It would seem that equality, objectivity and any public/private dichotomy are eroded as women come before the bench not so much as abstract citizens but as identifiably female.

Key Courtroom Players: Lawyers, Judges, Juries

It is useful to know something about the key players in the courtroom, in order to contextualize the court processes and sentencing outcomes described above. The following discussion focuses on lawyers, judges and juries. In keeping with one of the key themes of this book, we emphasize the significance of legal cultures and social identities and interactions, rather than the psychological or individual characteristics of the parties involved in any particular case.

Lawyers as professionals

Legal professions in adversarial countries have their origins in medieval England and are linked to the rationalization of law more generally. In the reigns of Henry III and Edward I, a series of changes affected litigation. Hearings became increasingly centralized, expert judges emerged, and cases were managed through a series of complex and unfamiliar rules and procedures. As a result, the ordinary citizen needed help and this was provided in the form of sergeants-at-law, who spoke for their clients in the court, and attorneys who were responsible for managing rather than pleading cases (Brand, 1992; Rose, 1998: 7). Originally sergeants and attorneys were friends or supporters of the litigants, with no formal skills or qualifications for appearing before the courts. Over time, some of these men appeared again and again for different parties, and became sought after for their expertise. Eventually, some men charged for their service, and so the 'proto-professional' lawyer emerged (Brand, 1992). In time, the right to appear was systematically recognized through statute and informal routine.

However, it is possible to argue that these roles developed into a coherent **profession** with the attendant culture, structures, privileges rather later. Starting with A. Carr-Saunders and P. Wilson (1933), a number of sociologists have debated the characteristics of a 'profession'. Those that are most commonly accepted as fundamental include (Carr-Saunders and Wilson, 1933; Cotterrell, 1984; Goode, 1957; Greenwood, 1957; Roach Anleu, 2000: 78):

- clearly defined educational expectations and entrance rules;
- a monopoly on theoretical knowledge and its application;
- autonomous work practices and professional regulation;
- professional associations representing a community of interest;
- an emphasis on the ideal of service rather than the blatant pursuit of profit.

The **ideal of service** is of particular ideological significance in the definition of lawyering as a profession. In part, service refers to protecting the interests of clients. Another facet of the concept encompasses a more generalized responsibility to ensure a just and stable legal order. Historically, this informed the perception that lawyers should not be driven by the profit motive, and that they had a responsibility to help those who could not otherwise easily access justice (this work was called *pro bono publico*). However, this remained the ideal rather than practice, and the poor were dependent upon the goodwill of patrons, the Church or the charitable consciences of individuals. Today the ethic of service is entrenched as an ideal, but is less obvious in any formal, binding expectations upon lawyers.

The service ideal is important for functionalist (see p. 13) interpretations of lawyering. This approach is exemplified in Talcott Parsons's work (1939, 1954). He argued that the professions generally contributed to the stability of society. The professional's concern for the public good stood as an example of the ideal attitude and behaviour for citizens generally, and this is a necessary role in light of the highly differentiated nature of society, and its unstable organic solidarity. Roger Cotterrell (1984: 91) notes, 'The theory implies an awesome responsibility of professions, to say the least.' Lawyers have a further, more specific role. They must integrate the legal system into the social system generally and bolster its authority so that its functions are more easily fulfilled (ibid.: 93).

The conservative functionalist perspective was later usurped by a critical focus from the 1960s onwards, one that emphasized the pursuit of professional interests. Sociologists began to argue that merely listing a series of attributes fails to locate the claims and structures of the professions within a changing political, economic and social context (Freidson, 1994). Rather than simply defining a profession, the characteristics we listed above are used to create a monopoly (Abbott, 1988; Larson, 1977; MacDonald, 1995). They are strategies that can prevent others from offering similar services and ensure the autonomous control over members and work practices. In so doing, lawyers buttress their own social status and financial and political power (Freidson, 1972). In a slightly different argument, Terence Johnson (1972) argues that professional power and expertise are ultimately used to support the interests of other elite groups. Ultimately, claims of altruism and service to the ends of the public good or the support of justice do not reflect the actual practice or aims of professionals. This **market control** or conflict perspective concludes that the legal profession is more focused on retaining benefits of their dominant position than any duty to serve justice.

If we look to perspectives of the actual practitioners, rather than the claims and structures of the profession itself, the sociologically ordained disjunction between service and self or professional interest is not so clear. On the one hand, there is evidence to suggest that law students are motivated by financial and other social rewards (Astin, 1984). Some studies also suggest that it is likely that students' service orientation will fade over the course of their studies (Erlanger and Klegon, 1978). However, concern for the public good and personal interest are not necessarily mutually exclusive. For example, some studies indicate the students do not accept that personal prosperity needs to be sacrificed on the altar of society's well-being (Granfield and Koenig, 1990; Halliday, 1994). In terms of professional practice, a research project involving one of the authors of this book (Western et al., 2001) pointed out that lawyers' service orientation is strong, but not as important as the financial rewards or intellectual interest that attached to their work. Perhaps not surprisingly, such studies suggest that whatever the structural and symbolic claims of the profession as a whole, the individuals who constitute it are motivated by a number of concerns.

Today, the possibilities for exercising professional power have been dramatically altered. A series of social and professional changes have suggested lawyers are entering a new world. Some of these transformations include:

- A state- and university-initiated growth in law schools and the number of students accepted by them, which undermines professional control over new members' entrance.
- The breakdown of monopolies and attempts to increase competitiveness in the profession.
- Increasing salaried employment. This undermines work autonomy by demanding that a practitioner's first loyalty lies with the interests of their employer, rather than the interests of the profession, and by determining the conditions and nature of the work (Lee, 1992).
- The development of large, global and nationwide law firms and inter-disciplinary practices. This is associated with Marc Galanter's (1983) concept of mega lawyering in which labour is specialized, and legal expertise is a product to be sold. The increasing profit orientation of law work stands in contrast to the ethic of service and orientation to the professional community – two of the pillars of traditional definitions of professionalism.

Lawyers in court: the significance of gender

Lawyers as a profession hold a great deal of power in society. However, in the context of court proceedings, they are constrained by the court processes, rituals and rules. In particular, their behaviour and claims are subject to the presiding judge. The following section describes the ways in which gender shapes people's experiences in court, this time focusing on how female lawyers are treated. Gendered interpretations of women's behaviour are particularly relevant in the context of professionals' courtroom interactions. The courtroom is a site in which professional ability, authority and control are displayed. The available findings suggest that gendered norms and presumptions impose limits on the strategies of female barristers arguing before the courts. According to Susan Martin and Nancy Jurik (1996: 136), 'The legal world clearly is filled with sexist jokes, disparaging or patronising treatment, inappropriate terms of address, remarks that call attention to a woman's gender, and other displays of disrespect.' Lilia Cortina and her colleagues (Cortina, et al., 2002) report that the majority of both men and women experience incivility or rudeness when practising in court. However, men are more likely to be subject to general rudeness; female advocates can expect a different type of treatment when arguing in court. The incivility that women experience is both general and gender-related (for a review of these points, see Bogoch, 1999a; Delfs, 1996; Martin and Jurik, 1996; Resnik, 1996).

- Women are more likely than men to be subject to comments about the personal appearance, and their success attributed to their sex or sexuality.

- White women are more likely than men to have their status as lawyers questioned by judges. This experience is even more common among women of colour.
- Stereotypes are used to categorize women. Elizabeth Delfs (1996) reports that images of cats were remarkably common. For example, arguing female attorneys were having a 'cat fight' or acting 'like cats'.
- Female lawyers are less likely to be addressed in formal and deferent terms by judges and witnesses. This can extend to the enforced, false intimacy of 'endearments' such as 'honey' or 'sweetie' which infantilize female attorneys and undermine their authority.
- Female lawyers are interrupted more frequently.
- Witnesses are interrupted more frequently when a female lawyer examines them.
- Judges are more likely to direct female lawyers, and to do so in ways that might undermine their professional reputation. Elizabeth Delfs (1996) reports that female advocates are more often presumed to be incompetent. She cites what one hopes is an extreme example, where a Florida judge asked a litigant, 'Are you satisfied with the representation you had at trial, even though she was a woman?' It beggars belief that such a comment would be made of a male representative.
- Judicial criticism is altered according to whether the recipient was a male or a female lawyer. Men are criticized for being too adversarial or aggressive, that is, they were too rigorous in conforming to the ideal lawyer. Comments directed towards women suggested disorganization and lack of professionalism.
- When witnesses are examined by a woman, judges are more likely to criticize the lawyers' questions and instruct them on more effective examination strategies.

Delfs (1996) concludes that sexist remarks and behaviours have three functions: (1) they maintain the maleness of law; (2) they belittle women as competitors; and (3) they symbolically return women to the domestic sphere. Bryna Bogoch (1999a) also argues that such behaviours and directions reproduce a gendered, hierarchical status quo. They undermine the professional status of women and might even affect their ability to perform competently.

A tension arises between female lawyers' need to be an aggressive advocate for their clients, and expectations that their behaviour will be womanly (Thornton, 1996; Kennedy, 1992). Bogoch (1999a) finds evidence to suggest that judges expect different, feminine behaviour from female lawyers, and may sanction those who do not conform. Patricia Esteal (2001: 219) has defined this as a 'paradox': if female barristers are to succeed 'they must display adversarial skills but by doing so, they are apt to be looked at askance for embodying masculine behaviour'. A man's actions might be described as passionate or vigorous but the same actions or demeanour when enacted by a woman may be interpreted as 'bitchy', cold or alternatively, over-emotional or partial (Delfs, 1996; Kennedy, 1992). In a high-profile example, the prosecutor in the O. J. Simpson trial, Marcia Clark, was seen to be pushy and aggressive. Some commentators believe that in response, she 'softened' her image, to avoid further alienating the jury and judge. Regardless of the truth of the matter, the very presence of the story highlights the different standards against which women are measured – there was no talk of the male defence lawyer, Johnny Cochrane, feminizing his approach by wearing a little more pink.

Despite their relative power and authority, female judges also report experiences of gender bias. Joyce Sterling (1993) found that male lawyers perceived female judges to be inferior on every measure to their brothers on the bench. Another study reported that one-third of female judges felt that they were not offered the same respect as male judges (Resnik, 1996: 971). Others report being addressed as Mrs, rather than Judge (ibid.). While these experiences may seem only minor, particularly when compared to the outcomes suffered by defendants or victims, they are useful in reminding us that gendered power in the courtrooms is ubiquitous and plays out on different levels, beyond the most obvious examples of witnesses and defendants and the court personnel.

Female judges: the possibilities of a 'different voice'

In light of court interactions and the ideologies behind sentencing decisions, some look to women to change the culture and implementation of the law. In particular, a long-held belief predicts that an increased number of women on the bench will change the substance of decisions and the process through which they are arrived at. This raises the question: can women make a difference to the ways in which people are judged? (see Box 4.3).

Box 4.3   Carol Gilligan and Women's 'Different Voice'

Carol Gilligan's (1982) work has been used to argue that more female judges will make a difference to court processes and outcomes. Gilligan identified a systematic gendered difference in boys' and girls' moral reasoning. This was evident their responses to a hypothetical moral dilemma in which a man cannot afford the medicine necessary in order to save his wife from dying. The question is asked: Should he steal the drug? Gilligan concluded that boys were more likely to approach this issue as a contest of rights, and judged the scenario by weighing the strength of competing interests. Gilligan termed this approach 'formalism'. In contrast, girls questioned the scenario in terms of connectivity, recognizing that actions occurred within particular contexts, and these needed to be taken into account. The girls sought to find a way in which the parties could negotiate an agreement. They were less likely than boys to abstract the issues or apply pre-existing general principles. Gilligan termed this perspective 'contextualism', and described it as an **ethic of care**. From these different approaches, Gilligan argued that men and women judged in different voices – men were rights-focused, and women emphasized a community of interest.

Gilligan's conclusions have attracted a lot of criticism. Some of these concerns are empirical: the differences between men's and women's approaches are not as clear-cut as they have sometimes been presented (see Walker, 1984). Additionally, the effects of class and ethnicity have not been systematically considered. On a conceptual level, some writers believe that emphasizing women's difference reinforces their subordination. It naturalizes the sentiments that are assumed to encourage their increased contributions to domestic labour, care for relatives and the like. Catherine MacKinnon has argued strongly against Gilligan's theory on these grounds. However, others have cautioned against MacKinnon's approach, on the basis that she is devaluing women's moral voice, a somewhat perverse outcome given MacKinnon's (1987: 39) own decrying of the silencing of women's voices (see for example, Cornell, 1991: 136).

How does an ethic of care compare to the liberal legal ideal?
Is this approach appropriate in the law and criminal justice system?

Carrie Menkel-Meadow (1984, 1985) has argued that increasing the number of women within the profession generally, including increasing the number of female judges, will create a justice system that is less oriented towards punishment and more to rehabilitation, with a greater emphasis on cooperation. In a similar vein, Suzanna Sherry (1986) studied the decisions of Sandra Day O'Connor, the first woman appointed to the US Supreme Court. Her decisions have often disappointed feminists in their conservativism but Sherry provides a different reading of the situation, concluding that Day O'Connor utilized a feminine paradigm and located people as members of a community, even if her politics are conservative. This was interpreted to reflect women's 'different voice' and a deviation from the liberal ideal of individualism upon which our legal tradition is based.

Other scholars have used the potential of a different voice in ways that do not strictly reflect Gilligan's original formulation, looking instead for any variations between men and women. Some have successfully identified a gender disparity. For example, Donald Songer and Kelly Crews-Meyer (2000) studied decisions relating to obscenity and the death penalty in the US State Supreme Courts. They report that women voted more liberally than their brother judges. Their influence extended beyond the simple act of decision-making, and their presence affected the decisions of the males with whom they shared the bench. Others suggest that female judges are somewhat more sensitive to gender discrimination, stereotypes and unacceptable, sexist and uncivil behaviour in their court rooms (Padavic and Orcutt, 1997).

However, there are some significant causes for cynicism over the possibilities of incorporating feminine values within a legal system dominated by the rule of law. Klein (1989: 20) points out that connectivity and nurturance may stand at odds with the expectation of impartiality in which the liberal legal conception of the law is rooted. Others have noted that a rape victim, for example, may not wish to be placed in any kind of community of interest with her attacker.

At an empirical level, many studies have generated evidence that counters any utopian hopes of a different judicial voice. These studies identify no differences, or only slight variations between male and female judges, or produce results that seem to suggest that women are harsher in their judgments. For example Sue Davis (1993) investigates whether female justices' voting patterns differed from their male counterparts in ways that reflected inclusiveness rather than individual rights; the findings only partially support claims of difference. Ralph Henham (1990) discusses British magistrates' attitudes towards a range of issues. He found only two significant differences: women emphasized law reform and the significance of deterrence as a sentencing objective, more than men. Peter McCormick and Twyler Job (1993) suggest that an appeal court with women is more likely to increase the sentence than an appeals court with all men on it. Taken together, these studies and others like them suggest that we must be careful in any claims of the potential differences between the judging processes of men and women, at least as they are played out in the formal legal arena.

There are a number of reasons that can be used to account for the lack of difference between male and female judges. First, women as well as men are socialized through a rigorous and standardized training process that inculcates particular world-views. Legal education and work experience emphasize traditional values of law, its role and the process of judging. This is significant given that only the elite of the legal profession can expect to reach the level of magistrate or judge. Success is at least partly the result of conforming to the rules and norms of the profession. In light of this, some researchers have argued that female judges are just like male judges, in terms of their class and ethnic background, their education and politics (Fineman, 1994; Thornton, 1996). Leading on from this point, it is simplistic to assume that being a woman equates to being a feminist. There are other ways to interpret criminal behaviour or interactions in the courts. We should not assume that female judges are sympathetic to the structural constraints against women leaving an abusive relationship, for example, or the privation that might drive a person to welfare fraud. Female judges are lawyers, not social scientists, and their perspectives are shaped through their particular disciplinary training.

It is also important to remember that we none of us are simply 'women' or 'men'. Our identities are located on multiple axes of class, ethnicity, religion, education, age and sexuality, as well as gender. These affect how we understand others' experiences as much as does our gender, and they may also affect the outcomes of any court case. Gender is only one dimension of inequality within the courts. We have pointed to the significance of race, and how it intersects with other socio-economic characteristics. Given these differences, even if the evidence supported the relevance of the standpoint perspective, any particular judge would be unlikely to be able to mirror the characteristics of those before her.

Even if female judges were perfectly neutral in their application of the law, the rules that are applied are arguably gendered (see pp. 62–72). If the law is an articulation of a male world-view, and buttresses patriarchal structures and male interests, then its neutral application will only continue systematic gender bias. The dominant positivist approach demands recognition of precedent, and finding rather than making law. The common law tradition requires continuity in decisions, with deviations being rooted in substantially different factual situations. What might seem to one judge to be an obviously discriminatory basis for reasoning may not in itself be grounds for overturning one hundred or so years of law. Most changes to law are incremental, not heroic.

Further, any arguments about women making a difference can only be extended to certain cases, and in certain contexts. Judges are not the sole players in any court proceedings. Other personnel are also involved. For serious crimes, with potentially more significant consequences for the defendant, the role of the judge may be limited to directing the jury, who decides questions of guilt or innocence. The same concerns that some writers hold about judges can be extended to the jury: they might be biased, sheltered, see the world from a masculine or patriarchal perspective, or suffer from a failure of imagination. The most objective – or the most feminist – judge in the world cannot effect change in realms beyond her legal influence.

Juries

The jury enjoys a privileged position in Western cultural imagination. When we think of a criminal trial, we are most likely envisaging a barrister addressing a panel of 12 men and women. But legally juries are rather less entrenched than they appear to be. Juries first appeared in England following the Norman conquest. In their original form they were comprised of worthy locals who had prior knowledge of the issues at hand. This stands in contrast to our current expectations of impartiality, facilitated by no or very limited knowledge of the case. Earlier, the independence of the jury was also a somewhat tenuous proposition, and those serving were often victimized by a state determined to achieve a conviction. Sally Lloyd-Bostock and Cheryl Thomas (1999: 8) describe the physical punishments that could be visited on recalcitrant juries, including imprisonment and starvation. The Star Chamber would seize the land and possessions of those who did not find an accused guilty. These practices were officially judged to be unlawful in 1670. In the Bunell case, jurors refused to return a finding of guilty against two Quakers who were charged with seditious assembly. In order to encourage a change of heart, they were locked away for two nights without 'food, water, fire, tobacco or chamber pot' (ibid.: 8). When this failed, they were fined, and two jurors refused to pay. The Lord Chief Justice finally held that only the jury were the **finders of fact**, and the judge had no position to interfere with or overturn this. This continues to be the presumption in contemporary practice so that it is up to the jury to determine which account of events is to be believed, and the finding of guilt or innocence that flows from this.

The long-term presence of juries does not equate to an unassailable right to be judged by one's peers. In England, for example, the right to a jury exists in only in legislation, and can be revoked or limited by Parliament (ibid.: 11). Yet until the middle of the nineteenth century, trial by jury was the only process available. Although the right to a jury trial is written into the US Constitution, until the 1968 case of *Duncan v. Louisiana* this was interpreted to apply only to Federal crimes (King, 1999: 43). In England, Australia and the USA, the right only extends to 'serious' offences. Additionally, offenders must usually opt for a jury trial. Practices also change: jury decisions can be unanimous or by majority; and the number of people on a jury is not set. What is in popular imagination a fundamental element of the criminal justice system is often rather marginal to the process.

Despite their usual absence, juries can play an important role in the criminal justice processes. The jury's fundamental role is the determination of the facts of the case. In adversarial systems, this means they become the impartial adjudicator of the evidence presented by the two sides (Israel, 1998: 35). They apply the facts to the law and in so doing, determine the guilt or innocence of the accused. Throughout this process, the members of the jury use their common sense to come to decisions. They are explicitly there as citizens, rather than legal experts. The centrality of common knowledge gives rise to an argument that the jury represents the conscience of the community and as a result, judgments serve the needs of the people, rather than the interests or preconceptions of the state and the elites. Through the same processes, juries also provide protection against oppressive states. In so doing, they are also seen to increase public trust in the system. Further, they are a source of education in the practices of the law. Finally, they remove the pressure that would otherwise be shouldered by judges. The panels allow judges to avoid the stress of determining the guilt or innocence of a stream of people (ibid.: 35–6). In short, these arguments emphasize the importance of citizens as a check on the power of the state.

Sociologists are rather less enthusiastic about the real possibilities of juries. Many see the purposes of a jury as fundamentally ideological and largely symbolic. They are acceptable to the extent that they do not substantially undermine the formal power of the courts (Mungham and Bankowski, 1976; Cotterrell, 1984: 328). Rather than limiting state power, juries legitimize its law and institutions because they are believed to be impartial. The claims of an expression of community conscience are also symbolic. Any articulation of community values occurs without a substantial and extended involvement of the public in the criminal justice process.

The idea that the juries play an ideological role can be further supported. In the first place, very few criminal trials are conducted in front of a jury (Duff and Findlay, 1997: 363; Israel, 1998: 35; Lloyd-Bostock and Thomas, 1999: 15). As we have already seen, many people simply plead guilty, or engage in plea bargaining before the case is heard before a court. Additionally, most charges do not attract the right or option of a jury trial. Even when they do, defendants may opt to be heard in front of a judge (King, 1999: 60). In light of this, Peter Duff and Mark Findlay (1982: 262) argue that a jury is a 'showpiece'. It dramatizes in a condensed, obvious and limited form the impartiality of the law, but its claimed checks and benefits do not extend far. Similarly, Doreen McBarnet (1979) describes two tiers of justice.

The higher tier is associated with jury trials and is enacted for public display. But as we have seen, most cases are processed through the lower courts, which have less symbolic value and involve the routinized application of bureaucratic process.

The ideological role of the jury is also important in light of systematic inequalities. It disguises the possibility that some groups are not being treated fairly because it claims that each person is judged by citizens like them. As we saw in Chapter 2, the question of 'like' is fraught with ambiguities, and it can be difficult to determine what social characteristics are relevant to questions of impartiality and common sense. These issues have been pertinent in debates over the composition of juries. In fact, with only a very few exceptions, there is no right to be tried before a jury that includes members of one's own ethnic group. In the USA prior to the Civil War, eligible jurors were effectively limited to white property owners or tax payers. Local law might require that they also be of intelligence or fair character. These characteristics were judged exclusively by sheriffs – the men in charge of rounding up jurors. They would use their discretion – usually unchecked – to generate a list of appropriate individuals. This process was obviously open to gross manipulation and discriminatory practices, and the resulting pool of potential jurors was homogenous, consisting of white, property-owning men. After the Civil War, Congress prohibited the disqualification of jurors on the basis of race, but this was rarely applied in Southern states, many of which continued the formal or *de facto* exclusion of Blacks. Throughout the 1930s, 1940s and 1950s, a series of court challenges ended in determinations that nothing but racial discrimination could explain the absence of Blacks on juries. But even following these decisions, only enough men to avoid appeal were included (King, 1999: 54–5). In England, before 1972 people were eligible for jury service only if they owned property of a particular value. Not surprisingly, the subsequent jurors were 'predominately male, middle aged, middle minded and middle class' (Lloyd-Bostock and Thomas, 1999: 21), a categorization that succinctly sums up the outcome in other countries as well. Historically, gender bias has also been a problem. As Susan Okin (1979: 261) has recognized, the right to be a juror is linked to citizenship rights and obligations. Given that women's claims to citizenship have been tenuous in the past, it is not surprising that women were legally prevented from jury service. The reasons were the 'usual ones' (Naffine, 1990: 11). It was argued that women needed protection from the ugly facts of crime and life. Further, judges decided that jury service undermined women's availability to fulfil their primary role as homemakers (see also Okin, 1979: 261). Only in 1973 were women granted the right to sit on juries in every US state.

Today, explicit racism and sexism have receded. Juries are now randomly chosen from lists of names. This is a surprisingly recent development. In the USA Congress adopted the random selection of people from voter lists in 1970. In state jurisdictions as well, they are now typically drawn from the electoral roll, or from other independently generated lists, such as licensed drivers. However, problems of structural bias continue to arise. The most obvious question is: are some groups systematically excluded from the relevant lists? We can answer this question through a brief consideration of the situation in Australia. Here, voting is compulsory, and theoretically, every adult aged 18 and over is a potential jury member. However some groups may be effectively excluded, even in the absence of deliberate bias or discrimination. Commentators have focused in particular on Aboriginal Australians. This group is often highly mobile, which can cause contact problems. Aborigines have disproportionately high rates of criminal convictions, some of which may disqualify them from being jurors. Geographical factors also play a part – people who live a long way away from urban centres may be excused from service, and other locations may not be included in the initial pool. Those who do not speak English are also disqualified (Israel, 1998: 43; White and Perrone, 1997: 118). The same kind of processes may be at work in England, where juries are drawn from the electoral roll but where nonetheless, women and ethnic minorities are under-represented on juries (Lloyd-Bostock and Thomas, 1999: 51). Social structural barriers thus continue to play a significant part in the application of justice.

The process of empanelling jurors has been open to manipulation on the part of both the defence and prosecution. Nancy King (1999: 54) relates that in earlier times, when not enough of those enlisted for jury service responded to their summonses, or those who showed up were drunk, bystanders made up the remainder. By carefully selecting the initial list, local officials could attempt to stack a jury with sympathizers, and a defendant could do the same by trying to control who attended and who was standing around to take the place of no-shows. Contemporary practices are not so lackadaisical, but the possibility of manipulation continues to cause concern. Prosecution has the power to remove jurors. Jurors are not excluded, but are returned to the pool, from whence they can be reselected for a different case. Political and public disquiet is more usually directed towards the defence's opportunity to challenge potential jurors through a vetting process that occurs prior to the swearing in of jurors. These pre-emptory challenges are informed by the need for unbiased and representative juries. It is perhaps more accurate to say that it allows the defence to ensure that evident biases complement their interests (Israel, 1998: 43). For example, challenge for cause allows the defence to reject a juror because they are biased. The power demands pre-existing evidence to support claims and as such is often not particularly useful to attorneys (Lloyd-Bostock and Thomas, 1999: 25). More common is the pre-emptive challenge, in which people are stood down with a simple 'no', no reason necessary. The extent of this power varies across countries. In England it is no longer available, after commentators raised concerns over the stacking of juries. In the USA, the power of veto remains a part of the extensive voir dire process in which advocates may be requested to justify their calls. In Australia the process continues, although the number of challenges is limited.

Mark Findlay (1994) questions the extent to which these processes contribute to any systematic advantage accruing to the defence. He conducted a study using observations of the challenge process and interviews with the defence lawyers. He concludes that there is no identifiable logic in the pre-emptive challenges. The process was partisan, imprecise, 'casual and arbitrary' (Findlay, 1994: 49). Lawyers challenged some people but not others who by all outward appearances seemed to belong to the same social categories. Because no questions are asked, the process relies on stereotypes, which are of course imprecise at best, and often plain wrong. At the end of the process there was no indication the jury was any more unbiased or impartial than it otherwise would have been, and the gender, ethnic and age composition was similar to that of the pool at the beginning of the process (ibid.: 51). The jurors themselves seemed to find the challenges confronting and alienating.

The expectation of circumscribed involvement in the criminal justice process is also evident in the criticisms directed towards juries over their 'wrong decisions'. Findlay (ibid.: 380) identifies a series of assumptions that form the basis of these complaints. In particular, it is claimed that juries do not understand the issues and they are composed of the wrong people. These critiques suggest that community conscience and common sense are most acceptable when they meet dominant needs and preconceptions. Beliefs that the 'wrong' type of people can sit on juries are evident in complaints that all the 'worthy' citizens – professionals and the like – are usually excused from jury duty, leaving only those who are not productively employed and thus presumably do not have the intellectual wherewithal necessary to follow and responsibly judge proceedings. This implies that juries should act like legal professionals even though this is not in fact their job (Mungham and Bankowski, 1976).

The limited available evidence suggests that that the above presumptions are not accurate. In terms of understanding proceedings, we can look to a 1993 British study where juries were asked if they had problems understanding evidence or following the judge's instructions. Most believed that they did not experience any problems. More than 90 percent claimed that they had found the evidence or instructions 'not at all' difficult or 'not very difficult' (Zander and Henderson, 1993, cited in Lloyd-Bostock and Thomas, 1999: 33). There are limitations to this study – we cannot know how much the jurors *actually* understood – but it suggests that citizens are not necessarily fazed by the arcane mysteries of the law.

The extent of jury control over their role is limited. In England and Australia for example, the judge sums up the evidence as well as instructing the jury on points of law. There is some belief that this may put pressure on the jury, particularly given the symbolic authority of the judiciary (Lloyd-Bostock and Thomas, 1999: 34) and, in all countries, judges have control over the kinds of evidence that are presented. This is not purely discretionary – systematic laws apply – but there remains space for judicial interpretation of the 'fit' between the evidence and the rules that guide it.

Nonetheless, juries can be independent. The most obvious example of this is **nullifications**, where jurors exercise discretion according to conscience and acquit a person even when the law and evidence would seem to indicate they are guilty. This occurs when the jury refuses to apply the law in a specific case, or refuses to apply what they see as a bad law, or protests against some other conduct or social condition applicable to the case. In the first two instances, this might include the refusal of Southern juries to convict those charged with violence against African Americans after the Civil War, or those in the Prohibition era who would let bootleggers go free (King, 1999: 51). Of course, it is difficult to know when nullification occurs and when juries 'get it wrong'. King suggests that this is in part because 'getting it wrong' is synonymous with 'I don't agree with the decision'. The legal experts remain the valid arbiters of the juries' responses and behaviours in identifying a nullification. Having made this point, it is also important to acknowledge that judge/jury disagreement is not the rule: Harry Kalven and Hans Zeisel (1966) found that juries and judges agreed in over 75 percent of cases. And ultimately, any possibility of subversion is limited through re-trials. For example, in the USA double jeopardy prohibits an accused of being tried twice for the same crime, but does allow a trial in a different jurisdiction (for example, in the State rather than Federal courts) or in civil, rather than criminal law.

The limited power wielded by juries informs the critiques that are directed against them, but these concerns are expressed in particular ways. Pat O'Malley (1983) and others have pointed out that many of the recent changes to jury practices, such as the implementation of majority decisions and the refusal of pre-emptory challenges, are informed by the need for administration and cost cutting. O'Malley (ibid.: 139) says that we are seeing 'a programme which facilitates the routine production of guilt in the adjudication process'. Rationalization is an efficient means of pursuing and achieving the aims of social control. But defining social control in terms of efficiency recreates it as a neutral 'technical operation' (ibid.: 140), not as an overt expression of state power.

Alternative Adjudication

Courts perhaps retain their primacy in public imagination and in jurisprudential thought. However, the range of formally recognized dispute resolution processes is widening. In these emerging forms, the often aggressive and silencing processes of the adversarial system are displaced. New procedures emphasize the need for all parties to 'have their say', through less confrontational interactions and a more informal context. Underpinning the introduction of these options is a hope that dispute resolution, as defined by Cotterrell, might be effected (see pp. 121–122).

The promise of these processes was first identified through anthropological studies of the decision-making of tribal groups. Richard Danzig (1973) wrote one of the key papers defining the approach in this area. He drew upon the tribal moots of a Liberian tribe, the Kpelle, as a model for Western mediation system. The Kpelle used a mediator who expressed the community consensus, usually in matters relating to marital disputes. People were encouraged to air their grievances and concerns in a familiar place and surrounded by familiar faces. Danzig argued that the same principles could be used to deal with a series of minor offences and disputes among members of a local community. In this way decisions acceptable to all parties, and catharsis, could be achieved by efficient, simple and accessible means.

In part because of these early and somewhat idealistic claims, there now exists a series of arbitration options in which the formality and ceremony of the courts are being replaced by looser arrangements that can ideally allow all parties to have their say and create outcomes to which everybody agrees. Richard Abel (1982: 2) lists a series of characteristics. Such dispute resolution forums tend to be:

- unofficial and de-coupled from state power;
- non-coercive;
- voluntary;
- decentralized;
- non-professional;
- ordered by democratic, flexible and contingent procedures that are determined by the needs of each case.

As such, mediation/conferencing are sometimes presented as the opposite of the criminal courts. However, in reality we find a number of composite forms.

In the criminal justice context, **alternative dispute resolution** most often takes the form of victim–offender mediation or family conferencing, and usually used in contexts where the offender is a juvenile. The emphasis on these procedures has been linked to restorative justice (see p. 190), a philosophy that is relatively popular with both liberals and conservatives. Liberals emphasize the less punitive ideology of the process; conservatives appreciate its low cost, the emphasis on personal responsibility, and victim empowerment. Both recognise that courts are not necessarily the most appropriate option for the settlement – as opposed to the adjudication – of disputes. In the courts, people may leave the process dissatisfied, feeling that their needs and experiences have not been heeded. Additionally, mediation and other alternatives have the potential to counter the expense of the formal court system, and the length of time it takes for a matter to come to trial. It is also hoped that offenders are more likely to fulfil their obligations when they have had a role in formulating responsibilities that are meaningful to them.

Although comparatively flexible, a general structure shapes the interactions in alternative dispute resolution. Take a family group conference. After the criminal act, the offender admits to their wrongdoing, and they, their family and the victim are invited to attend a 'meeting of two communities of care' (Braithwaite, 1999: 17). At this conference, there is a discussion of the crime and its consequences on all of the interested parties, and negotiation and agreement on what needs to be done to repair the damage. People have a chance to tell their stories in ways with which they feel comfortable, but a mediator facilitates the process as a whole.

John Braithwaite (1999) claims that conferences are 'structurally fairer' than court cases. In particular, he points to the personnel involved. In the courts, the dominant players are there to inflict maximum damage upon their opposites – that is the nature of the adversarial system. But in mediation, those involved communicate and explain, rather than throw doubt on the veracity of competing accounts. Braithwaite – perhaps a little optimistically – believes that participants are 'expected to be fair and therefore tend to want to be fair. They tend not to see their job as doing better at blackening the character of the other than the other does at blackening theirs' (1999: 41). Ideally, people are empowered rather than controlled by lawyers and formal rules of interaction. Additionally, because procedure is flexible, conferencing can be adapted to different cultural contexts. Braithwaite (ibid.: 86) suggests that this generates 'undominated speech', and there is a lot of freedom for people to work through problems in a way that is meaningful to the cultures and the communities involved. In contrast, a criminal trial is based on consistency, the need for procedural justice and the universal and objective application of a single law, irrespective of its relevance to victims and offenders.

Many studies have shown high levels of satisfaction among the participants. For example, Mark Umbreit (1992) found that 89 percent of offenders believe the conferencing process is fair, compared to only 78 percent in unmediated conferences. Some victims feel better as a result of the conference process (Strang and Sherman, 1997, cited in Braithwaite, 1999), although a substantial minority feel worse. For example Paul McCold and Benjamin Watchel (1998, cited in Braithwaite, 1999) report on a US study in which 96 percent of victims assigned to conferencing were satisfied with the process and its outcomes. This stands in contrast to the 79 percent of those who went to court. Victims of crime are also more likely to believe that the process is fair, their opinion regarding the issues is considered, and the offender is held accountable for their actions. This is not surprising when we consider that the conferencing procedure is designed to allow people to describe and explain their experience. It stands in contrast to the rules of evidence and conduct in the courts where victims are witnesses and the telling of their stories is constrained by defence and prosecution counsel. Conferencing allows a more useful and integrated role for the victims of crime.

In light of the above figures, we might conclude that conferencing is the ideal way of 'giving back' the crimes that have been 'stolen' by the state. However, some sociologists are less enthusiastic about the processes. They see the same old relations of power replayed in a new context, in an only slightly different arrangement. Some are concerned that the ideology of conferencing renders anger, resentment or revenge illegitimate. For example, Jennifer Brown (1994: 1274) concludes that this can make victims feel disenfranchised, as though their feelings are not worth anything and they are simply tools in the reintegration of the offender. In a similar argument, Sara Cobb (1997) believes that the process may 'domesticate violence', reinterpreting it within a new framework that blunts its meaning, and dissolves the category of victim, failing to recognize the material, physical and emotional hurt that people have suffered. While these concerns hold a theoretical resonance, we must remember the studies mentioned above, which overwhelmingly report high levels of victim satisfaction with the process.

Other commentators remain unconvinced that the processes do in fact allow all voices to be heard and considered equally. In the first place, formally trained mediators are not part of the relevant community, but possess greater symbolic authority than other participants and have developed their own ideologies of an 'appropriate' or 'acceptable' outcome. In their role of facilitating communication and reaching a resolution, they may act as pseudo-judges or try to talk participants into standardized outcome options despite their wishes (Roach Anleu, 2000: 135). Power inequities are potentially even greater when the police officers act in the role of mediators, so that the authority of the state is obviously manifest. Additionally, Kathleen Daly (1996, cited in Braithwaite, 1999) reports that in the conference she studied, the family of the offender had the greatest influence in deciding an appropriate response. The second greatest influence was that of professionals, and then the offender. Victims' desires were the least significant in the process, although this may reflect the limited number of victims who chose to be involved in the conferencing process. Similarly, Braithwaite (1999: 97) points out that despite the rhetoric, it is the parents of the offender, rather than the offender, who most often decide who will be part of the 'community of care' lending support in the conference. But while this breaches the ideological presumptions of the process, we must note the high degree of satisfaction on the part of offenders. It may be that the benefits are relative, so that even when the full promise of the process is not met, conferencing is still a more inclusive and empowering option than the courts.

Other concerns relate to an absence of procedural justice. For example, an admission of guilt is necessary in order to begin the process. Those who are not fully cognizant of their rights may be pressured to admit their guilt in order to avoid a traumatic court appearance. Similarly, offenders may not be aware of the legal defences that might excuse or explain their behaviour and which might in a court lead to a mitigation of their plea, or a finding of not guilty. Additionally, because of the idiosyncrasies of those involved, conferencing will not lead to similar outcomes for similar offences – this breaches the promise of certainty offered by precedent. Indeed, the outcomes may be repugnant to the ideals that underpin the process. Braithwaite (1999) relates an instance where the victim and offender's family enthusiastically adopted a punishment whereby the young man was required to wear a T-shirt emblazoned with 'I am a thief'.

Additionally, courts ultimately retain jurisdiction over the offenders and their victims. Admissions and negotiations may later be used in court proceedings if the process breaks down – a worrying possibility in light of the absence of safeguards to procedural justice. The courts also have the power to alter the decisions of the conference parties should they be too obviously contrary to the principles of justice. Braithwaite (ibid.) describes one outcome where the initial agreement had the offender paying for the plastic surgery of his victim, who had been left scarred as a result of an attack. The court overturned this outcome and imposed a jail term in its stead. The victim's only recourse to paying his surgery costs was an already existing public compensation fund, which did not cover his needs. Examples like this suggest that the entrenched authority of the courts is not substantially countered in these alternative resolution processes, just as 'alternatives to prison' are ultimately underpinned by the prison system (see pp. 185–188).

A contrasting argument holds that informal justice is essentially second-rate justice for those who do not have the resources to be heard in the court system (Roach Anleu, 2000: 131). Richard Hofrichter (1987: 195) argues that removing low status cases clears otherwise over-extended courts, but does so for the benefit of elites, so that their own interests may be achieved more efficiently. Options such as conferencing are an addition to, rather than a replacement for, those forums already in existence. There have also been cases where dominant groups use restorative justice for their own ends, and in the absence of any recognizable law. In the context of critiquing neighbourhood justice centres (which address a broad range of non-criminal disagreements), Hofrichter (1987) argues that local elites use these processes to maintain social control, and sanction those who breach local norms. Braithwaite relates an instance in which conferencing was used to forbid a young man from seeing his girlfriend, and remove him to a different province in order to facilitate this outcome. There is also concern that it might be used by indigenous elders to control – and sometimes tyrannize – young people in the group, or apply indigenous law that is not recognized by the Western legal system (1999: 96).

There is also a problem of the gendered division of the caring activity. On the one hand, conferencing and restorative justice generally have been lauded as a space where women's voices can be heard. For example, in Daly's (1996, cited in Braithwaite, 1999) study, a minority of offenders were women, but women constituted the majority of victims, victim supporters and offender supporters. These figures suggest that women are well and truly incorporated into the processes in a way in which they are not in formal court hearings. On the other hand, women are bearing a disproportionate burden of restorative justice, through their gendered caring roles which – as might be expected – are unpaid and not officially recognized (Daly, 1996, cited in Braithwaite, 1999).

Box 4.4   Truth Commissions

Truth Commissions are informed by the same assumptions as those underpinning conferences on a more modest scale. They have a surprisingly long history, being used to investigate war crimes after the Balkan wars in 1912 and 1913, and in response to World War I and World War II. More recently and famously, Truth Commissions have been held in Guatemala, El Salvador, South Africa and East Timor.

Truth Commissions are not focused on prosecuting and punishing individual actions and they are not strictly informed by liberal legal ideals. Instead they uncover abuse, oppression and violence in a way that contextualizes discrete events within broader social processes. Perpetrators are encouraged to admit their crimes, the damage they caused and seek reconciliation with their victim, victims' families and society in general. Victims and their perspectives are central to the process. Those who suffered from the wrongs are offered the chance to explain their experiences outside of the constraints of formal court procedures, come to terms with their losses and forgive those who hurt them. These accounts generate a record of events that places individual crimes within a social history and context, and ensures that shameful events are recorded and remembered.

The South African Truth and Reconciliation Commission is one of the most famous of these bodies. It was created following the formal dismantling of Apartheid after decades of civil unrest and political violence, much of it perpetrated by the state trying to maintain white minority rule. The aims of the Commission were informed by the principles of restorative justice. They included the creation of 'as complete a picture as possible of the nature, causes and extent of gross violations of human rights; ... affording victims an opportunity to relate the violations they suffered; the taking of measures aimed at the granting of reparation to, and the rehabilitations and the restoration of the human and civil dignity of, victims of violations of human rights'. In so doing, it was hoped that the relationships between different groups could be re-formed. These echo in more inspiring and momentous language, those of the family conferencing processes discussed previously.

How do the aims of Truth Commissions contrast with those of adversarial legal systems? Does their usefulness outweigh their limitations?

Media Representations of Law

In light of the omnipresence of the media in contemporary society, it is useful to conclude this chapter by considering how legal practices and cultures have been represented in films and on television. It has been argued that such shows have a broader social relevance. In the first place, the changes in representations of the law and its personnel may be loosely reflective of broader developments in social ideologies and definitions of right and wrong (Friedman, 1989: 1589). Conversely, the large numbers of films and television shows generally conform to similar tropes and narratives and use a set stock of images, which leads to the 'naturalizing' of the text. That is, particular messages come to be understood as 'common sense', so that people take them for granted rather than critically reflect upon them (Papke, 1999: 477). Stark (1987: 230) puts it bluntly: 'Prime time television drama has the power to change – and in fact has changed – the public's perception of lawyers, the police, and the legal system.'

Popular culture is also the source of many people's knowledge of the law. Citizens receive technical and legal information: what are the laws, what happens in court, what are our legal rights? (Stark, 1987). David Harris (1993) lists a series of concerns over the misinformation disseminated through popular culture. It has been argued that fictional shows are guilty of:

- promoting unrealistically high standards for police, particularly in terms of their scientific and investigative abilities;
- creating a perception of a violent world;
- encouraging the belief that people get away with crimes;

- misrepresenting whites as the most common victims of crime;
- reducing the court system to a series of formal rules.

This is important because, as Lawrence Friedman (1989: 1592) notes, it is not the law itself but representations of the law that affect behaviour. In other words, the public acts on the basis of what they think the law is, rather than on actual legal principles. Some writers have suggested that the positive portrayals of lawyers that occasionally saturate the market can encourage people to enrol in law school (Menkel-Meadow, 1999; Spitze, 2000: 732). Additionally, they may affect the kind of lawyers people wish to become (Menkel-Meadow, 1999: 3). This is most notable in the instance of the melodrama *L. A. Law*, first screened in the 1980s and 1990s, and the 'golden age' of lawyer representations in the 1950s. At another level, television and films provide a means by which individuals can interpret the social world (Papke, 1999). For example, portrayals of lawyers reflect and buttress popular expectations. Others go further and argue that our viewing practices contribute to how we see multiple groups in society. In the case of legal shows, these include the meanings of 'man' and 'woman', 'criminals', and 'race' identities (Howarth, 2000: 477). However, having made these observations, it is important to note the distinction between a show as a programme – a commodity that is fixed and stable – and the show as a text. The text promotes particular readings of the world, but cannot directly construct them: readers interact with the text in order to refine or subvert the meanings incorporated within it (Fiske, 1987).

Why are legal dramas so popular? Some authors have noted that the narrative arc and characters are necessitated by the demands of drama. In order to be involving, shows must have conflict and a story. This is particularly the case for television, which is heavily reliant on weekly dramas for its content. Placing the protagonist within recurring 'dramatic' problems would become unbelievable if the main character was, for example, a dentist or a plumber. There are a limited number of professions that are presumed to be involved in real-world drama on a regular basis. Police and lawyers are two that, in the public imagination at least, provide a believable basis for on-going excitement and tension. Stark (1987) notes that the narrative of a crime story in particular is suitable for television. It incorporates good versus bad with clear winners and losers and an unambiguous morality, all of which can be comfortably resolved in a half-hour or one-hour format.

But the demands of the format alone cannot explain the particular and limited images that populate the stories. Characters and stories are not chosen because they are inherently dramatic but because they incorporate dominant social norms and are shaped by prevailing mythologies. Anglo popular culture has often romanticized crime, in part because the law has been an obvious embodiment of crown or state oppression (Stark, 1987: 236). In the American context there developed morally ambiguous tales of the Wild West gun-slinger, heroes who were themselves often embroiled in legally marginal activities. England has had Robin Hood; in Australia bushrangers such as Ned Kelly are the most iconographic examples of the criminal as hero. Then last century, detective novels emerged. Like the earlier cultural types, the detective was often in competition, if not in direct conflict, with the police (ibid.: 237). These tense relationships were even more pronounced in the hard-boiled private eye of the 1920s. Thus, the early history of the crime genre has been marked by a suspicion of the forces of law and order.

The tenuous position of the police began to change in the 1930s. Radio shows reflected and contributed to the public's faith in key law and order institutions. This was buttressed when television exploded onto the suburban scene. Weekly shows dominated the programming and these demanded a series of dramatic situations that could be played out and resolved in a limited time frame. Joe Friday, the protagonist of *Dragnet*, is the example *par excellence* of the crime fighter of this period. He carried a badge, worked in a team, served the public, and seemed to have no personal vices or life beyond police work. According to Stark (ibid.: 245), this type of representation resonated with the viewing public because of changing class aspirations. Working classes were more closely aligning their identity to that of the middle classes and this change included the rejection of anti-cop sentiment. These attitudes also fitted to developments in law enforcement agencies, which were undergoing reforms and professionalization following their earlier scandals.

The media rehabilitation of the police existed in tension with another theme. Spitze (2000: 732) argues that the 1950s and the 1960s were notable for the portrayal of 'hero' lawyers who battled against the odds in order to achieve justice for a deserving client. The greatest example of this was the indefatigable Perry Mason, who each week reasoned, investigated and argued through a series of adventures that resulted in an acquittal for his falsely accused client. In this formula, lawyers' success came at the expense of the police. If defence attorneys were always right, the police who charged their clients must always be bumbling and ineffectual.

The traditional police shows gradually faded until they all but disappeared in the 1960s. However, this did not equate to a subversive presentation of dominant legal and normative codes. Instead, attorneys, secret agents and private eyes were used to reinforce the message that the law was good and right. The shows and their leading players were conservative in their portrayal of a presumed community of values, nostalgia and apolitical readings of crime, law and order (Stark, 1987: 255). Lawyers evolved into benevolent patriarchs. They attempted to fix their clients' human as well as legal problems but they were also authority figures. However by the late 1960s the heyday of the golden era of television lawyering was over. Cops were back and this time around, they were cool. For example the ex-hippies of the *Mod Squad* ('One black, one white, one blonde') bridged the abyss between counter-culture and law enforcement. Such officers were hip, not straights or squares but as with the earlier denigration of police, the latent messages were conservative. Funky clothes were not translated into radical politics or any real attempt to critique legal institutions and enforcement practices. As the 1970s boogied on into the 1980s, a new and slightly less conservative consideration of crime began to emerge. Police shows continued to represent law officials sympathetically but this marched alongside explorations of social issues, albeit in a non-confronting way. Nonetheless, many of the earlier messages remained. Television police were themselves often in breach of procedural justice but escaped critique, given the continuing emphasis on 'justice', which has consistently been defined as nabbing the bad guy. Stark concludes that many of these shows are 'light on the law, and heavy on the order' (1987: 282). Lately, we have seen a return of the lawyer as hero in shows such as *The Practice*. But the representation is neither ubiquitous nor independent of context. Joan Howarth (2000) argues that contemporary shows often represent lawyers and the procedural rules of the legal system as a hindrance to more significant substantive justice outcomes (Grant, 1992, cited in Howarth, 2000: 489). On police or prosecutor shows such as *Law and Order*, defence attorneys are constructed as sleazy and opportunistic, or at best naïve with a misplaced faith in the people they represent. In these instances, the heroic is represented by prosecutors, who, according to Papke (1999: 483), have re-emerged in courtroom and police dramas.

Questions over the role and usefulness of television have also arisen in the context of 'reality television' and the broadcasting of court processes. Shows such as *Judge Judy* and *People's Court* where people come before a television judge to resolve their disputes are one example of 'reality television', although the label is perhaps loosely applied. These shows are interesting in the ways they render the dramaturgical processes of court so transparently clear. Kimberlianne Podlas (2001) came to the conclusion that syndicated court reality television affects the expectations of viewers. In particular, those who watched a lot of these types of show were more likely to expect judges to be active, ask questions, and interpret judges' silence as an opinion on the veracity of litigants' stories. Podlas expresses concern that if silence is interpreted as belief in the truth of the story, jurors will hold a pro-prosecutor bias, given that they present their accounts first, to a silent judge. But perhaps the pre-eminent example of reality TV is *Court TV* (Courtroom Television Network), which provides continuous live coverage of trials. Its format allows the opportunity to present a more coherent picture of how a trial is actually conducted, with all the banality and tediousness that are usually attendant. It also provides experts who interpret the significance of events and arguments, rendering them into a language that the layperson can appreciate. 'Court TV' also has the same potential as the fictionalized version. It still tends to show the more extreme, lascivious or celebrity studded trials. After all, it is a commercial channel and it needs to encourage people to watch what can be a fundamentally uninteresting process. Further, it abstracts the court processes from the interconnected institutions of the criminal justice and legal systems (Harris, 1993). The case of the televized O. J. Simpson trial showed the problems that can attend such trials as well as the advantages that come from an open display of judicial process.

It should be no surprise, then, that the televizing of trials is also the subject of intermittent debate. This is usually accepted in the USA but is seen as somewhat more problematic in other jurisdictions, largely on the grounds that it does not afford the defendant a fair trial, and media scrutiny may disrupt the proceedings. But a number of benefits have been argued. Some believe in the educative function of televizing trials – through watching, people develop an appreciation of how the procedures actually work. It might make the justice process transparent and limit the possibility of miscarriage of justice. It will facilitate the accountability of the criminal justice system to the public, by providing people with accurate information with which to judge its processes and outcomes. It allows people to see how at least some of their tax dollars are being spent. In effect, television becomes one of the few sources of information easily available to citizens.

Conclusion

Within pre-eminent jurisprudential approaches and popular cultural representations, courts are the centrepiece of the justice process. They provide a forum for the resolution of disputes and dramatize the ideals of objectivity, equality and justice. However, in practice, their role is rather more ambiguous. The rationalization of the criminal justice process in the course of modernity has transformed the role of courts so that the management of sentencing has replaced the earlier adjudication functions. The adversarial procedures and subsequent judgments often reinforce pre-existing relations of power and social inequalities. In light of these difficulties, alternative dispute resolution processes might offer new possibilities for justice. And as we have seen, their promise is not always fulfilled. A series of structural disadvantages and cultural prescriptions belies the guarantees of liberal legal philosophy. What is perhaps more surprising to readers who are by now familiar with sociological preoccupations such as ethnicity, class and gender, is the absence of data that consistently supports obvious discrimination. But, then, the book has shown that criminal justice is a series of connecting practices, institutions and ideologies. These are not easily unravelled and so their discriminatory effects are not obvious or effortlessly addressed. This is obvious in the interaction between legal precepts and adjudication, between police practice and court process. And as we shall now see, the effects flow on to the systems of punishment and rehabilitation adopted in contemporary society.

Study Questions

1 'Perhaps the most common complaints of litigants at all levels of the legal process are that they did not get a proper opportunity to tell their story and that the judge did not get to the real facts of their case' (Conley and O'Barr, 1990: 172). Discuss the formal and informal rules of communication that create this situation. Is it possible to change the dynamics of courtroom interaction within the adversarial system? Is it desirable that we do so?
2 Visit a courtroom and consider how authority and power are reproduced. Consider these processes with reference to:

   • the gender of those in the court;
   • the layout of the court;

- the ways in which people interact;
- behaviours that may subvert this process.

3 Undertake a role-play. First, allow someone to tell a story in his or her own words. Then appoint someone as a counsel and have them interrogate the narrator:

- How does this change the dynamics of the narrative process?
- Is it possible to maintain control over the narrative?
- How would the interaction differ from that in a courtroom?

4 Consider processes such as family conferencing and mediation. Do they conform to the Western liberal legal ideal? Is it important that they do?

5 Debate the statement 'More women will make a difference' with reference to court procedures and outcomes.

Glossary of Key Terms

alternative dispute resolution – Cases are removed from the adversarial and hierarchical court and managed through flexible and non-coercive processes.

chivalry – Male judges treat women more leniently than men because they see them to be in need of protection.

different voice – Originates in Gilligan's experiments. It has been applied in the context of the criminal justice system to suggest that women and men may have different ways of judging court cases or other conflicts.

discrimination – People are judged or treated with reference to legally irrelevant considerations. Direct discrimination refers to the deliberate considerations of inappropriate or extra-legal factors. Indirect discrimination occurs when structural and institutional processes and expectations are not purposefully designed to treat people differently, but this is nonetheless the outcome. Contextual discrimination refers to the differential outcomes and treatments.

doubly deviant – Criminal women breach social norms in two ways: (a) they have broken the law; and (b) in so doing they have transgressed definitions of feminine behaviour.

ethic of care – Associated with Gilligan's discussion of a 'different voice'. Women are more likely to judge issues recognizing connections and relationships between people.

executive discretion – The discretionary power exercised by administrative bodies in contexts such as parole decisions.

finders of fact – Juries are responsible for determining the usefulness and accuracy of the evidence presented in court. Conversely, judges are responsible for considering matters of law that might arise.

'focal concerns theory' – Judges pursue a series of priorities when sentencing, but must do so with incomplete knowledge. They draw on assumptions and stereotypes to fill in the gaps.

ideal of service – Lawyers' rhetorical/cultural emphasis on (a) protecting the interests of individual clients; and (b) ensuring a just society and stable legal order.

judicial discretion – Flexibility in sentencing held by judges.

liberation hypothesis – Minorities are treated more harshly, comparative to whites, when they commit lesser offences, because the less serious the crime, the more discretion available to the judge, and the more likely they are to draw upon extra-legal considerations and stereotypes.

Madonna–whore dichotomy – Positions women on opposite ends of a spectrum, as either perfect or sinful.

mandatory sentencing – A policy where prison terms are legislated for particular offences. Sometimes linked to '*three strikes legislation*'.

market control – Emphasizes lawyers' attempts to maintain the benefits of monopoly at the expense of any duty to serve justice.

nullification – Jurors act in accordance with their conscience rather than strictly according to the law, and acquit a deserving defendant.

organizational perspective – Prosecution and sentencing policies are in part directed towards the simplification of the criminal justice system. This end is achieved by the differential and ultimately discriminatory application of policies.

profession – Sociologists argue that law is a profession because of its control of training and legal knowledge, autonomous work practices and regulation and an emphasis on service, rather than the blatant pursuit of profit.

question–answer format – The dominant mode of language in the courts. Witnesses' comments are determined by the questions of lawyers; they have little control over what they talk about, and how.

rationalization – Process by which cases are being channelled out of the courts in order to save the time and costs associated with the prosecution of a defendant.

real rape and not real rape – Real rape is taken seriously. It occurs when a woman is violently assaulted by a stranger. Rape is not real, and thus not reprehensible, when a woman is seen to be somehow deserving of the attack.

sentencing – The process in which a criminal is allocated a penalty.

sentencing guidelines/sentencing grids – To be used by judges, these aim to make sentencing more accountable and consistent.

status offences – Legal adult behaviour is criminalized when undertaken by juveniles.

'three strikes legislation' – Policies that mandate a prison term for repeat offenders. The term comes from baseball, where a batter who fails to hit the ball three times in a row is given out.

'truth in sentencing' – Legislation mandating that punishments handed down by a court are literally 'true', a full term is served and they are not subverted by executive discretion during parole decisions.

Suggested Further Reading

In light of the array of topics addressed in this chapter, the following is somewhat of a grab-bag of potentially interesting readings. To start, Cassia Spohn (2000) provides and excellent overview of the changing findings on discrimination in sentencing processes, Kathleen Daly's (1994) book on gender and discrimination is also very interesting. Ngaire Naffine (1990) and Patricia Esteal (2001) present questions of gender in an accessible way. In terms of language and power in the courtroom, Cooke's (1995) article is approachable and engaging; Matoesian's (1993) book is a more sophisticated and challenging but very rewarding read. Turning to the media, Stark's (1987) article on changing images of police and lawyers is fascinating for the range of shows he has covered – and presumably watched.

Suggested Websites

The following allow access to overviews of court structures and practices:

http://www.cjsonline.gov.uk/publications/current.html   For information on the English criminal justice system generally, you can access the document, The Criminal Justice Process – who's involved.

http://www.courttv.com/   The site of *Court T.V.* provides an interesting glimpse into the range of trials covered. Similarly, check out also http://www.judgejudy.com/home/home.asp – the Judge Judy site.

http://law.emory.edu/FEDCTS/   The Emory School of Law also provides this service for the Federal courts in the US context.

http://www.nla.gov.au/oz/gov/leg.html#crtcom   The National Library of Australia provides a gateway to useful Australian court sites, which in turn provide basic information on the structure, purpose and history of the relevant courts.

5   Punishment

Once a person has been found guilty, or has admitted their wrongdoing, the contemporary legal landscape offers a broad range of options. While prisons continue to be a significant presence in popular imagination, political claims and legal processes, other outcomes are also available. Along with prisons, these alternatives are often imposed in a context of debate and controversy. The lack of agreement over appropriate sanctions reflects the more general confusion over underlying philosophies of punishment.

Philosophies of Punishment

Those found guilty by the courts are liable to punishment. In the Western world there are a number of contending philosophies behind the idea of punishment. We start by looking at these. **Retribution** refers to the idea that a price should be paid for crime. Under this model a crime is seen as a moral affront to society and the punishment as a justified outcome for this violation. In a sense society has a normative duty to see that the punishment balances out the harm done by the criminal. Retributive theories of punishment often draw upon Old Testament theories of 'an eye for an eye' and suggest that punishments have to be in some way proportional to the severity of the offence. Theories of **deterrence** or **reductivism** suggest that the aim of punishment is to prevent crime. According to a leading early advocate of this position, the great eighteenth-century Italian criminologist, Cesare Beccaria (1995), punishments have to make offending unattractive by exacting a price greater than the possible benefits of such action. This kind of model operates with an understanding of the human actor as rational and calculating. If appropriate penalties are codified, potential criminals will work out the equation of probable gains versus probable losses and opt for a life of conformity. Deterrence can work in two ways. General deterrence refers to the belief that a punishment will dissuade the public at large offending. Hence we sometimes understand a sentence as 'making an example' of a particular wrongdoer. Specific deterrence involves the punishment of a given individual in the expectation that this will prevent that particular person from offending in future. A judge might hope, for example, that a tough sentence will turn a juvenile offender away from a life of crime. Aside from questions of deterrence, reductivist approaches also assert that offending can be reduced simply by removing malefactors from circulation, thus eliminating their opportunities to commit crimes. If criminals are in prison or under intense surveillance in the community, they will find it difficult to re-offend. The philosophy behind all this is known as **incapacitation**. Approaches focusing on reform or **rehabilitation** suggest that the aim of punishment should be to bring about a moral or behavioural change in the offender. In the contemporary era this approach sees punishment as an opportunity for interventions involving health care, education, counselling and training in the expectation that these might turn a bad person into an upright citizen.

Today ideologies about deterrence seem to play the major role in the justification of punitive sanctions against offenders. Yet, amazingly enough, there is little evidence for this (Nagin and Paternoster, 1991). Efforts to demonstrate deterrence usually try to establish a correlation between severity and certainty of penalty and crime rates within a given jurisdiction. For example, we might compare rates for drug offending before and after tough new anti-drug laws are established, or perhaps compare states with divergent sentencing policies. Studies of this kind have usually demonstrated either no support or very limited support for deterrence theory. More sophisticated attempts to look at deterrence try to measure perceptions and mental processes. This is because, according to deterrence ideology, potential offenders weigh up the benefits and risks of crime, or experience fear of possible punishment. Getting at perceptions is methodologically very difficult. In prisons we have a sample of those who were not deterred. A more representative sample would include people who did not commit crimes because they were deterred. Investigating 'non-events' such as this is always problematic and usually involves asking respondents to recall decisions about past episodes where they were tempted to commit a deviant act or else asking for responses to hypothetical scenarios. Such strategies are seriously flawed because they rely on selective and faulty mental processes rather than capturing the real-time, real-world experience of criminal decision-making.

Notwithstanding these difficulties, the research looking into deterrence has generated some consistent findings.

- Potential and actual offenders seem to be more concerned that they will be shamed by family and friends than punished in the criminal justice system. This reality has fed into ideas about reintegrative shaming and restorative justice that we discuss on pp. 189–190.
- Perceptions relating to the risk of getting caught may well be more important to offenders than those relating to the severity of punishment. In other words, criminals give priority to whether or not they will get away with a crime.
- Thoughts about punishment have a low priority in the decision whether or not to commit a crime. Many crimes are spontaneous and impulsive and others habitual. There seems to be no rational calculation of costs and benefits as specified in deterrence ideologies. The work of Jack Katz (1988), for example, has argued that people commit crime for emotional and moral reasons, not for rational gain.

- Those who do not commit crime seem to be constrained by morality rather than fear of formal sanctions. For most of us it is unthinkable to commit a major crime because to do so would be wrong.

These kinds of results lend indirect support to the diverse theoretical positions that suggest contemporary punishment has little to do with controlling crime and criminals and might have more to do with broader social processes of which criminal justice actors are unaware. We reviewed some of these in the first chapter – most notably work in the traditions established by Durkheim, Foucault and Marx.

Prisons

Even though most offences do not result in prison sentences, the prison has such symbolic centrality that it is usually the first thing that comes to mind when we think about punishment today. In Chapter 1 we looked at Foucault's work on the origins of the prison and how it can be understood in theoretical terms as part of the broader societal shift towards modernity (see pp. 28–32). Here we explore a series of issues that are more specific to the study of prisons in contemporary sociology.

Box 5.1   Prisons and Remand Centres: A Question of Terminology

It is amazing how often 'prisons' and 'remand centres' are conflated in everyday language and how few students know the difference. This section sorts out the distinction. A *prison* is a place where you will find convicted criminals. A *remand centre* is a place where people are held pending trial or sentencing. These are often run by distinct organizations. Hence in the United States a remand centre might be run by the sheriff's office and a prison by a Department of Justice. A considerable proportion of the people behind bars are on remand, not in prison. This can often create confusion when looking at official statistics on rates of incarceration and imprisonment.

The History of the Prison

An exploration of the history of the prison brings us to the understanding that (like courts and the police) they are a curious accretion of contradictory and competing ideologies and practices. Prisons have emerged as a key component of the criminal justice system during the past 200 years. The conventional history of the prison is one that ties them to the growing power of humanitarian ideologies (for an alternative view, see the discussion of Foucault on pp. 28–32). With the rise of the

Enlightenment, punishments such as death and torture came to be seen as barbaric by criminologists like Cesare Beccaria. Advocates and administrators of prisons often had religious motivations. They believed that procedures such as hard labour, solitary confinement and enforced attendance at worship would lead people to repent their sins and become morally reformed. The belief was that lack of discipline and faith were responsible for crime. As the saying goes, 'the devil makes work for idle hands'. For these sorts of reasons early prisons were sometimes known as 'penitentiaries' – a word whose root lies in 'penitence'.

The Walnut Street Jail in Philadelphia, opened in 1773, is often cited as an early exemplar of an institution carrying a prison ideology of this kind (Rothman, 1995). Although it looks like a harsh place to modern eyes, it was established largely through the efforts of citizens concerned about the cruelty of the then existing punishments. Quaker philosophies had a significant impact upon the prison. It was believed that quiet contemplation would lead to penitence. Inmates were held in solitary confinement in small cells where they also worked. They would be let out only to attend religious ceremonies. This model was later copied elsewhere in the United States and is sometimes referred to as the **'Pennsylvania System'**. Ideas similar to those of the Pennsylvania system could be found world-wide. Thus, half a globe away in the Port Arthur penal colony in Tasmania, Australia, ideas about convict separation were taken to extremes. Here prisoners had to wear hoods to obscure their identities whenever they were outside their cells and were forbidden to talk to one another. Identified by numbers, inmates had to wear their hoods on the way to and from religious worship. Only within the chapel could they remove them. Here they were separated from each other by wooden screens. They could look only forwards at the preacher with possibilities for mutual interaction minimized.

During the first part of the nineteenth century new systems came into place that allowed work to take place collectively during the day. At night prisoners returned to individual cells arranged in galleries within prison blocks. Silence and discipline remained central principles and solitary confinement was still used as punishment for those who broke rules. This regime is sometimes known as the **'Auburn System'** after the Auburn Prison in New York where it was developed. Everyday life in such prisons was resolutely militaristic. David Rothman (1995: 110) provides a vivid description.

> At the sound of a horn or a bell, the guards opened the cells and the prisoners stepped onto the deck and then in lockstep went into the yard. In formation they emptied their night pails, which they then washed; they took a few more steps and placed the pails on a rack to dry. They then move in lockstep to the shop and worked on their tasks while sitting in rows on long benches. When the bell rang for mealtime, they grouped again in single file, passed into the kitchen, picked up their rations … [and] ate their meals while, by regulation, sitting erect with their backs straight.

Fierce debates erupted between advocates of the Auburn and Pennsylvania systems. Apologists for the Auburn systems suggested that it was more cost-efficient, while supporters of the Pennsylvania model argued the newcomer had compromised the purity and austerity of their approach. The Auburn template eventually became prevalent, but towards the end of the century such ideological tussles began to look irrelevant given empirical realities of 'overcrowding, corruption and cruelty' (Rothman, 1995: 152). Reform movements started up which slowly pushed prison life towards the form we see today. Pivotal to these was the Elmira Reformatory in New York which opened in 1876 and offered education and vocational training. Inmates were graded and rewarded with privileges. During the twentieth century other innovations fell into place. Recreation was allowed among prisoners during the day and educational and therapeutic programs were introduced. Religious elements became weaker and prisons were increasingly shaped by secular belief systems such as those of managerialism, psychology, health sciences and academic criminology. Prison design and activity today reflect such changes in ideology. There is a strong focus on reducing security within the prison but maintaining it on the perimeter. It is thought that a 'campus'-style prison will improve prisoner behaviour better than a repressive institution of walls and bars. Such changes have been made possible through the use of new technologies such as security cameras and the re-skilling of prison officers so that they can use interpersonal abilities to maintain order.

Box 5.2   Sheriff Joe Arpaio: A Shift to the Right

Although ideologies may become dominant and then recede, they are not necessarily completely displaced. The practices and policies of Sheriff Joe Arpaio highlight some of the contested claims over the purpose of prisons and their appropriate administration.

Some believe that prisons, and the criminal justice system in general, have become ineffective as they are soft on criminals and offer conditions that are too attractive. One controversial advocate of this position is Sheriff Joe Arpaio of Maricopa County, Arizona. He has instituted a series of reforms within his jurisdiction that have attracted the attention of the media world-wide. These include:

- having inmates wear old-fashioned striped convict uniforms with pink underwear so they feel humiliated;
- serving food that is perfectly nutritious but looks disgusting, most notably a green bologna. The Sheriff also claims to serve the cheapest meals in any US Jail at 45c per person.
- banning pornographic magazines, coffee, smoking and unrestricted television from prisons;
- working male inmates on chain gangs;
- working female inmates on chain gangs (the Sheriff says he believes in gender equality);
- setting up a jailhouse webcam to increase shame and deter crime;
- housing inmates in a Tent City, complete with 60 ft observation tower and a pink neon 'Vacancy' sign.

Critics claim that Sheriff Arpaio has violated human rights and has implemented an inhumane prison regime. Despite his tough side, Sheriff Arpaio also prides himself on close ties with the community. One of his programs involves housing juveniles in a replica of his Tent City jail, dressing them in prison uniforms and subjecting them to random searches so they get a taste of life inside and turn away from crime. This is known as S.M.A.R.T., which stands for Shocking Mainstream Adolescents into Resisting Temptation. His Posse Reserve involves 3,200 citizens who do things like look for 'deadbeat parents' and try to stamp out prostitution. You can check out his activities at: www.mcso.org/

Are there any similarities between the above practices, and the Auburn and Pennsylvania systems, and more contemporary alternatives and ideologies?
Can you predict the criticisms of Sheriff Arpaio that might be made by an advocate of labelling theory or Braithwaite's 'reintegrative shaming' (pp. 189–90)?

Looking at the history of the prison from the vantage point of social theory, we can see several connections with the themes we explored in Chapter 1. Broadly speaking, we can explain the existence of the modern prison in terms of its congruence with the values and social systems of modernity. It is a rational and bureaucratic institution controlled by the state – a reality that can be explained with reference to the work of Weber on the shift away from local and *ad hoc* administration of the law (see pp. 36–37). The prison also allows punishment to involve the whole individual and fits in with Foucault's ideas about shifts in forms of social power from the body to the soul (see pp. 28–32). If we turn to the question of culture, the prison is consistent with Elias's views on the need to hide punishment from public view and eliminate its more brutal attacks on the body (see pp. 37–39). In short, the cultural and administrative shifts associated with modernity laid the groundwork for this particular criminal justice institution. They made it both organizationally possible and normatively desirable as the pivotal and emblematic form of punishment.

Do Prisons Work?

In answering this question we need to think about what it might mean. The first thing to understand is that prisons are based upon conflicting aims and objectives. Meeting all of these at the same time might be an impossibility. As a form of punishment, prisons do indeed seem to work. Felons do not want to go there and they are glad to get out. They also do a good job in terms of incapacitation. Media stories on jail-breaks are newsworthy precisely because they happen so rarely. For this reason, prisons also work as a means of preventing crime. They take offenders out of the community and in effect make it impossible for them to offend (at least outside of the prison).

When it comes to reforming the criminal so they do not to commit crime, however, prisons are less effective. Although prisons punish, they do not seem to deter or rehabilitate. **Recidivism** is the technical term used for offenders who re-offend. Prisons seem to do little to prevent this and we find that around 50–60 percent of people in prison have been there before. Rates of offending within prison are also high. Statistics suggest that around 50 percent of prisoners have broken a prison rule at some point. Critics claim that recidivism and rule breaking take place because punishments are not tough enough. Others suggest that prisons need to focus more on reform. This is currently done via **correctional programs**. These vary widely in design, implementation and philosophy and can take the following forms.

- Educational opportunities and life skills (e.g. obtaining a high school diploma, learning a trade). The object here is to improve opportunities and life chances, perhaps leading to a job and a stake in conformity.
- Medical interventions (e.g. drug detoxification). These programs try to eradicate the clinical conditions that lead to offending behaviour.
- Therapeutic and counselling interventions (e.g. sex offender programs, substance abuse programs, anger management programs). These aim to encourage personal growth and reflexivity, allowing individuals to understand, recognize and modify patterns of offending behaviour.

Some suggest such programs are an afterthought in the prison system. They cost money to run and are often the first item to be cut when budgets begin to look tight. Access to programs can be especially difficult for women prisoners. Because their numbers are small, it can be difficult to justify extra expenditure on targeted interventions. Moreover, conflicting priorities and clashing objectives mean programs have little chance of working in the broader, hostile prison environment. For example, Russell Dobash, R. Emerson Dobash and Sue Gutteridge (1986) report a 'chum' system existed in the Scottish prison that they studied. This meant that younger inmates were expected to team up with a prison officer who would be their mentor and confidante, thus contributing to a therapeutic environment. Such a system was jeopardized by other aspects of the prison officer's role: the fact that they had to exercise discipline, strip search inmates after visits and report rule infractions. It has been widely argued that placing people in a planned environment and in isolation from the wider society makes them dysfunctional. In prison everything is laid on – food, lodging, work. There is little need for everyday survival skills of the kind required in the outside world. Critics also assert that isolating the prisoner from family, work and the wider community and immersing them in a concentrated criminal subculture creates stigma and a sense of oppositional identity that does not help them reintegrate upon release (see discussion of labelling theory, pp. 26–28, and prison culture, below). Although there is widespread dispute over the best way to organize prisons and prison programs, there is general agreement that more evaluations need to be conducted of specific programs to find out just what works and what doesn't.

From the perspective of critical sociology, prison programs have been interpreted as yet another attempt at social control rather than as creative and genuine efforts to help. For example, when Dobash et al. (1986) looked at the Scottish women's prison, they argued that ideals behind psychiatric and drama therapy programs arose from stereotypes. These suggested that offending women were mentally ill or disturbed and were driven by biological forces and emotions rather than reason. Institutional attempts to modify behaviour and personality could be read in Foucauldian terms as something that has 'enlarged the net of discipline and woven it still finer by extending surveillance and control to even the most intimate and mundane aspects of daily life' (ibid.: 158). They point out that women were obliged to monitor themselves and appear polite and compliant in order to fit in with the norms of the therapeutic regime. Failure to become a 'good woman' – essentially complying with middle-class norms – would result in punishment. Similarly, work programs centred around the idea that the women had failed as wives and mothers. Skills training centred largely on domestic activities and on the needs of the institution. Hence women could work in cooking and cleaning roles, keeping costs down in learning to become the 'good woman'.

The idea that prisons failed to rehabilitate came to a head with the rise of the doctrine of '**nothing works**' and the belief that there was no evidence that treatment programs were successful (Martinson, 1974). The idea that 'nothing works' is probably mistaken. Meta-analyses of various programme evaluations suggest that correctional programs have modest effects, especially those oriented around cognitive/behavioural skills development (Gaes et al., 1999). However, the idea has been influential. Conservative critics argued that punishment was insufficiently severe to bring change in prisoners and during the 1980s retributive policy started to make headway in tandem with wider 'law and order' debates and policies. At the same time, according to David Garland (1991), the search continues among criminologists to locate a guiding philosophy or *raison d'être* for prisons other than simple punishment. Put simply, prisons exist and continue to be used, but there is no coherent or overarching framework explaining why we have them, how they should be organized and what they should do with offenders.

Regardless of issues of recidivism, reform and mission, many argue prisons are quite simply a bad idea. They are cruel and brutalizing. They are also very expensive. The cost of incarcerating a person in a medium or maximum security prison is around US$20,000–40,000 per annum. This is not very different from the average wage. In the USA the budget equates to around $25 billion that has to be spent every year on keeping people locked up (Blumstein and Beck, 1999). For these sorts of reasons some criminologists have advocated a policy of using the prison only for dangerous and repeat offenders – typically those involved in organized and/or violent crime. This ideology is known as **selective incapacitation**. Such an initiative is supported by the belief that the majority of serious crime is committed by a small pool of repeat offenders. If they can be identified and put away, then crime rates should drop significantly. However, controversy exists over whether such a group exists, and if so, how it can be defined and identified. In extreme cases, ideologies of selective incapacitation have been tied to thinking about indefinite sentences for dangerous individuals. The idea here it to take volatile offenders out of action permanently if they can be shown to be an enduring threat to the community. At the other end of the scale, selective incapacitation has been broadened out to a wider range of crime than was perhaps intended and tied to philosophies of mandatory sentencing. Such thinking, as we have seen, has been attacked with reference to themes of proportionality and due process.

Some suggest we need to think about the costs of prisons not only in terms of their impact on offenders or on the taxpayer, but also in terms of their impact on others. John Hagan and Ronit Dinovitzer (1999), for example, attempt to itemize the consequences of imprisonment on the children of the inmate. These can include 'the strains of economic deprivation, the loss of parental socialization through role modelling, support, supervision and the stigma and shame of social labelling' (ibid.: 123). They suggest that children can consequently suffer adverse mental health, increased involvement in delinquency and educational failure. There are also what Hagan and Dinovitzer call 'collateral costs' not only to individuals but to collective forms of human and social capital. These can be thought of in part as opportunity costs, with socially beneficial activities forsaken when available money is spent on prisons. In California, for example, the state spends $6,000 per annum on each college student but about $34,000 per year on each prison inmate (ibid.: 130). In addition, as the next section outlines, minority communities as a whole lose social capital as an entire generation of members are locked away, only to be further socialized into deviant subcultures.

Prison Populations

Census information shows that prison populations tend to be comprised of repeat offenders who have been charged with serious offences such as robbery, assault and drug dealing. These are mostly male, from working-class or poor backgrounds. They are usually aged under 30 years. Minorities tend to be dramatically over-represented. These patterns can be illustrated with reference to Australia (ABS, 1998). In 1997 some 28 percent of prisoners were aged under 25. Indigenous people made up 18 percent of the prison population, even though Aborigines are only 2 percent of the wider population. Women made up only 6 percent of Australian prisoners. Some 58 percent of inmates had been incarcerated before, suggesting that prison does not deter or reform very well.

A major problem for some developed economies over recent years has been the growth of prison populations. This is particularly acute in the United States where currently around two million people are incarcerated in jails and prisons – about one person in every 145 US residents (Bureau of Justice Statistics, 2002). Between 1925 and 1975 the US prison population remained remarkably stable at around 110 inmates per 100,000 population. There followed a period of rapid increase in the

1980s and 1990s (Blumstein and Beck, 1999). During the 1990s alone the American prison population doubled, with currently 450 people per 100,000 in prison. This rate is from six to ten times greater than for similar developed countries (Garland, 2001c: 1–3). Of perhaps greater concern is the way that this growth has centred largely on young black urban males. In the United States in 1996 the imprisonment rate for Blacks was 8.2 times that of whites (ibid.: 23). Around one in three black men aged from 20–29 years of age is under some kind of punitive supervision and at current rates about 1 in 3 black males can expect to serve some time during their life span. In 2001 an estimated 12 percent of black males aged in their twenties or early thirties were locked up, compared to only 1.8 percent of whites (Bureau of Justice Statistics, 2002). In other words, policies of incarceration can be seen operating against an entire social group. A negative outcome of this is that prison is seen as an ordinary experience for a large proportion of the population, criminogenic norms are routinized, and inequalities based upon prison are added to those related to race and class.

The literature explaining the rising prison population points to a series of factors which are not mutually exclusive (Caplow and Simon, 1999; Mauer, 2001):

- Tougher sentencing guidelines and legislation such as 'three strikes' and 'truth in sentencing'. This has increased inputs to prison and delayed release.
- Police efforts to control drugs and gangs in urban settings. This was linked to the Reagan era 'War on Drugs' and the arrival of crack cocaine in the 1980s.
- Sensationalist media reporting on crime and negative images of offenders. This has resulted in a moral panic and a climate that supports tougher sentencing (for discussion of this concept see pp. 17, 103).
- A reactionary political climate that encourages fear of crime and the rise of a private corrections industry coupled with a 'crime control' ethos, influencing expectations of government.
- The imposition of new managerial and financial systems in the US Justice system making rapid growth possible in prison populations.
- Rising crime rates. This is a point of controversy as it is difficult to distinguish offending rates from arrest and conviction statistics, especially for drug-related crimes. However, it is *prima facie* plausible to suggest that rates of drug offending increased during the 1980s and 1990s.
- Increasing social inequality leading to the emergence of a permanently excluded urban underclass who are driven to crime.

Blumstein and Beck (1999) provide perhaps the most detailed empirical report on this trend in the United States. They show that there has been a significant rise in the number of violent offenders incarcerated, especially sexual assault and aggravated assault, but that these trends are dwarfed by a massive increase in drug-related convictions. They suggest that 'drug offending is the major component of the overall growth' contributing 33 percent to the total growth in incarceration (ibid.: 21) and is largely responsible for the over-representation of African-American males in the prison system. They go on to look in more detail at criminal justice process. They find no evidence that the increase is due to improved policing methods, leading to more arrests, but point instead to patterns in sentencing as a crucial factor in growing prison populations. There has been more frequent use of the decision to incarcerate and increasing use of longer sentences, in part, reflecting the impact of mandatory sentencing, tougher penalties in the legislation and 'truth in sentencing' legislation that results in delays until release. Parole violations have also increased, with violators accounting for 35 percent of all prison admissions.

Other explanations look less to proximate causes and are more theoretical in orientation. Katherine Beckett and Bruce Western (2001) have developed the influential idea that in the United States social welfare and incarceration form part of a single **policy regime**. This perspective draws on earlier work such as the critical theory of Rusche and Kirchheimer (1939) (see pp. 20–21) and David Garland (1985) which suggests that penal policy is linked to wider social and political contexts. In this view, all governments face the problem of dealing with marginal populations as a task of social control. They can respond either through welfare systems that aim at inclusion and improvement of life chances, or through exclusionary and punitive measures. Hence, reduced social programme spending might generate a compensatory increase in criminal justice budgets. Beckett and Western suggest that there has been a shift in the policy regime over recent decades. Spurred on by the impetus of conservative Reagan-era reforms, welfare-based programs are giving way to those focused on incarceration. By statistically comparing American states, they were able to show that those with Republican Senators, large populations of the poor and African Americans and less generous welfare programs were those that adopted exclusionary policies. These findings broadly supported their hypothesis.

Loïc Wacquant (2001) has situated such patterns within a broader context of specifically racist social control. He sees the prison replacing the ghetto as a instrument of caste control. Using Foucault's idea of the carceral continuum (see p. 30), he suggests that the ghetto has become more like a prison (the 'hyperghetto') and the prison more like a ghetto, with both used to control a minority population made marginal by capitalism. According to Wacquant, the apparatus of state control has invaded the ghetto, replacing that of communal self-organization. Ghetto institutions such as housing projects and schools come to resemble prisons, with extensive use of security technologies, random searches, curfews and wire fences. Prisons, meanwhile, have become more like the ghetto with gangs divided along race lines and underground economies that circulate drugs. These serve to reproduce inequality as inmates are deprived of rights to cultural, economic and political participation.

An alternative, although perhaps complementary, explanation has looked in more detail at cultural beliefs and the role of the media. Thomas Mathiesen (2001) suggests that the rise of television has been vital in offering a precondition for mass imprisonment. He identifies three major factors here. First, television works through succinct images rather than text that can provide detailed coverage of a full range of issues. Second, there has been a change whereby information is presented as entertainment – a package that crime fits particularly well. Third, people have become dependent on television and do not seek alternative sources of information. As a result, Mathiesen suggests, television culture has broken down the normative defences that might have scaled back mass imprisonment policies. Beliefs of a humanitarian nature are pushed to the side by stereotypes, elaborate and systematic debate has been sidelined and the legitimacy of penal policy is decided by 'burlesque television shows' (2001: 32). (For further discussion of the media and criminal justice, see this book pp. 23, 115–117, 159–163.)

The Experience of Prison and Prison Culture

Contrary to news reports and sensationalist stereotypes, prisons do not provide a state-subsidized country club for criminals. Classic studies of life in prison show them to punish and to do this quite effectively, although often in ways not intended by formal prison policy. As Gresham Sykes (1958) pointed out some decades ago in his seminal work, there are real 'pains to imprisonment' which attack an individual's sense of self-identity and self-belief. Although the history of prisons can be read as one of reforms and reformers and, in the long run, conditions have been continually upgraded, they still manage to punish in several ways.

- Prisons deprive offenders of their liberties, such as freedom of movement and freedom of association. Life in prison is subject to rules, timetables and lack of privacy. Sykes suggests that the inmate is reduced from adult to child status. They have to obey instructions, show deference and are subject to arbitrary power.
- They deprive offenders of wider social contact. This can create a feeling of rejection by society. Research suggests that women prisoners in particular find imprisonment harsh when it cuts them off from family ties, perhaps even their own children. This makes it difficult to fulfil the domestic and maternal role expectations that are held of women (Dobash et al., 1986).
- They offer harsh and generally unpleasant living conditions characterized by objective material deprivation. This can lead to low self-esteem in a society where wealth and lifestyle are seen as evidence of success.
- Inmates are deprived of heterosexual relationships. The result can be a challenge to the prisoner's sense of gendered identity.
- There is continual psychological damage and trauma. There are constant dangers of assault and sexual assault. Many inmates live in fear. Sykes refers to this as the 'deprivation of security' and notes that feelings of anxiety are widespread.

Studies of life in prison from around the globe have been mostly conducted in male prisons. The following discussion pertains largely to this context. The big picture research finding is that a common **prison culture** exists (Sykes, 1958; Toch, 1977). This can be seen as a collective and adaptive, but also problematic response to a hostile and artificial environment. Inmates must not show weakness or fear or they will be victimized. Newcomers are often tested to see if they are prepared to fight for their rights. If they fail, they may be subject to physical, psychological and sexual abuse. Even those who pass the test might be picked upon in future by another prisoner looking to improve their own status by attacking a hard target. Gangs consequently form to offer inmates protection and a sense of belonging. In the United States there are estimated to be over 100 gangs in prison. These tend to be segregated along racial lines. Well-known gangs include the Aryan Brotherhood (whites); La Nuestra Familia and the Mexican Mafia (Chicano) and the Black Guerrilla Family (Black). Gangs will often form complicated alliances or have long-running feuds and vendettas with each other. Because of their organized character, they have caused problems for prison administrators. Gangs are often behind much of the crime, corruption and disorder that takes place in prisons. From the perspective of the inmate, however, they can be a good thing, bringing some security and feelings of solidarity. This can come at a price, as a key feature of gangs is a hierarchical structure, with the leaders demanding obedience and continually humiliating and abusing weaker inmates.

Box 5.3   Prisoner Roles

In his work Sykes (1958) suggested that the distinctive language or argot of the prison provided an insight into the culture of the institution and in particular the roles the inmates play. Although the terms might change over time or cross-nationally, the findings still hold up pretty well and suggest the world-view through which inmates think about prison life. A *rat* or *squealer* is a person who provides information to the authorities. In so doing, this person has violated the code of silence and solidarity that links the inmates. The *centre man* is a person who bends over backwards to help institution officials. He is likewise a figure of contempt. The *gorilla* is a person who uses force or bullying tactics to get what they want, such as sex or cigarettes. The *weakling* is his victim – a person who gives in rather than fights. *Merchants* and *peddlers* are involved in selling goods. They violate norms of gift giving and reciprocity. *Wolves* are aggressive homosexuals and *punks* are their unwilling victims. *Fags* and *queens* voluntarily adopt homosexuality and often exhibit womanly mannerisms and behaviour. Wolves are seen as 'masculine' while punks, fags and queens are understood as failing to be true men. *Ball busters* make life difficult for authorities. They question orders and start fights even though they know this will bring punishment. Rather than being seen as a hero, they are unpopular with inmates as they threaten the negotiated order of the prison and can bring down collective sanctions that affect everyone else. The *real man* manages confinement with fortitude. He is stoic, retains his dignity and plays it cool. The *tough* is a person who is unstable and always willing to fight if confronted. By contrast, the *hipster* is a fake and fraud. They try to appear tough and relentlessly seek peer approval.

What kinds of rules or characteristics of prison culture are suggested by Sykes's typology?

Prisons also have a defined underground economy. Sex, drugs, money and cigarettes are traded among inmates and between them and staff. There are continual possibilities for corruption and so prisons are, ironically, a major locus of criminal activity. Prisoners also share moral codes. There are strong injunctions against snitching to guards. Hence victims of abuse know it is best to keep quiet. These norms and symbolic classifications extend to the classification of inmates. Paedophiles in particular are seen in a negative light and are targets for victimization. By contrast, murderers, armed robbers and persons known for violence are held in high esteem. They are seen as 'real criminals', as a 'bad ass' or 'hard man'.

Box 5.4   Philip Zimbardo's Prison Experiment

The importance of seeing interactions and roles as part of a culture rather than the outcome of individual, deviant personalities, is evident in the famous Stanford prison experiment.

In the summer of 1971 the always controversial and imaginative psychologist Philip Zimbardo (1972) conducted an experiment that suggests that systems of authority and terror tied to prison culture spontaneously arise in prison contexts. Mature and emotionally stable students were randomly assigned to roles as guards and prisoners. The prisoners were picked up by the police and subject to searches and fingerprinting before being locked up in a basement at Stanford University that had been fitted out as a mock prison. It did not take long before some of the guards became brutal and others did not intervene to stop them. Prisoners adopted survival tactics and some became psychologically disturbed. After a riot the guards became friendly with some of the prisoners and struck deals. This made it easier to maintain control – a situation known as negotiated order (see below pp. 182–183). The behaviours of the participants share many of the same characteristics of those in actual prisons. The most amazing fact was that these results were obtained even though the people involved knew that it was just an experiment.

Zimbardo has set up an excellent website which details what happened and draws parallels between his experiment and research findings on real prisons (http://www.prisonexp.org).

Why does Zimbardo's experiment indicate that the rules and interactions that characterize prisons are structural or cultural rather than the amalgamation of a set of individual psychological patterns?

Violence remains a central feature of prison life and culture (Cohen, 1976). Estimating the exact prevalence of violence is difficult due to problems of access, reporting and definition and the literature frequently boils down to discussion of the inadequacies of various imperfect studies or the differences between diverse prison systems. Institutions are unlikely to want negative publicity and inmates may not wish to cooperate with outsiders by filling in a survey or participating in an interview. According to Lee Bowker, prison rape is quite common (1980: 2). He cites a study conducted in Philadelphia in 1966–68 suggesting that around 4.7 percent of inmates had been victims of a sexual assault. Of the estimated, 2000 assaults in the study, only 26 were eventually reported to the Philadelphia police department. Figures from British studies are not dissimilar. Data from the 1980s suggests rates of sexual attack ranging from 3 percent in an open prison through to 13 percent in a maximum security prison (Bottoms, 1999: 218). Rates for violent assault were similarly diverse, with only 2 percent of inmates in the open prison claiming they had been attacked, compared to 30 percent in the maximum security context.

Albert Cohen attributes the prevalence of violence and sexual assault to a number of factors. The youth of inmates means that they have less stake in conformity (family, job, etc.) and are probably also 'less secure in their reputations for undoubted virility' (1976: 10). These facts reduce the incentive to conform and increase the incentive to prove their manhood through fighting and domination. Second, there is a **subculture of violence** that exists within and without the prison and may well be shared by low-ranking prison staff as well as inmates. This has several components. A 'machismo complex' places an emphasis on male honour and the need for combat to defend this. There is a preference for 'private justice' rather than the use of official channels to resolve disputes. Physical strength and its display in efforts at the domination of others are at the core of social relationships in prisons. Assaults and rapes in prison should be understood in this context as efforts to dramatize power. Social relationships from outside the prison can also play a role in encouraging violence – especially those related to gang membership. These largely cultural factors are facilitated by a number of structural contingencies. Prisons are places where the organizational priority is the maintenance of order. A bureaucratic and impersonal social system exists which does not facilitate rich and rewarding human relationships. Prisons are also 'traps'. In everyday life, avoidance (just walking away) is a means of dealing with disputes and reducing tensions. In prisons this is not an option. Finally, prisons are built around deprivations: food, sex, money, cigarettes. The black markets that emerge to satisfy these needs are likely to produce disputes that cannot be resolved by appeal to authorities as in ordinary business life.

Lee Bowker (1980) provides a useful review of the various forms of violence in prison and their meanings within prison culture, arguing that rape is part of a dynamic of power and fear. Dominant individuals build their status by orchestrating rapes and forcing newcomers into submission. For victims 'devaluation of the self is swift and severe' (1980: 16). Other forms of violence in prison are driven by diverse motives: revenge on a 'snitch', disputes over contraband, gang vendettas, righteous punishment of the paedophile or simply the search for status as a 'real man'. *Psychological victimization*, much of it riding on fears of physical victimization, is also a key feature of prison life. Bowker suggests that psychological games are a routine and efficient way of building status. These might include threats, insults, gossip and nasty practical 'jokes' which aim at humiliating the other person. *Economic victimization* involves activities such as loan sharking, theft, and demanding protection money. *Social victimization* involves prisoners being victimized as they are members of a group rather than because of their individual characteristics. Bowker reports that whites, members of the middle class and child sex offenders are often victimized and speculates that many such assaults are a form of revenge for collective injustices suffered outside the institution. Finally, we have to remember prison staff can be both perpetrators and victims of violence.

Prisons as a Negotiated Order

Aside from documenting deprivations and a pervasive culture of violence, studies of prison life also indicate the centrality of interactions between staff and inmates. Common sense tells us that guards have power and the inmates do not. Sociological studies informed by symbolic interactionism (see p. 27) suggest otherwise. In conversation, prison guards will often mention that the inmates run the place. They are only half-joking. In the day-to-day life of the prison the major priority of the officer is to maintain order and stability, to keep a lid on things, to keep things quiet. In order to accomplish this aim they have to rely upon the goodwill (or at least cooperation of the inmates).

In his classic text *The Society of Captives* Gresham Sykes (1958) points out that prisons differ from other organizations in that structures of power are not supported by normative pillars. There is no sense of obligation or duty or internalized morality among the prisoners as there might be in, say, the army or a school or hospital. Consequently 'custodians find themselves confronting men who must be forced, bribed, cajoled into compliance' (ibid.: 47). Violence can be used to deal with major disturbances but is inefficient for ensuring everyday conformity with instructions. The use of force can also set a precedent which is dangerous for the physically outnumbered guards. Yet the guards need the prisoners to behave. A rowdy cell block is simply interpreted by management as a sign that the guards are not able to do their job properly. The result is a situation of **negotiated order** (See Box 5.5). This means that officers will turn a blind eye to minor misdemeanours or tolerate and work with informal structures of power such as gangs. As Sykes puts it the 'best path of action is to make "deals" or "trades" with the captives ... the guard buys compliance and obedience in certain areas at the cost of tolerating disobedience elsewhere' (ibid.: 57). In extreme situations the situation can eventuate in which power shifts towards the inmates and they resist efforts at control. The guard is threatened with blackmail (e.g. a letter to the prison governor detailing regulations they have broken) should they try to clamp down on abuses.

Box 5.5   The Macquarie Harbour Penal Settlement: An Example of Negotiated Order

The following provides an example of negotiated order even in the most extreme and brutal of conditions. Established in 1822 on the island of Tasmania, the Macquarie Harbour Penal Settlement was arguably the most remote and harsh in the world. This was a prison labour camp for secondary offenders – an intentional hell on earth for convicts who had broken the law *after* transportation from Britain to Australia. The colony was situated in a wilderness area on a coastline facing Antarctica. At times the colony nearly starved as supply ships could not get through the rough seas for months on end. There were no maps of the mountainous interior and those who escaped had to resort to cannibalism to try to survive. Prisoners were housed on an island in the harbour, with the worst criminals chained up and confined to an exposed rock 40 yards long and 8 wide. Suicide and murder were common.

The prison was in effect a slave labour camp dedicated to logging valuable timber from the surrounding, almost impenetrable bogs and forests. Subsequently the convicts were employed making ships. It is here that the negotiated order takes over. The original ships were of poor design and workmanship and were made very slowly by the prisoners. But things suddenly changed. In 1828 some 8,004 lashes were given as punishment compared to 800 in 1829. This shift corresponded with the arrival of a new master shipwright who selected and trained talented men. Some 96 ships and boats were built between 1828 and 1833, many to advanced designs, making this the most productive shipyard in Australia. Prison conditions improved correspondingly with existing documents and archaeological records suggesting extra rations, a blind eye turned towards trade in contraband and better living conditions eventuating despite orders to the contrary from the State Governor. A letter of 1830 even suggests prisoners wanted to be transferred to Macquarie Harbour from other convict stations. All the evidence points to a negotiated order. The prisoners worked hard in return for a liveable prison. The on-site prison administration gave the prisoners what they wanted in return for a profitable supply of ships. And the master shipwright obtained a state-subsidized laboratory to experiment with boat design and construction.

Source: Davey (1998).

Women in Prisons

Women in prisons face many of the same issues as men. For example, power relations within the prison are comparable to those found in male prisons: guards are authoritarian and prisoners are ostensibly powerless and subordinate with very little freedom to organize or individualize their lives. Illegal drugs are prevalent, and much of the prison routine is oriented (unsuccessfully) towards limiting their supply and use. Contact with family and support networks is limited and can be revoked as punishment. The programs and facilities offered are rarely enough to encourage rehabilitation or provide meaningful and marketable skills for when a prisoner's sentence ends.

However, a number of gender-specific issues are also evident. First is the issue of classification. In Australia, women are more likely than men to end up in maximum or medium-security prisons. This does not reflect the nature of their crimes, but the lack of facilities available: there are more women with minimum-security classifications than there are available places in minimum-security prisons (McCulloch, 1988). This mixing of security classifications is also evident other jurisdictions (Crawford, 1988, in Morash et al., 1994). Thus those who have no past criminal history, or who have been convicted of only minor offences are forced to negotiate a more oppressive environment (Esteal, 2001: 79). Morash et al. (1994) point out that mixing security classifications also makes it impracticable to offer facilities and programs that require a less restrictive environment.

The specific needs of female offenders are also problematic. High proportions of women prisoners have suffered family abuse as children and/or as adults, and significant percentages have a history of drug or alcohol abuse (Morash, et al., 1994; Esteal, 2001: 79). Proper programs are necessary in order to deal with the consequences of these experiences. But smaller, low-security prisons are marked by the offer of fewer programs (Morash et al., 1994). In addition, the low numbers of incarcerated women means that it is not efficient to offer a wide range of educational, skills development, rehabilitation and therapy programs (Morash et al., 1994; Esteal, 2001: 80). Some studies suggest that women have better access to mental health treatment than men (Morash et al., 1994) but others have generated less promising results for medical care generally (Bershad, 1985). A very high proportion of women have dependent children, which reflects women's position as primary child carers. Many prisons do not allow children to live with their mother. Patricia Esteal (2001: 90) reports that in her study of women in prison, every mother described her absence from her children and her worries about their well-being as the worst element of imprisonment.

The subculture of the women's prison also varies, compared to that of men. Some early studies of women in prison indicated the development of pseudo-kinship networks that to some extent replace those lost through their incarceration (Giallombardo, 1966; Ward and Kassebaum, 1965). Rose Giallombardo (1966) describes the function of these relationships as creating a stable social structure, demarcating some women as 'off limits' sexually, providing source of friendship and a means of socialization into the prison culture. Lesbian relations were also important in allowing the women to develop intimate and secure relationships. Barbara Owen's (1998) more contemporary work lends support to these earlier conclusions. However, Lori Girshick (1999) found that these were by no means widespread, and many women frowned upon 'playing family' and sexual relationships. Through in-depth interviews in one US state institution, Kimberley Greer (2000) noted that friendships and sexual relationships were the most common forms of connection among women in prison, but were viewed ambiguously, even by those involved in them.

The majority of women described themselves as 'loners', and generally friendship was seen as a risky and transitory proposition. Kinship relationships were not widespread. Greer concludes that women adopt a primarily individualistic focus on 'doing time'.

Greer's work in particular echoes Patricia Esteal's (2001: 80) description of the three dominant principles of women's prison culture. The first rule is 'Don't trust' – prison practices and expectations are changed seemingly at random and confidences are often violated. The second rule is 'Don't talk'. Female prisoners do not report the abuse or their fellow inmates, nor do they 'dob' or 'snitch' on guards. Further, they fail to acknowledge their own difficult history of abuse. The third rule is 'Don't feel' – women often 'shut down' emotionally. Esteal concludes that the rules reflect those in dysfunctional families and that prisons perpetuate rather than address the conditions and culture that may have led to offending.

Intermediate Sanctions

We have already mentioned that when we think of punishment, the prison is the first thing to come to mind. It is clearly the major symbol of the penal system. Yet most offenders do not go to prison. In Australia, for example, around three times the number of people in prison are currently under some kind of community supervision. When another form of punishment is given, this is referred to as **intermediate sanctions** or sometimes as **community corrections**. It should be noted that these terms and their boundaries are frequently contested. In particular, it is often noted that community involvement in 'community corrections' is minimal. A commonly used distinction in the literature on this topic is between **front end** alternatives, which in effect divert offenders away from a prison term, and **back end** alternatives which are used at the end of a prison sentence, typically drug parole. Options within the rubric of intermediate sanctions/community corrections include the following:

- Probation: This option is often imposed instead of a jail term. Here the offender must meet with a probation officer on a regular basis. There are often restrictions and expectations upon behaviour. For example, there may be periodic tests for drug and alcohol use, the offender must hold down or look for a job, they must not go to certain areas or associate with certain people. Violation of these conditions can see the offender sent to prison. The system of **parole** is a variation on this. The term comes from the French for 'promise' or 'word of honour'. It is often used at the end of a prison sentence to assist with the reintegration of the prisoner into society. The prisoner will be released before the end of their term so long as they fulfil certain conditions. The transition to life outside the prison appears to be difficult. A California study found that in 1997 around 65 percent of prison admissions were of parole violators (Petersilia, 1999: 483). As we have already discussed, over recent years parole systems have come under attack, such hostility often arising when a parolee commits a horrific attack that is reported in the media (see pp. 137–138). Legislation has progressively wound back the use of discretionary parole in favour of mandatory sentence terms and parole officers have lost much of their rehabilitation and social work role to become more involved in tasks of surveillance. These might include enforcing curfews or conducting random drug tests.

- Community Work Orders: Often used for minor offences, this can require a person to put in a certain amount of time on community projects. For example, they might be involved in building a park, planting trees, or painting a playground.
- Periodic Detention: This involves detention in stages to minimize harm to the offender or their family. A typical situation will see someone holding down their job during the week but being locked up at the weekend.
- Home Detention: Here the offender is confined to their house. They may be checked up on by random visits or phone calls. More recently forms of electronic monitoring have been introduced. These make use of a device that is attached to the body.
- Suspended Sentences: Here the sentence is given but will not be activated so long as the offender conforms to certain conditions. For example, a minor drug offender might be required to undergo drug testing. They will be sent to jail only if they fail to test clean or if they break another law.
- Fines: These are the most common form of penalty. For example, in New South Wales, Australia, they made up around 80 percent of sentences in low-level criminal courts. They are less common in higher courts where more serious cases tend to be heard (Findlay et al., 1999: 225). Fines are popular because they offer several advantages.

  - They can be adjusted according to the facts of the case.
  - They bring in revenue rather than requiring expenditure.
  - They are simple to administer.
  - They involve less stigma or harm to the offender than other punishments. For this reason they are especially popular for low risk offenders.

Having said this, large numbers of fine defaulters end up in jail. These people are often poor or simply disorganized. For more affluent people paying a fine is not usually a problem. Hence fines are a form of punishment that tends to discriminate against the poor. For this reason more recent initiatives have attempted to calibrate the size of the fine to the offender's income as well as to the nature of the offence. Such a system is in place in Finland, where it has led to the world's biggest traffic fines, especially for senior executives and dot.com millionaires. At the time of writing the record is held by Mr Anssi Vanjoki, a senior executive with Nokia, who earns $5.2 million every year. His fine for doing 46.5 mph in a 30-mph zone was $103,000!

Advocates suggest that intermediate sanctions have a number of advantages, including:

- They allow the prison to be a 'last resort', thus protecting minor offenders from the potential harm of imprisonment.
- They provide judges with a range of sentencing options. For minor offenders prison seems too harsh.
- Prison is expensive, intermediate sanctions may allow tax-payers to save money.
- They may do a better job at rehabilitating the offender.
- They can be used to reduce prison overcrowding, for example, through early release to community correction schemes.

Although intermediate sanctions are sometimes thought of as 'alternatives to prison', it is worth remembering that they are still backed up by the eventual possibility of confinement. Offenders who fail to live up to the terms and conditions of such a punishment (e.g. a fine defaulter) may be liable for a prison sentence. Intermediate sanctions are also intimately tied to the prison system through the parole system. Their purpose here is to ensure the transition of offenders to ordinary life, hence they are loaded with both punitive and reintegrative functions.

Some critics have pointed out that the increasing provision of intermediate sanctions has not led to reduced prisoner numbers. So-called 'alternatives to prison' have not contributed to decarceration but rather have been used in addition to existing policies of imprisonment. Hence, rather than thinking of such activities as an 'alternative' to prison, it is better to see them as part of an ever expanding continuum of practices aimed at reforming criminals and punishing crime. Looking from a distance we can understand the growth of community corrections as tied to the growth of the welfare state and to the rise of welfare ideologies and administrative functions in criminal justice during the twentieth century. These link justice to the language games of social work and blur the boundaries between the criminal justice system and those of broader regulatory programs in the area of social administration. Hence there is a focus not so much on providing support to offenders as on monitoring and regulating potentially dangerous populations through the provision of an apparatus of surveillance and administration.

This line of negative evaluation has been especially strong among criminologists influenced by poststructuralism and neo-Marxist criminology. Stanley Cohen (1979) offers perhaps the best known of these. He suggests that although they may seem positive and progressive we should really think about such policies in terms of **net widening**. In effect, they will allow more and more people to be pulled into the punitive and administrative systems of the state by changing social and administrative definitions of deviance and offering alternative low threshold entry points into the criminal justice system. As segregated and walled institutions, prisons provided clear boundaries around the deviant. Now it is hard to see where the deviant and the normal are to be separated. Consequently the rise of community corrections allows the expansion of state power to be hidden. Cohen (1979: 54) writes 'it will be impossible to determine who exactly is enmeshed in the social control system – and hence subject to its jurisdiction and surveillance – at any one time.' Because they are seen as 'soft', alternative punishments also allow such control to be masked. It is disguised and socially acceptable because it draws upon a range of knowledges. Hence, 'Systems of medicine, social work, education, welfare take on supervisory and judicial function, while the penal apparatus itself becomes more influenced by medicine, education, psychology.' (ibid.: 58). Cohen sees a bleak future in which a Foucauldian 'punitive city' arises that is dominated by a raft of judicial and welfare institutions whose ultimate extent and true power are difficult to evaluate (see p. 30). The growth of community corrections has not been without its critics on the Right as well. In public opinion such policies are sometimes seen as insufficiently punitive for some categories of offending and as not offering protection for the community by incapacitating violent offenders. Such concerns have provided a major brake on their ability to be used for middle-order offences (Zdenkowski, 2000: 170–1).

The Death Penalty

At the other end of the scale from intermediate sanctions is the death penalty, which still exists in the United States. The exact crimes for which death is applicable as a punishment vary from state to state in America, but in most cases a simple murder is not sufficient to receive the penalty. What is required is a more serious offence such as murder for gain (e.g. during an armed robbery), murder of a police officer, murder tied to a sexual offence, or a drug-related murder. Despite Hollywood stereotypes, the typical recipient of the death penalty is not a cool and calculating serial killer. They tend to be from a poor background, have a delinquent past tied to a broken home and poor educational attainment (Carter, 1965). Typically, they have a history of offending which gradually becomes more and more serious and will have spent many spells in prison before the crime that sees them killed. This is usually a bungled robbery in which someone gets shot.

Over history the death penalty has reflected societal trends in modernity, becoming more bureaucratic and technologically mediated. Studies of the administration of the death penalty have pointed to the way that staff are trained so that it runs smoothly and with minimum mental anguish. In *Death Work*, Robert Johnson (1990) shows that the final hours of the inmate are governed by routines. Staff and inmates follow a precise timetable that includes activities like a final shower, last meal, goodbyes in a situation of intensive surveillance. Johnson reports that most prisoners go to their deaths in a quiet and resigned state – a radically different situation from the expressive public executions of previous centuries (see pp. 17–18, 28). Prison staff are mostly concerned to be 'professional' and to follow procedures to the letter. They will have rehearsed these many times before the real execution. It is arguably the case that this concern for professionalism enables staff to deal with the psychological consequences of killing another person.

Despite the availability of such a bureaucratically mediated death, the punishment has come to be seen as inherently barbaric in most Western developed nations – a perception that can be explained in terms of the work of Elias on the civilizing process (see pp. 37–39). The United States is the exception to the general trend of dispensing with violent penalties directed against the body. The death penalty in America is supported by a number of justifications. Some argue that it is consistent with morality of natural justice – that the punishment should resemble the crime. This, of course, is the philosophy of *lex talionis* or 'an eye for an eye'. Others claim that the death penalty has a strong deterrent effect on potential murderers.

Critics retort that the death penalty is brutal, barbaric and often botched and that there is no substantial evidence of deterrence. To the contrary, the United States has an abnormally high murder rate when compared to other OECD countries. In recent years particular attention has been given to the racist application of the death penalty. Evidence seems to suggest that African Americans in particular have been disadvantaged. For example, Blacks who kill Whites seem to have the greater odds of receiving the death penalty than Whites who kill Blacks, Whites who kill Whites or Blacks who kill Blacks (Keil and Vito, 1989). The causes of this disparity are disputed. Some point to racism in the criminal justice system, especially among police, judges and prosecutors. Others, however, suggest that factors such as poverty may be at play. On average African American people are poorer and this might impact upon their ability to pay for good legal support when defending their case. The case of sporting legend O. J. Simpson is a case in point. During the 1990s Simpson was indicted for a double murder and there was a strong raft of evidence against him. He was, however, a millionaire and his legal 'dream team' were able to discredit the evidence, showing that one of the police officers investigating Simpson was a racist who might have planted a bloody glove. Simpson was found not guilty. It is doubtful that a poorer African American would have been able to mount such an effective defence.

New Initiatives in Punishment

In the course of this chapter we have touched upon diverse critiques of existing punishments as ineffective, too cruel or too soft, incoherent or simply too expensive. The search is always on for new ways of doing things. We conclude the chapter by reviewing a couple of new initiatives.

Reintegrative shaming

Pioneered by John Braithwaite (1989), the idea of **reintegrative shaming** suggests we need to radically rethink the process and philosophy of punishment. He claims that most existing punishments are stigmatizing. They confer a deviant identity upon the criminal and cut them off from the community. Consequently they might contribute to crime rather than eliminating it (see pp. 26–27). Braithwaite suggests that what is needed is shaming followed by reintegration. Shaming involves communicating to the offender that what they have done is morally unacceptable. The second phase, reintegration, involves efforts to forgive and welcome the offender back into the community and seeks to provide a set of internalized moral constraints against offending. The aim here is generally to build support and so suggest that blame does not belong only with an individual but can be thought of as a failure of a wider collectivity. Braithwaite points to the fact that reintegrative shaming goes on throughout our society in everyday life. Within the family, for example, children are told that something they have done is wrong and then told that they are still loved. He also suggests that it is common in Japan, where the criminal justice system values confession followed by re-acceptance. Only the most serious offenders are imprisoned, and Japan has a very low crime rate.

Ideas about reintegrative shaming have been important since the 1990s, particularly in the sphere of juvenile justice where it finds a fit with welfare ideologies. The idea here is to divert the young offender from a criminal path and provide positive sources of esteem and sentiments of belonging. This typically works through a system of conferencing in which representatives of the victim, police, social work and family discuss the crime with the delinquent and try to arrive at a negotiated solution (see pp. 154–159).

Braithwaite is less sanguine about the potential of reintegrative shaming to work with a small minority of hardened criminals. These might find support from criminal networks and find a sense of belonging in a deviant identity. People who are strongly immersed in deviant subcultures (e.g. some gangs) might not care what the wider society or even their family thinks. Psychopaths and those with certain kinds of mental illness may also be resistant to the moral dynamics of reintegrative shaming. Concerns also need to be raised about due process. In Japan, for example, there is strong pressure placed upon the accused to confess and attempts to claim innocence are seen in a negative light as resistance to social norms. The result can be a harsher penalty for those who do not express contrition.

Ideas about **restorative justice** have risen in influence alongside ideas about reintegrative shaming. Central to this philosophy are ideas about repairing harm and resolving conflicts rather than punishing the offender and allocating blame. Typically some form of victim/offender mediation takes place in which the police, social workers and family also play a role. The idea is to share experiences, come to an understanding of harm and arrive at a collectively agreed solution. Examples of this include the Wagga Wagga Juvenile Cautioning Program in Australia and the system of Family Group Conferences in New Zealand.

Private prisons

Whereas there seems to be widespread support for reintegrative shaming (at least for juveniles and minor offences), the privatization of prisons has caused some of the most heated debates of recent times in the criminological community (James et al., 1997; Sparks, 1994). This can refer to a range of things from the subcontracting of laundry, food, education and health services through to the construction, ownership and management of entire prison complexes. Many of the lower-level forms of privatization have been around for a long time and contention usually surrounds developments at the other end of the scale. The period since 1980s has seen the rise of major corporations such as the Corrections Corporation of America (CCA) and Wackenhut as major players in the corrections area. For example, in 1986 controversy erupted when CCA proposed running the entire Tennessee prison system for an annual fee of $250 million. The private prison industry is largest in the United States where around 95,000 prisoners, or 7 percent of inmates are held in privately operated facilities (Bureau of Justice Statistics, 2002). However, Australia is the country where the idea has been most enthusiastically adopted. Some 28 percent of Australia's prisoners are held in privately managed prisons (James et al., 1997: 11). The ideological groundwork for such shifts was laid in the 1980s, with 'tough on crime' policies combining with a neo-conservative groundswell that the private sector could solve social problems more efficiently than the state.

Arguments in favour of privatization of prisons point to the failures of the public system and suggest that new strategies are needed. It is claimed that competition will lead to improved services. The involvement of the private sector will also generate fresh ideas, sidestep bureaucracy and improve flexibility. However, James et al. (1997: 8) suggest that 'the most decisive practical consideration influencing the appeal of private-sector management of prisons was cost'. Savings, it was hoped, could be attained by adopting more efficient management and surveillance techniques, enhancing workforce flexibility and providing in turn a benchmark for measuring the public sector.

Critics, however, are sceptical that real cost savings and real benefits will eventuate (Bowditch and Everett, 1987; Harding 1997). They believe that:

- Pressure to reduce costs will impact upon the quality of care, especially in the area of programme delivery. Overcrowding may also be encouraged. In effect, prison corporations will cut corners to return a profit to their shareholders.
- Private prisons will try to select only the best prisoners, leaving more difficult cases to the public system. Evidence for this is the fact that most private prisons are minimum-security institutions.
- Levels of staff training will be reduced. This endangers both staff and inmates and will compromise the quality of service provision in prisons. Moreover, privatized prisons are a way of confronting and challenging trade unions. They have casualized labour, undermined industrial award conditions and career paths.
- There are moral and philosophical problems in profiting from punishment. Theories about the 'social contract' (see pp. 12–13) suggest that punishment on behalf of the people should be by the state.
- Accountability and public scrutiny are reduced as 'commercial-in-confidence' legal clauses are invoked by profit-making concerns.

Fears that privatization will lead to lower standards means that a great deal of effort goes into constructing contracts. These have to spell out in meticulous detail what is expected of the private prison operator, how much they will be paid for particular services and what the penalties will be for non-compliance. Rigorous programs of inspection also fall into place to check that standards are being maintained. This activity amounts to a big hidden cost of privatization and may wipe out the savings made from free market efficiencies.

In recent years the literature has moved on from hypothetical statements on possible benefits and disadvantages towards evaluation. It is now widely acknowledged that insufficient high quality research has been conducted to see whether or not privatizing prisons is a good idea. The available evidence is equivocal. Many studies seem to be poorly designed or prejudiced by ideological or institutional bias. Investigations should ideally use matched pairs. This involves comparing prisons that are similar in all respects except for management. Locating suitable pairs is difficult. One study suggests that private facilities do indeed save money. Sellers (1993) compared facilities in Pennsylvania, New Jersey and Tennessee found an average inmate *per diem* cost of $46 in private prisons and $74 in publicly operated facilities. However, several other studies have not identified any cost savings (see James et al., 1997: 24–5). Investigating the 'quality' of prison administration is even harder with disputes over the definition and measurement of quality. A study of the Wolds prison in the United Kingdom, which is run by Group 4, showed a number of positive outcomes. For example, remand prisoners were unlocked for 14 hours a day and a survey showed widespread satisfaction with living conditions and facilities. Some 58 percent of prisoners at Wolds though it was better than other remand facilities, compared to only 41 percent at an otherwise similar state-run institution, Woodhill (ibid.).

Conclusion

This chapter has reviewed sentencing and corrections and indicated many areas in which there are current concerns. It has also placed these in a theoretical context and suggested ways in which a sociological perspective can help us reflect upon what is happening and why. It is clear that there are no easy answers when it comes to the problem of arriving at appropriate and effective punishments. Yet perhaps knowing the right questions to ask is more important. The diverse themes we have explored here provide a starting place for this activity.

Study Questions

1 What are the characteristics of prison culture? How are these reflected in prison language?
2 Several trends related to prisons arguably reflect the growing influence of law and order politics. What are these?
3 What are the alternatives to prison? Why should we have these? Debate the pros and cons of using these more widely.
4 Outline the contradictory aims at play in sentencing and corrections.

Glossary of Key Terms

Auburn System – A prison philosophy emphasizing the need for militaristic discipline and work.

back end – A term referring to exit from a component of the criminal justice system. In the case of prisons, this might refer to parole or release policies.

community corrections – Forms of punishment that keep the offender in the community and out of prison. Often used synonymously with 'intermediate sanctions'.

correction program – Interventions designed to prevent prison inmates re-offending.

deterrence – The philosophy that argues that punishment should try to reduce crime levels by making the costs of crime outweigh the benefits. General deterrence is directed to the public at large; specific deterrence to the individual offender.

front end – A term referring to entry into a component of the criminal justice system. For prisons this might refer to sentencing policies or sentencing rates.

incapacitation – An approach advocating taking criminals out of circulation and thus preventing them offending.

intermediate sanctions – Punishments that fall short of a prison term, typically things like fines, home detention and community service orders.

negotiated order – A form of social order that depends less on official rules and more on informal norms and agreements. In prisons, these are usually between staff and inmates.

net widening – Criminal justice policies that bring more people into the criminal justice system.

'nothing works' – The influential, but perhaps erroneous view, that programs in prisons fail to reduce recidivism.

Pennsylvania System – An early prison philosophy emphasizing the benefits of solitary confinement and repentance.

policy regime – A term that refers to the style and priorities of the state or criminal justice system in implementing social policy.

prison culture – The informal culture of prison life held by inmates.

recidivism – Repeat offending by convicted offenders.

reductivisn – See *deterrence*.

rehabilitation – The philosophy that argues that punishment should aim to reform criminals into law abiding citizens.

reintegrative shaming – An approach to justice that focuses on the moral dimensions of crime. Offenders are first made to feel shame and then encouraged back into the community.

restorative justice – A philosophy that argues the aim of justice should be to repair harm. This usually involves taking a big picture approach rather than focusing on the individual offender.

retribution – The philosophy that argues that punishment should exact a price for crime.

selective incapacitation – The view that prison should be used as a last resort for containing only the most serious offenders.

subculture of violence – A local cultural form that emphasizes the normality and desirability of violence as a means of resolving dispute and accords status to those accomplished in violent acts.

Suggested Further Reading

It is impossible to recommend any survey texts on prison and punishment. Those that exist tend to be in the area of justice administration and are aimed at practitioners rather than providing a sociological perspective. Hence they are full of descriptions of roles and responsibilities, corporate structures, etc. However, many of the works referred to in this chapter are accessible to a student audience. We particularly recommend *The Society of Captives* by Gresham Sykes (1958), which is a telling if slightly dated analysis of prison life. David Garland's (1991b) collection on mass imprisonment in the United States provides a taste of contemporary work in the penal area that combines social theory with data. Pratt (2002) provides a theoretical account of the prison and its ties to culture and modernity. Harding's (1997) book on private prisons, and Johnson's (1990) study of 'death work' have similar virtues. Various government reports, many available on the Internet, are an important research tool. Journal articles on prisons are less common than those on policing, but can still be found in the major academic outlets such as *Criminology* and *Justice Quarterly*. Many specialist journals such as *The Prison Journal*, *Corrections Today* and *Corrections Management Quarterly* tend to be oriented towards practitioners and are likely to be of most interest to those engaged in applied social science. *Punishment and Society* is the pivotal journal for those interested in theoretically informed discussion of corrections.

Suggested Websites

The various government agency sites listed here provide access to reports and policy documents on line. They can be especially good for locating statistics. The other sites are of educational value or provide an insight into the operation of various players in the corrections field.

http://www.aic.gov.au/ Australian Institute of Criminology. Some worthwhile reports and papers can often be located at this website.

http://www.homeoffice.gov.uk/   British Home Office. By clicking around you can usually find some good material here on corrections policy as well as statistics and evaluation reports.

http://www.prisonexp.org   This site offers a fascinating look at Zimbardo's prison experiment, see p. 180.

http://www.usdoj.gov/   United States Department of Justice. It is usually possible to access up-to-date statistics and reports here.

http://www.wackenhutcorrections.com   Wackenhut is a major player in the private prison business. This site provides an idea of the range of services they offer and, indirectly, an insight into the language and world-view of the corrections industry.

6 Conclusion

Law, Criminal Justice and the Sociological Perspective

Here at the end of this book, we are in a position to return to the themes of the Introduction. Having read the previous chapters, readers will be able to judge for themselves the statements and speculations we wish to make in closing. At the outset we made the case that a sociological perspective is necessary for a more complete understanding of law and the criminal justice system. But just what is this 'sociological perspective'? Fundamentally, it is about explanations, not descriptions or doctrines. Sociologists cast a critical eye over the social world. They re-evaluate taken-for-granted presumptions, irrespective of whether these are found in common-sense perspectives, political claims or the knowledge bases of other disciplines. This activity does not always entail rejecting prior conclusions, but by and large sociologists hold that insights into the ways the world works should always be tested with empirical evidence and that our understanding must be rooted in systematically collected data. Thinking 'how could it be otherwise?' also furthers re-evaluation. This activity, often fostered by theoretical models and a comparative perspective, allows us to challenge assumptions by stretching our minds to other, potentially more insightful or interesting possibilities (see Willis, 1995: 78–80). Such intellectual practice allows us to debunk the received wisdom that often guides thoughts and action. Debunking means that we contest the ways in which people generally think; in the words of Peter Berger (1963), we 'see through' popular opinion and official explanation. As both Willis (1995: 82–3) and Berger point out, at times this can lead to controversial and unpopular conclusions and recommendations. But it also has the potential to generate exciting and innovative ways of viewing and confronting our world. In this book we have attempted to provide the resources necessary for this activity. Our ambition has been to not only to provide information but also to destabilize complacent certainties and to encourage both scepticism and creative, critical thinking. Let us review how a sociological perspective can accomplish this task.

As you have read this book it has no doubt become clear to you that sociological visions are plural and contested. However, they also share some family resemblances, a set of frequently encountered properties that crop up time and time again, regardless of paradigm disputes. These commonalities have anchored many of the lessons we have tried to present in this book with respect to the issue of 'how to think' about law and criminal justice. First, we have pointed to an *imperative to move beyond explanations that ground outcomes in individual and collective volitions and plans*. In other words, sociologists generally hold that things do not come about simply because people, groups or organizations want them or think they are a good idea. Explanations cannot be found just by looking in people's heads. There are structural forces and cultural forms that make their choices possible and thinkable. The prison, for example, did not emerge simply because in the eighteenth century Caesare Beccaria and others like him came to the conclusion there was a need for humane, predictable punishments to replace prior barbarisms. We need to consider the origins of the culture that shaped this vision: the Enlightenment rationalism and the 'civilizing process' identified by Elias (pp. 37–39; Prett, 2002); the presence of religious traditions, architectural forms, technologies and know-how that made prisons a workable option for the relevant bodies (pp. 169–172); the centralization of regulatory power in the state that enabled such large-scale enterprises to replace local forms of justice (pp. 36–37); and the wholesale transformation of forms of power towards those of a disciplinary society (pp. 28–31). The efforts of people and their initiatives always have the potential to make a difference, but this is a human agency that takes place in a wider socio-historical context of which the actors might be unaware.

The next, related point is that the sociological perspective tends to be *structural rather than individual*. Whereas psychologists are interested in explaining how people act with reference to brain function and personality, the sociologist is more concerned with the network of relationships into which they are embedded, their roles, their membership in aggregate categories such as those of race and gender, and their location within a broader social structure of which they may have only a limited, practical awareness. Arguing for a science of society, Emile Durkheim called these supra-individual determinants of human actions and possibilities 'social facts' and argued that the task of sociology was to uncover their form and function. Such a vision sees individuals as less sovereign, less in control of their destinies than we might imagine. Rather, their identities and actions are shaped by forces of a more collective stamp. In the contents of this book we can see such a perspective at work. The actions and attitudes of the police, for example, were shown to be shaped by their social role as order maintainers and occupational socialization into a police culture (pp. 88–93). To explain how they behave, we need to look at these social facts, not at the individual lives and personalities of the millions of police officers around the world. Likewise we can understand what goes on in the prison by pointing to theoretical understandings from Goffman on total institutions, Foucault on discipline or Sykes on inmate roles (see pp. 27–28, 28–32, 178–179). In the work of each of these authors the individual is displaced from the centre of analysis. Indeed, the very sense of self that the inmate has is shown to have been socially constructed by the processes and cultures of the institution. To begin an explanation by pointing to individuals and without taking into account how they are themselves shaped by social forces would be to misrecognize what is in fact a dependent variable. As a concrete example, sexual assault does not take place in prisons because they are full of predatory homosexuals. Rather, it is the setting of the prison, its inmate roles and its organization that generate the patterns of violent sexual activity (pp. 180–182).

A third property we often find in sociological explanations is an appreciation of the *unintended consequences of action*. This can lead to a strongly ironic vision in which outcomes of actions eventuate that are the opposite of those wished for. In a diluted and more common form, we find arguments that the results of action are often simply unanticipated or that the actions make less difference than their initiators might suppose. There are several reasons why this could be so. Actors cannot know how others will respond to their strategies. They might be ignorant of some facts or blinded by ideologies or common sense to the systemic implications of their choices and strategies. This book has been replete with examples of such a process. For example, the Kansas City Patrol Experiment demonstrated that although the police believed routine motorized patrol reduced crime and fear of crime, it made no difference to either (pp. 98–99); racial disparities in sentencing appear to arise as an unintended consequence of the application of informal decision-making rules as judges attempt to be fair (pp. 129–133); well-intentioned efforts to get Battered Woman Syndrome accepted by the courts may have perpetuated stereotypes of women as not fully rational (pp. 67–68, 136). The lesson here is to investigate the outcomes of actions rather than to assume that these align neatly with the intentions of their sponsors.

The characteristics listed above are part of a *search for higher order explanation*. This involves developing theoretical models that can recognize common underlying social patterns even as they identify and account for diverse particulars across cases. This is a complex task, one that requires digging a little deeper than what Charles Tilly (2000) calls the 'standard stories' of everyday explanation in the effort to identify the true causes of actions and outcomes. While 'standard stories' involve visions of motivated actors and deliberate decisions, sociological explanations point to structural relationships and hidden social forces. Let's illustrate this. A classic case of an analytic framework allowing for higher order explanation is Marxism, with its claim that class struggle and material interests underlie phenomena as diverse as the operation of police discretion, the drafting of legislation and the practice of mass imprisonment (pp. 19–24, 103–104, 177–178). To have accounted for these in terms of, respectively, the latest policy initiative from the police chief, the desire of parliamentarians to control crime and the actions of judges in the court system might have intuitive appeal but it would stop short of the full story. From the Marxist perspective, each of these more immediate causes can be better understood as simply the concrete mechanism of an underlying set of determining structures: the role of the legal and criminal justice systems as a state apparatus responsible for ensuring favourable conditions for the reproduction of capitalism and controlling dissent. Mobilizing these kinds of higher order accounts, perhaps using Marxism, perhaps rival paradigms, enables us to look at situations in new ways. We can now ask questions that take us beyond the myriad details of the particular issues and personalities at stake such as we might find in a newspaper account and insert these into a more comprehensive vision of social order and history. We gain a critical distance, an altitude from which we start to see the outline of the forest and not just a tree here and a tree there.

In searching for these higher order explanations, sociologists are aware that an account or description, no matter how elegant, is not the same as a truly convincing explanation. *Empirical research* allows suppositions to be tested and contributes to a solid empirical foundation for knowledge. It hammers theory against the bedrock of reality, and thus ensures that we do more than tell plausible stories. Some sociologists are positivists, arguing that research should be scientific and allow us to collect a set of verifiable, objective data. Others claim that meaning is fundamental to our inquiry and that our methods must come to terms with this by interpreting human actions and cultural systems. These contrasting positions mirror differences in how people understand knowledge – this is known as epistemology – but both reflect the sociological need to explain the workings of society with reference to empirical facts, rather than simply trade in ideas from the comfort of an armchair. The means of collecting the data we need are diverse. Through your reading you may have identified two broad approaches within sociology. The first uses qualitative methods, gathering information that is not easily transformed into numerical data, often with the aim of translating and distilling the interpretive frameworks of the subjects. There are multiple ways in which this project can proceed. Some researchers have committed to ethnographic projects, observing social life 'in the field' where interactions between sociologists and their subjects are less formally structured than in most other research contexts. Erving Goffman's *Asylums* (1968) is a classic of the genre. To investigate the lives and interpretations of asylum inmates, Goffman spent a year working within an institution, attempting to develop a holistic account of how that world was experienced (see p. 27). Other approaches use texts. For example, judges' written decisions are a resource for describing the world-views that underpin legal reasoning processes (Esteal, 2001); the transcribed verbal exchanges in courts can help us trace relations of power and constructions of reality in that setting (Eades, 2000). The second way of studying the world uses quantitative procedures. Numerical data is useful for identifying patterns over large populations and pinning down the relationships between variables (see for example, Spohn et al., 1985; Steffensmeier et al., 1998). Both qualitative and quantitative methods have their positive attributes and their weaknesses. Qualitative studies have been extremely useful in developing an appreciation of the texture of social life, the ways in which it is negotiated and interpreted in different and sometimes contradictory ways. Thus, it is able to provide information on *why* people do the things they do. On the other side of the ledger, qualitative work is often small-scale and it is difficult to argue that the findings are generalizable to a broader population. Good quantitative work allows us to identify relationships between social facts, calculate the likelihood of future outcomes or events, and extrapolate the findings of a particular study. This approach also has its limits, most notably, a difficulty in studying and presenting the nuances of meaning, the interpretative practices through which people make sense of their world and respond to it. These different approaches and methods are subject to mutual critique and contestation. Yet taking a broader view, each fits within the more global vision of sociology as an empirical and not simply speculative activity.

Through the deployment of systematic research we are able to test perceptions that need questioning, document realities that need to go on the public record and uncover the world-views that lead to particular forms of behaviour. It is precisely because research methods key inquiry to the 'real world' in this way that they have become effective, albeit in often limited and indirect ways, in allowing social science to make claims upon policy. Consider, for example the representative contributions of the following studies and the ways that each might inform the operation of criminal justice: Steffensmeier et al.'s use of statistical techniques on sentencing data to show that racial disadvantage in sentencing does not manifest in a blanket way as we might suppose but is overwhelmingly concentrated on young, black males (pp. 131–132); Bowker's efforts with survey research to uncover the rates of sexual assault in prisons (pp. 181–182); Findlay's qualitative investigation of the processes of jury selection (pp. 152–153). Each of these provides an evidentiary base to enable our intellectual inquiry to become more precisely targeted. From each policy, initiatives may be put into place, including education, prevention or shifts in procedure. In short, convincing data can enable the perspective of sociology to move beyond the groves of the academy and into the realms of decision-making.

In addition to illustrating these bases of the sociological perspective, discussion in this book has been ordered by the argument that laws and criminal justice systems do not exist outside of the relationships, structures and ideologies of a society. Rather, their form, aims and outcomes are intrinsically connected to a broader social environment. Consequently, we have emphasized in particular the importance of *visions of modernity* as a pivotal intellectual resource for thinkers looking to connect the specific object of their inquiry on law or criminal justice to an encompassing terrain. We have indicated how the past few centuries have witnessed growing rationalization, secularization and professionalization (Weber); the emergence of a disciplinary society (Foucault); changing moral and cultural sensibilities (Durkheim, Elias); the centralization of state power and control (Weber, Giddens); the rise of social relations mediated by capitalism (Marxism); and how each of these was manifested in a new set of institutions, cultural codes and practices. We have seen in the course of this book that prisons, formal legal codes, lawyers and professionalized police, for example, can all be seen as expressions of these unfolding properties of modernity. They involve specialization, technology, large-scale organizations, formal rules of procedure and a rationalization of action. We might add that criminological knowledge has itself long been caught up in the unfolding of modernity with its use of scientific method, reason and secular explanation and its home in the post-Enlightenment university system. When not simply an ivory tower exercise, applied research tends to be closely tied to modernity's justice agencies and institutions. This is thanks to the role of the state in funding and sponsoring research programs (Savelsberg, 1994; Savelsberg et al., 2002).

At the same time as showing that a concept of modernity must be central to our efforts at understanding the structure and function of social control systems, we have repeatedly documented limits to its reach. This kind of critique is reflected in diffuse ways in materials scattered throughout this book. At an empirical level, we have seen how sociological research has problematized claims that people are treated in accordance with those universalistic and impartial legal principles that embody the ideals of modernity. Studies on policing, for example, have emphasized the racist and sexist nature of police culture. This world-view contributes to a series of outcomes, from differential policing to police brutality, that do not fulfil the promises of enlightenment values such as equality before the law (pp. 104–108). Looking to the courts, we have noted similar concerns. There are suggestions that groups are subjected to different presumptions and concerns when being judged and so, for example, increasingly refined statistical techniques have been used in the attempt to uncover bias in sentencing outcomes (pp. 131–132). Using a more interpretive approach, writers have described the not fully rational processes in which members of particular groups are represented and judged through legal discourse (pp. 139–141). In short, studies of contemporary policing and court processes, to mention just two arenas, highlight the incomplete institutionalization of modernity's ideals and principles in the concrete activity of criminal justice institutions.

Some analyses of contemporary practices in the criminal justice system provide grounds for a more fundamental critique, one that questions not only empirical shortcomings relative to the promise of modernity, but also the ability of its standard operating procedures to bring substantive justice. For example, formal rules of procedure and the rationalization of action are being undermined through calls for alternative dispute resolution and conferencing (pp. 154–159). Advocates see mainstream adjudicative justice as impersonal and its binary logic of victims and offenders as flawed. What is needed, they argue, is an effort to reintroduce meaning into a more local and informal, less bureaucratic justice system. And so we are seeing a proliferation of procedures that emphasize context and negotiation over formal rules and the marginalization of traditional players, notably judges, in favour of victims' powers to contribute to the outcomes of the process (pp. 154–159). Community policing is similarly proposed as an antidote to the legalistic, technologically mediated and overly bureaucratic realm of reactive policing routine (pp. 99–101). At least on paper, authority over the actions and priorities of police have been delegated to the community, rather than centralized in the state. In a sense these can be read as an affirmation that traditional systems of social control (see pp. 9–11) to some extent got it right and modernist social control has taken us off track.

The classical claims of modernity are also under attack on more abstract philosophical and theoretical fronts. In Chapter 2 we saw how the guiding principles of liberal jurisprudence are questioned (pp. 50–51, 61–78). For example, 'rationality', 'objectivity', 'rights' are defined by some as problematic. Rather than protecting individuals from the rougher currents of social life – tyranny, exclusion, bias or arbitrary decision-making – they cast them adrift on a sea of hidden agendas and relations of power. The theoretical bases for these arguments are diverse. For example, our discussion has noted the prevalence of feminist rejections of equality – one of the fundamental pillars of the legal system, and an ideal most of us would intuitively support (pp. 62–66). Feminist theorists argue that equal treatment before the law is a legal fiction. It has been developed with reference to a subject who is to all extents and purposes, male. And not just any male – Ngaire Naffine (1990: 53) among many others points out that he is the middle-class, white, able-bodied male who has been imbued with a world-view and logic that do not necessarily reflect the realities of those groups who fall outside of this very specific template. The failed promise of 'human rights' provides another illustrative example of these concerns (pp. 72–78). They were represented as offering universal protection in the face of the limits of citizenship rights. Such claims have been questioned on the basis of their incoherence, their Eurocentrism and the continued exclusion of some groups. Similar concerns have been raised in regard to other organizing concepts of the modernist world-view such as objectivity (pp. 66–68) and the public/private dichotomy (pp. 69–72). Postmodern approaches have taken this line of thinking to its limits (pp. 32–35). Here we find a rejection of doctrines on the existence and relevance of objectivity, the desirability and possibility of reason and the certainty of progress through knowledge.

Whether we use it as a tool for imposing conceptual order on our data or subject it to withering critique, modernity provides a starting point from which to launch our inquiry into contemporary law and criminal justice. For this very reason we need to keep a weather eye on the horizon for signs of transformation in the social order. Less prevalent than accounts of modernity, but becoming increasingly pivotal to contemporary sociology and social theory have been efforts to develop visions of our current age as somehow qualitatively different from that of high modernity. Discussions of postmodernity, risk society and globalization are usually organized around such a motif. These accounts have emerged from the philosophical critique of modernism and modernity and/or from awareness of empirical shifts in the social world that require a new set of theoretical models. While scholars are far from in agreement that we have indeed made the transition to a radically new epoch, there do seem to be good grounds for claiming that the Western world today is in many ways different in its logic of operation from even the mid-twentieth century. Reviewing such theoretical arguments and situating some of the material from this book within them would seem to be an appropriate way to conclude our study. This is an activity that can sensitize us to the themes and realities that will provide the broader social context for criminal justice activity in the twenty-first century.

Pivotal over recent years as an aspect of contemporary society and social thought has been the growth of social discourses that engage in a *critique of the Enlightenment world-view*. This held that truth, reason, planning and science could bring continuing social progress towards a good society. Today these concepts and claims are treated with suspicion. We have already noted that sociologists working in critical paradigms such as feminism, Marxism or critical race theory have long argued that the claims made for modernity are not supported by the experiences of marginalized groups. Concerns are also evident in popular thought, with modernity linked to negative outcomes such as the mind-numbing bureaucracies and state control of Kafkaesque totalitarianism, the growing meaninglessness of social life and the spread of environmental pollution. Theorists of postmodernity reflect upon or embody these themes. The French philosopher, Jean-François Lyotard (1984) identified a 'postmodern condition' and spoke of the end of the philosophical 'grand narratives', both liberal and Marxist, that had offered a comprehensive vision of the world and steered social action, suggesting we had lost faith in these. Likewise, Zygmunt Bauman (1989) has argued that modernity was an era that was obsessed by the urge to classify and regulate, and that reason thereby led to a process of Othering. That which was negatively coded or did not fit the mould was subject to control and repression, with the Holocaust the purest expression of this logic. According to Bauman, we need a new and more flexible logic in our lives, one that can lead to respect for difference and tolerance of 'strangers' – those who do not seem to fit our classifications. We can also point to the work of Foucault (1975) as symptomatic of this structure of feeling. Although not a postmodernist, he did launch a sustained attack on the culture and institutions of post-Enlightenment Europe demonstrating how new forms of reason, technology and professionalization led to greater levels of control and authority. This exercise in what we might call the hermeneutics of suspicion has had a profound influence on social thought with its imperative that we look for the dark side of modernity, the cloud behind each silver lining where power is lurking.

A suspicion of modernity, then, looks set to be a growing feature of our social life as well as our intellectual life. It is one whose implications for law and criminal justice we traced just a few paragraphs ago when discussing the limits of modernity's reach. A further characteristic of the dawning postmodern era, it has been argued, has been the *growing dominance of signs, symbols and cultural representations* in structuring all aspects of social life. The argument has been made that we live in a 'semiotic' world where images proliferate and the political and economic life of society are increasingly oriented around the production and reception of discourses. We are all familiar, for example, with the superficial fads and fashions of consumer capitalism and the fact that spin doctors in politics can come to shape policy rather than simply engaging in post-facto public relations activity. This perspective of culture unchained reached its apogee in the work of Jean Baudrillard (1983) who suggested that the distinction between reality and representation is now so blurred that we live in a world of **simulation**. This means the 'real' world has come to reflect symbolic patterns in settings like themed communities, amusement parks and wars that resemble video games. Baudrillard's point is a perhaps a little exaggerated. Nevertheless there may well be a germ of truth to what he argues. In various places in this book we have indicated the importance of media representations of crime and criminal justice. Even when fictitious, these can have real-world implications. For example, they might shape fear of crime more than real crime rates or perpetuate stereotypes about criminal groups, the courts and the police. These might influence policy in turn as public opinion calls for 'tough on crime policies' (see pp. 103, 137–138). Even more consistent with Baudrillard's position is the fact that criminal justice activity is increasingly structured around the performance of activities that circulate and reproduce particular signs and images. This is most clearly the case with the police. Zero tolerance policing and other 'quality of life' policing strategies are all about confronting crime and fear of crime by manipulating visual cues in the urban landscape as much as confronting criminals (pp. 101–103). Community policing and schemes like neighbourhood watch are based on the positive mythology that attaches to the signifier of 'community'. Activity is organized around the pursuit of this mythical beast and the hope that a simulated police/community intercourse might evolve into a more genuine coupling (pp. 99–101). Reality crime shows and public relations campaigns involve the circulation of mediated images and narratives that break down barriers between crime control and information production. Celebrity trials are perhaps the arena where the intensely mediated qualities of contemporary justice are most clearly visible. When well-known personalities like entertainer Michael Jackson or sports icon O. J. Simpson are in the dock, separating out the screen image from the character of the 'real' person becomes problematic, and court room events start to resemble installments in a fictitious crime drama (McKay and Smith, 1995).

A third leitmotif of our future will be a *growing awareness of risk and the rise of risk management strategies*. Reaching its seminal formulation in German sociologist Ulrich Beck's (1992) articulation of '**risk society**', which he developed with reference to the dangers of environmental pollution, this argument holds that life today is lived in a condition of profound uncertainty. Consequently efforts to contain and deal with risk become more and more central in daily activity and administrative effort. Many of Beck's claims, including his definition of risk, have been disputed. Nevertheless, at the most fundamental level, his work is useful for bringing to our attention what has proved to be a surprisingly omnipresent dimension of social life. Certainly criminal justice systems, to take the example relevant to this book, have always been in the risk management business. The modern police emerged in part to deal with the risks of urbanization (pp. 84–86). Alternatively, we might argue that the buttresses to judicial independence are designed to head off the risks of the corruption of justice (pp. 48–49). It can be argued, however, that some of the most rapidly expanding contemporary crime control techniques, institutions and discourses manifest a new and more explicit orientation towards risk discourse. The roll-back of the state in recent decades and the continuing rise of capitalism have seen privatized solutions to risk management coming to the fore at the same time as fear of crime has grown (Garland, 2001a). The burden has moved onto organizations that engage in what Garland has called the 'criminology of everyday life'. Their crime control strategies function according to an actuarial logic and emphasize prevention through changes to routines and spatial environments, and the dollar costs of victimization. The morality of breaking the law, arguments over retribution and need for individual rehabilitation have been marginalized as concerns. We have seen this approach most clearly at work in discussions of private policing (pp. 112–115) and the ways that places such as shopping malls and airports try to minimize the costs of crime. It is also reflected in the emergence of what some have called the 'new penology' (Feeley and Simon, 1992) in which the organizing principle of punishment is actuarial rather than moral or welfarist and its objective is the management of the risks associated with 'dangerous classes' rather than the treatment of individual offenders.

Finally, we need to consider the *impact of globalization* on future decades as a context within which social control operates. Social theorists such as Roland Robertson (1992) and Arjun Appadurai (1996) have indicated how growing interconnectedness in terms of trade, culture and politics has radically altered the complexion of the globe in recent decades. Nations are less sovereign than before, identities more hybrid, flows of information and goods over borders accelerated. This process has obviously boosted both transnational crime and the criminal justice organizations such as Interpol that are attempting to deal with this. More subtly and profoundly it has led to increased reflexivity about justice systems. The collision of cultures through information exchange and the growing heterogeneity of populations due to transnational migration and the emergence of diasporic communities has created a set of conditions in which the taken-for-granted qualities of Western justice thinking have been questioned. In both its implementation and its core logic it is more likely to be seen as particularistic rather than universalistic, as an imposition rather than a social contract, and as arbitrary rather than necessary. Calls for parallel recognition of indigenous and religious codes that we discussed earlier (pp. 56–57) are symptomatic of the urge to question the liberal model of justice. They indicate the paradoxes of universalism that confront efforts towards 'equality' and 'rationality' when such Western legal concepts conflict with alternate belief systems and ways of life. Furthermore, debates about the unequal treatment of racial and migrant minorities in spheres like sentencing, imprisonment and police discretion (pp. 129–133, 176–178, 104–106) raise explicit questions about the possibilities for the impartial administration of justice and the logic of its operation that might be obscured in monocultural settings. Globalization, then, generates possibilities for the immanent critique of dominant forms of law and criminal justice in terms of outcomes as well as more conceptual challenges to core logics and concepts. When combined with postmodern and poststructural agendas and social movement pressures, a radical questioning and destabilization can eventuate.

So, as we write, law and criminal justice sit at the intersection of modernity and a budding social order that has yet to unfold but whose properties we can begin to foresee. It will be a world characterized by the growing critique of reason, the search for meaning and claims of difference; the proliferation of mediated images, identities and simulations; the awareness of risk and efforts to control this; and increasingly heterogeneous flows of people, capital and ideas as globalization accelerates. The implications of such transformations remain to be seen. We cannot assume that the bureaucratic state and its legal-rational armature will vanish overnight simply because we live in a changing world. Indeed, there is every reason to believe that its technologically and managerially enabled administrative and surveillance systems will have increasing significance in future years. Yet because law and criminal justice remain expressions of the society in which they operate, subtle shifts in the logic and operation of social control are both emergent and inevitable. Identifying their symptoms and thinking through their implications will be the task at the centre of criminological agendas, both theoretical and applied, over the next few years. The sociological perspective will help us meet this challenge.

Study Questions

1 Identify crime stories in a newspaper. Using your sociological knowledge provide a 'higher order explanation' for the material you have identified that places the events in a theoretical perspective.
2 Is sociology a useful tool for understanding law and the criminal justice system? Are some approaches potentially more useful than others?
3 Which of the 'postmodern' assaults on the justice systems of modernity seems to you to be more important and why?
4 What evidence can you find for the claim that the project of modernity remains incomplete in the criminal justice arena?

Glossary of Key Terms

postmodernity – The era after modernity which some believe we have now entered.

'risk society' – The term coined by Ulrich Beck to describe the current social era in which, he claims, dealing with unknown risks has become a dominant organizing principle.

simulation – The process in which the 'real' world comes to resemble models, plans and myths. The distinction between reality and representation becomes blurred.

Suggested Further Reading

Students should look at Murphy's (1997) *The Oldest Social Science? Configurations of Law and Modernity*. For a critical commentary on the sociological linkages of law and society, David Garland's (2001a) *The Culture of Control* offers an account of how the established practices of penal welfarism under modernity have been challenged in recent years. For a simple account of postmodernism and postmodernity, look at the last two chapters in Smith (2001). For a consideration of how these are playing out in the legal field, refer to Margaret Davies (2002) *Asking the Law Question: The Dissolution of Legal Theory*.

Bibliography

Abbott, Andrew Delano (1988) *The System of Professions: An Essay on the Division of Expert Labor.* Chicago: University of Chicago Press.

Abel, Richard (1982) Introduction, in Richard Abel (ed.), *The Politics of Informal Justice.* New York: Academic Press.

Aceves, William J. (2000) Liberalism and International Legal Scholarship: The Pinochet Case and the Move Toward a Universal System of Transnational Law, *Harvard International Law Journal*, 41, 129–99.

Adams, Kenneth (1983) The Effect of Evidentiary Factors in Charge Reduction, *Journal of Criminal Justice*, 11, 525–37.

Allen, Hilary (1984) At the Mercy of Her Hormones: Premenstrual Tension and the Law, *m/f*, 9, 19–44.

Allen, J. (1988) The Masculinity of Criminality and Criminology: Interrogating Some Impasses, in Mark Findlay and R. Hogg (eds), *Crime and Criminal Justice.* Sydney: Law Book Company.

Althusser, Louis (1971) *Lenin and Philosophy and other Essays.* New York: Monthly Review Press.

Alvarez, Jose E. (2002) Globalization and the Erosion of Sovereignty in Honor of Professor Lichtenstein: The New Treaty Makers, *Boston College International and Comparative Law Review*, 25, 213–35.

Appadurai, Arjun (1996) *Modernity at Large: Cultural Aspects of Globalization.* Minneapolis: University of Minnesota Press.

Arrow, Dennis W. (1997) Pomobabble: Postmodern Newspeak and Constitutional 'Meaning' for the Uninitiated, *Michigan Law Review*, 96(3), 461–89.

Astin, A. (1984) Pre-Law Students: A National Profile, *Journal of Legal Education* 34, 75–84.

Australian Bureau of Statistics (1998) *Prisoners in Australia 1997.* Canberra: Australian Bureau of Statistics.

Bailey, William G. (1989) *The Encyclopedia of Police Science.* New York and London: Garland.

Barry, Anita (1993) Constructing a Courtroom Narrative: A Lawyer-Witness Duet, in Mushhira Eid and Gregory Iverson (eds), *Principles and Prediction: The Analysis of Natural Language.* Amsterdam: Benjamins.

Barlow, Hugh D. (1996) *Introduction to Criminology.* New York: HarperCollins.

Baudrillard, Jean (1983) *Simulations.* New York: Semiotext(e).

Bauman, Zygmunt (1987) *Legislators and Interpreters: On Modernity, Postmodernity and Intellectuals.* Ithaca, NY: Cornell University Press.

Bauman, Zygmunt (1989) *Modernity and the Holocaust.* Ithaca, NY: Cornell University Press.

Bauman, Zygmunt (1992) *Intimations of Postmodernity.* London and New York: Routledge.

Bayley, David (1994) *Police for the Future.* Oxford: Oxford University Press.

Beccaria, Cesare (1995) *On Crimes and Punishments.* Cambridge: Cambridge University Press.

Beck, Ulrich (1992) *Risk Society.* London: Sage.

Becker, Howard S. (1967) Whose Side are We On? *Social Problems*, 14(3), 239–47.

Becker, Howard S. (1973) *Outsiders.* Glencoe, IL: Free Press.

Beckett, Katherine and Western, Bruce (2001) Governing Social Marginality: Welfare, Incarceration and the Transformation of State Policy, in David Garland, (ed.), *Mass Imprisonment: Causes and Consequences.* London: Sage, pp. 35–50.

Berger, Peter L. (1963) *Invitation to Sociology: A Humanistic Perspective.* Garden City, NY: Doubleday.

Berman, Harold J. (1983) *Law and Revolution: The Formation of the Western Legal Tradition.* Cambridge, MA: Harvard University Press.

Berman, Harold J. and Reid, Charles J. (1994) Roman Law in Europe and the Jus Commune: A Historical Overview with Emphasis on the New Legal Science of the Sixteenth Century, *Syracuse Journal of International Law and Commerce*, 20, 1–29.

Berman, Harold J. and Reid, Charles J. (1996) The Transformation of English Legal Science: From Hale to Blackstone, *Emory Law Journal*, 45, 437–505.

Berns, Sandra (1992) Regulation of the Family: Whose Interests Does it Serve? *Griffith Law Review*, 1(2), 152–209.

Berns, Sandra, Baron, Paula and Neave, Marcia (1996) *Gender and Citizenship.* Canberra: Department of Employment, Education and Training.

Bernstein, Marver (1955) *Regulating Business by Independent Commission.* Princeton, NJ: Princeton University Press.

Bershad, Lawrence (1985) Discriminatory Treatment of the Female Offender in the Criminal Justice System, *Boston College Law Review*, 26, 289–348.

Bittner, Egon (1990) *Aspects of Police Work.* Boston: Northeastern University Press.

Black, Donald (1976) *The Behavior of Law.* New York: Academic Press.

Black, Donald (1980) *The Manners and Customs of the Police.* New York: Academic Press.

Blumberg, Abraham S. (1969) *Criminal Justice.* Chicago: Quadrangle Books.

Blumstein, Alfred and Beck, Allen J. (1999) Population Growth in US Prisons, 1980–1996, in Michael H. Tonry and Joan Petersilia (eds), *Prisons.* Chicago: University of Chicago Press, pp. 17–61.

Blumstein, Alfred, Cohen, Jacqueline, Martin, Susan E. and Tonry, Michael H. (1983) *Research on Sentencing: The Search for Reform.* Washington, DC: National Academy Press.

Bogoch, Bryna (1999a) Courtroom Discourse and the Gendered Construction of Professional Identity, *Law and Social Inquiry*, 24, 329–75.

Bogoch, Bryna (1999b) Judging in a 'Different Voice': Gender and the Sentencing of Violent Offences in Israel, *International Journal of the Sociology of Law*, 27(1), 51–78.

Bottomley, Stephen and Parker, Stephen (1994) *Law in Context.* Leichardt, NSW: Federation Press.

Bottoms, Anthony A. (1999) Interpersonal Violence and Social Order in Prisons, in Michael H. Tonry and Joan Petersilia (eds), *Prisons.* Chicago: University of Chicago Press, pp. 205–82.

Bowditch, Christine and Everett, Ronald S. (1987) Private Prisons: Problems Within the Solution, *Justice Quarterly*, 4, 441–53.

Bowker, Lee H. (1980) *Prison Victimization.* New York: Elsevier.

Bowling, Benjamin (1999) The Rise and Fall of New York Murder: Zero Tolerance or Crack's Decline? *British Journal of Criminology*, 39(4), 531–54.

Boyle, James (1998) Anachronism of the Moral Sentiments? Integrity, Postmodernism and Justice, *Stanford Law Review*, 51, 493–527.

Boyle, Raymond (1999) Spotlighting the Police: Changing UK Police-Media Relations in the 1990s, *International Journal of the Sociology of Law*, 27(3), 229–50.

Bradley, David (1996) Contemporary Police Education in Australia, in Duncan Chappell and Paul Wilson (eds), *Australian Policing: Contemporary Issues.* Melbourne: Butterworths, pp. 85–110.

Braithwaite, John (1989) *Crime, Shame and Reintegration.* Cambridge: Cambridge University Press.

Braithwaite, John (1999) Restorative Justice: Assessing Optimistic and Pessimistic Accounts, *Crime and Justice*, 25, 1–127.

Brand, Paul (1992) *The Origins of the Legal Profession.* Oxford: Blackwell.

Brereton, David (2000) Policing and Crime Prevention: Improving the Product, in Duncan Chappell and Paul Wilson (eds), *Crime and the Criminal Justice System in Australia: 2000 and Beyond.* Melbourne: Butterworths, pp. 121–36.

Broderick, John J. (1973) *Police in a Time of Change.* Morristown, NJ: General Learning.

Brogden, Mike (1987) The Emergence of the Police – The Colonial Dimension, *British Journal of Criminology*, 27(1), 4–14.

Brogden, Mike and Shearing, Clifford (1993) *Policing for a New South Africa.* London: Routledge.

Brophy, Julia and Smart, Carol (1985) *Women in Law.* London: Routledge and Kegan Paul.

Brown, Jennifer M. (1994) The Use of Mediation to Resolve Criminal Cases: A Procedural Critique, *Emory Law Journal*, 43, 1247–309.

Brown, Jennifer M. (1998) Aspects of Discriminatory Treatment of Women Police Officers Serving in Forces in England and Wales, *British Journal of Criminology*, 38(2), 265–82.

Brown, Michael K. (1981) *Working the Street*. New York: Russell Sage.

Brown, Richard Harvey (1994) Rhetoric, Textuality, and the Postmodern Turn in Sociological Theory, in Steven Seidman (ed.), *The Postmodern Turn: New Perspectives on Social Theory*. Cambridge: Cambridge University Press, pp. 229–41.

Bull, David and Strata, Erica (1994) Police Community Consultation, *Australian and New Zealand Journal of Criminology*, 27(3), 237–49.

Bureau of Justice Statistics (2002) *Prison and Jail Inmates at Midyear 2001*. Washington, DC: U.S. Department of Justice.

Byrnes, A. (1992) Women, Feminism and International Human Rights Law: Methodological Myopia, Fundamental Flaws or Meaningful Marginalisation? *Australian Yearbook of International Law*, 12, 205–240.

Cain, Maureen and Harrington, Christine B. (eds) (1994) *Lawyers in a Postmodern World: Translation and Transgression*. New York: New York University Press.

Calavita, Kitty and Seron, Carol (1992) Postmodernism and Protest: Recovering the Sociological Imagination, *Law and Society Review*, 26, 765–71.

Caplow, Theodore and Simon, Jonathan (1999) Understanding Prison Policy and Population Trends, in Michael H. Tonry and Joan Petersilia (eds), *Prisons*. Chicago: University of Chicago Press, pp. 63–113.

Cappelletti, Mauro and Weisner, John (1978) *Promising Institutions, Book 1*. Alphenaandenrign: Sijthoff and Noordhoff.

Carlen, Pat (ed.) (1976) *The Sociology of Law*. Keele: University of Keele.

Carlen, Pat (1983) *Women's Imprisonment: A Study in Social Control*. London: Routledge and Kegan Paul.

Carr-Saunders, A. M. and Wilson, P. (1933) *The Professions*. Oxford: Clarendon Press.

Carter, Robert M. (1965) The Johnny Cain Story: A Composite of Men Executed in California, *Issues in Criminology*, 1, 66–76.

Cashmore, Ellis (1991) Black Cops Inc., in Ellis Cashmore and Eugene McLaughlin (eds), *Out of Order: Policing and Black People*. London: Routledge, pp. 87–108.

Cashmore, Ellis and McLaughlin, Eugene (eds) (1991) *Out of Order: Policing and Black People*. London: Routledge.

Chambliss, William J. (1964) A Sociological Analysis of Vagrancy, *Social Problems*, 12(1), 67–77.

Chambliss, William J. (1975) Toward a Political Economy of Crime, *Theory and Society*, 2(2), 149–70.

Chan, Janet (1997) *Changing Police Culture: Policing in a Multicultural Society*. Cambridge: Cambridge University Press.

Chappell, Duncan and Wilson, Paul (1986) *Australian Criminal Justice Systems – The Mid 1980s*. Sydney: Butterworths.

Chappell, Duncan and Wilson, Paul (1996) *Australian Policing: Contemporary Issues*. Melbourne: Butterworths.

Chappell, Duncan and Wilson, Paul (2000) *Crime and the Criminal Justice System in Australia: 2000 and Beyond*. Sydney: Butterworths.

Charlesworth, Hilary, Chinkin, Christine and Wright, Shelley (1991) Feminist Approaches to International Law, *American Journal of International Law*, 85, 613–53.

Chesney-Lind, Meda (1974) Juvenile Delinquency and the Sexualisation of Female Crime, *Psychology Today*, July, 4–7.

Chiricos, Theodore and DeLone, Miriam (1992) Labor Surplus and Punishment: A Review and Assessment of Theory and Evidence, *Social Problems*, 39(4), 421–46.

Church, Thomas W. (1976) Plea Bargains, Concessions and the Courts: Analysis of a Quasi-experiment, *Law and Society Review*, 10(3), 375–401.

Cobb, Sara (1997) The Domestication of Violence in Mediation, *Law and Society Review*, 31(3), 397–440.

Cohen, Albert K. Cole, George and Baliley, Robert (1976) *Prison Violence.* Lexington, MA: Lexington Books.

Cohen, Albert K. (1976) Prison Violence: A Sociological Perspective, in Albert K. Cohen, George Cole and Robert Baliley (eds), *Prison Violence.* Lexington, MA: Lexington Books, pp. 3–22.

Cohen, Stanley (1973) *Folk Devils and Moral Panics.* London: Paladin.

Cohen, Stanley (1979) The Punitive City: Notes on the Dispersal of Social Control, *Contemporary Crises*, 3(4), 341–63.

Conklin, John E. (1992) *Criminology.* New York: Macmillan.

Conley, John and O'Barr, William (1990) *Rules versus Relationships: The Ethnography of Legal Discourse.* Chicago: University of Chicago Press.

Connell, R. W. (1995) Sociology and Human Rights, *Australian and New Zealand Journal of Sociology*, 31(2), 25–9.

Cooke, Michael (1995) Interpreting in a Cross-Cultural Cross-Examination: An Aboriginal Case Study, *International Journal of the Sociology of Language*, 11(3), 99–111.

Cornell, Drucilla (1991) *Beyond Accommodation: Ethical Feminism, Deconstruction and the Law.* New York: Routledge.

Cortina, Lillia M., Lonsway, Kimberley A., Megley, Vicki L., Freeman, Leslie V., Collingsworth, Linda L., Hunter, Mary and Fitzgerald, Louise F. (2002) What's Gender Got To Do With It? Incivility in the Federal Courts, *Law and Social Inquiry*, 27, 235–66.

Cotterrell, Roger (1984) *The Sociology of Law: An Introduction.* London: Butterworths.

Cotterrell, Roger (1989) *The Politics of Jurisprudence: A Critical Introduction to Legal Philosophy.* London: Butterworths.

Cotterrell, Roger (1992) *The Sociology of Law: An Introduction.* 2nd edn. London: Butterworths.

Cotterrell, Roger (1998) Why Must Legal Ideas be Interpreted Sociologically? *Journal of Law and Society*, 25(2), 171–92.

Crawford, Charles, Chiricos, Theodore and Kleck, Gary (1998) Race, Racial Threat, and Sentencing of Habitual Offenders, *Criminology*, 36, 481–511.

Daly, Kathleen (1989) Rethinking Judicial Paternalism: Gender, Work-Family Relations, and Sentencing, *Gender and Society*, 3(1), 9–36.

Daly, Kathleen (1994) *Gender, Crime and Punishment.* New Haven, CT: Yale University Press.

Danet, Brenda and Bogoch, Bryna (1980) Fixed Fight or Free-for-all? An Empirical Study of Combativeness in the Adversary System of Justice, *British Journal of Law and Society*, 7(1), 36–60.

Danzig, Richard (1973) Toward the Creation of a Complementary, Decentralized System of Criminal Justice, *Stanford Law Review*, 26, 1–54.

Dateman, Susan and Scarpatti, Frank R. (eds) (1980) *Women, Crime, and Justice.* New York: Oxford University Press.

Davey, Richard (1998) *Sarah Island: The Penal Settlement.* Strahan, Tasmania: Australia Foundation for Culture and the Humanities.

Davies, Margaret (1994) *Asking the Law Question.* Sydney: Law Book Company.

Davies, Margaret (2002) *Asking the Law Question. The Dissolution of Legal Theory.* Pyrmont, NSW: Lawbook.

Davis, Angela (1998) Prosecution and Race: The Power of Privilege and Discretion, *Fordham Law Review*, 67, 13–67.

Davis, Kenneth C. (1969) *Discretionary Justice.* Baton Rouge, LA: Louisiana State University Press.

Davis, Sue (1993) Do Women Judges Speak in 'A Different Voice?' Carol Gilligan, Feminist Legal Theory and the Ninth Circuit, *Wisconsin's Women's Legal Journal*, 8, 143–73.

Delfs, Elizabeth. A. (1996) Foul Play in the Courtroom: Persistence, Cause and Remedies, *Women's Rights Law Reporter*, 17, 309–39.

Delgado, Richard and Stefancic, Jean (1992) Images of the Outsider in American Law and Culture: Can Free Expression Remedy Systematic Social Ills? *Cornell Law Review*, 77, 1258.

de Lint, Willem (1999) A Post-Modern Turn in Policing: Policing as Pastiche, *International Journal of the Sociology of Law*, 27(2), 127–52.

Dingwall, Robert and Lewis, Philip (1983) *The Sociology of the Professions: Lawyers, Doctors and Others.* London: Macmillan.

Dixon, Jo (1995) The Organizational Context of Criminal Sentencing, *American Journal of Sociology*, 100(5), 1157–98.

Dobash Russell P., Dobash, R. Emerson and Gutteridge, Sue (1986) *The Imprisonment of Women*. Oxford: Basil Blackwell.

Donzelot, Jacques (1979) *The Policing of Families*. New York: Pantheon Books.

Douglas, Roger (1980) Sentencing and the Suburbs, I: Theft and Violence, *The Australian and New Zealand Journal of Criminology*, 13, 241–62.

Drass, Kriss A. and Spencer, J. William (1987) Accounting for Pre-sentencing Recommendations: Typologies and Probation Officers' Theory of Office, *Social Problems*, 34(3), 277–93.

Duff, Peter and Findlay, Mark (1982) The Jury in England: Practice and Ideology, *International Journal of the Sociology of Law*, 10(3), 253–65.

Duff, Peter and Findlay, Mark (1997) Jury Reform: Of Myths and Moral Panics, *International Journal of the Sociology of Law*, 25(4), 363–84.

Durkheim, Emile [1912] (1968) *The Elementary Forms of Religious Life*. London: Allen and Unwin.

Durkheim, Emile (1973) *Moral Education*. New York: Free Press.

Durkheim, Emile [1893] (1984) *The Division of Labor in Society*. New York: Free Press.

Durkheim, Emile (1992) *Professional Ethics and Civic Morals*. London: Routledge.

Dworkin, Ronald M. (1986) *Law's Empire*. Cambridge, MA: Belknap Press.

Eades, Diana (2000) 'I Don't Think it's an Answer to the Question': Silencing Aboriginal Witnesses in Court, *Language in Society*, 29(2), 161–95.

Edwards, Susan M. (1996) *Sex and Gender in the Legal Process*. London: Blackstone Press.

Eid, Mushhira and Iverson, Gregory (1993) *Principles and Prediction: The Analysis of Natural Language*. Amsterdam: Benjamins.

Elias, Norbert [1939] (1978) *The Civilising Process*. Oxford: Basil Blackwell.

Emsley, Clive (1996) *The English Police*. London: Longman.

Engels, Friedrich (1969) Letter to Conrad Schmidt, October 27, 1890, in Lewis S. Feuer (ed.). *Karl Marx and Friedrich Engels: Basic Writings on Politics and Philosophy*. New York: Anchor, pp. 439–45.

Erikson, Kai (1966) *Wayward Puritans*. New York: Wiley.

Erlanger, Howard S. and Klegon Douglas A. (1978) Socialization Effects of Professional School: The Law School Experience and Student Orientation to Public Interest, *Law and Society Review*, 13(1), 11–35.

Erlich, Eugen (1936) *Fundamental Principles of the Sociology of Law*. New York: Arno Press.

Esteal, Patricia (2001) *Less Than Equal. Women and the Australian Legal System*. Chatswood, NSW: Butterworths.

Evans-Pritchard, E. E. (1976) *Witchcraft, Oracles and Magic Among the Azande*. Oxford: Clarendon Press.

Everett, Ronald and Nienstedt, Barbara (1999) Race, Remorse and Sentence Reduction: Is Saying You're Sorry Enough? *Justice Quarterly*, 16(1), 99–122.

Farrington, David P. and Morris, Allison M. (1983) Sex, Sentencing and Reconviction, *British Journal of Criminology*, 23(3), 229–48.

Feeley, Malcolm M. and Simon, Jonathan (1992) The New Penology: Notes on the Emerging Strategy of Corrections and its Implications, *Criminology* 30(4), 449–474.

Feinberg, Joel. and Gross, Hyman (1980) *Philosophy of Law*. Belmont, CA: Wadsworth.

Feldman, Stephen M. (2001) An Arrow to the Heart: The Love and Death of Postmodern Legal Scholarship, *Vanderbilt Law Review*, 54(6), 2351–78.

Feuer, Lewis S. (ed.) (1969) *Karl Marx and Friedrich Engels: Basic Writings on Politics and Philosophy*. New York: Anchor.

Fielding, Nigel (1988) Competence and Culture in the Police, *Sociology*, 22(1), 45–64.

Fielding, Nigel (1995) *Community Policing*. Oxford: Clarendon Press.

Findlay, Mark (1994) *Jury Management in New South Wales*. Carlton, Vic.: Australian Institute of Judicial Administration.

Findlay, Mark and Hogg, R. (eds), *Crime and Criminal Justice*. Sydney: Law Book Company.

Findlay, Mark, Odgers, Stephen and Yeo, Stanley (1999) *Australian Criminal Justice*. Melbourne: Oxford University Press.

Fineman, M. (1994) Feminist Legal Scholarship and Women's Gendered Lives, in Maureen Cain and Christine B. Harrington (eds), *Lawyers in a Postmodern World: Translation and Transgression*. New York: New York University Press.

Fiske, John (1987) *Television Culture*. London, New York: Routledge.

Foucault, Michel (1975) *Discipline and Punish*. London: Penguin.

Foucault, Michel (1990) *The History of Sexuality*. New York: Vintage Books.

Freidson, Eliot (1972) *Professional Dominance*. New York: Atherton Press.

Freidson, Eliot (1994) *Professionalism Reborn*. Cambridge: Polity Press.

Friedman, Lawrence (1978) Access to Justice: Social and Historical Context, in Mauro Cappelletti and John Weisner (eds), *Promising Institutions, Book 1*. Alphenaandenrign: Sijthoff and Noordhoff.

Friedman, Lawrence (1989) Popular Legal Culture: Law, Lawyers and Popular Culture, *Yale Law Journal*, 98, 1579–605.

Friedman, Lawrence M. and Percival, Robert V. (1976) A Tale of Two Courts: Litigation in Alameda and San Benito Counties, *Law and Society Review*, 10(2), 267–301.

Fuller, L. (1958) Positivism and Fidelity to Law – A Reply to Professor Hart, *Harvard Law Review*, 71, 630–72.

Gaes, Gerald G., Flanagan, Timothy L., Motiuk, Laurence L. and Stewart, Lynn (1999) Adult Correctional Treatment, in Michael H. Tonry and Joan Petersilia (eds), *Prisons*. Chicago: University of Chicago Press, pp. 361–426.

Gaete, Rolando (1991) Postmodernism and Human Rights: Some Insidious Questions, *Law and Critique*, 11(2), 149–70.

Galanter, Marc (1983) Mega-Law and Mega-Lawyering in the Contemporary United States, in Robert Dingwall and Philip Lewis (eds), *The Sociology of Professions: Lawyers, Doctors and Others*. London: Macmillan.

Garfinkel, Harold (1956) Conditions of Successful Degradation Ceremonies, *American Journal of Sociology*, 61, 420–4.

Garland, David (1985) *Punishment and Welfare: A History of Penal Strategies*. Aldershot: Gower.

Garland, David (1991) *Punishment and Modern Society*. Oxford: Oxford University Press.

Garland, David (2001a) *The Culture of Control: Crime and Social Order in Contemporary Society*. Chicago. University of Chicago Press.

Garland, David (2001b) *Mass Imprisonment: Causes and Consequences*. London: Sage.

Garland, David (2001c) Introduction: The Meaning of Mass Imprisonment, in David Garland (ed.), *Mass Imprisonment: Causes and Consequences*. London: Sage, pp. 1–3.

Gatrell, V. A. C. (1996) Crime, Authority and the Policeman State, in John Muncie, Eugene McLaughlin and Mary Langan (eds), *Criminological Perspectives*. London: Sage, pp. 383–91.

Giallombardo, Rose (1966) *Society of Women: A Study of Women in Prison*. New York: John Wiley.

Giddens, Anthony (1981) *The Nation State and Violence*. Berkeley, CA: University of California Press.

Gilligan, Carol (1982) *In a Different Voice: Psychological Theory and Women's Development*. Cambridge, MA: Harvard University Press.

Girshick, Lori B. (1999) *No Safe Haven: Stories of Women in Prison*. Boston: Northeastern University Press.

Goffman, Erving (1968) *Asylums*. London: Penguin.

Goldstein, Joseph (1960) Police Discretion Not to Invoke the Criminal Process: Low Visibility Decisions in the Administration of Justice, *Yale Law Review*, 69, 543–70.

Goode, William (1957) Community Within a Community: The Professions, *American Sociological Review*, 20, 194–200.

Gouldner, Alvin (1973) Foreword, in Ian Taylor, Paul Walton and Jock Young (eds), *The New Criminology*. London: Routledge and Kegan Paul, pp. ix–xiv.

Graber, Doris (1980) *Crime News and the Public*. New York: Praeger.

Granfield, Robert and Koenig, Thomas (1990) From Activism to Pro Bono: The Redirection of Working Class Altruism at Harvard Law School, *Critical Sociology*, 17(1), 57–80.

Graycar, Regina and Morgan, Jenny (1990) *The Hidden Gender of the Law*. Leichardt, NSW: Federation Press.

Greene, Judith A. (1999) Zero Tolerance: A Case Study of Police Policies and Practices in New York City, *Crime and Delinquency*, 45(2), 171–87.

Greenwood, C. (1957) Attributes of a Profession, *Social Work*, 2, 45–55.

Greer, Kimberley (2000) The Changing Nature of Interpersonal Relationships in a Women's Prison, *The Prison Journal*, 80(4), 442–68.

Hagan, John (1974) Extra-legal Attributes and Criminal Sentencing: An Assessment of a Sociological Viewpoint, *Law and Society Review*, 8(3), 357–83.

Hagan, John and Bumiller, K. (1983) Making Sense of Sentencing: A Review and Critique of Sentencing Research, in Alfred Blumstein, Jacqueline Cohen, Susan E. Martin and Michael H. Tonry, (eds), *Research on Sentencing: The Search for Reform*. Washington, DC: National Academy Press.

Hagan, John and Dinovitzer, Ronit (1999) Collateral Consequences of Imprisonment, in Michael H. Tonry and Joan Petersilia (eds), *Prisons*. Chicago: University of Chicago Press, pp. 121–62.

Hagan, John, Nagel Ilene and Albnonetti, Celesta (1980) The Differential Sentencing of White-Collar Offenders in Ten Federal District Courts, *American Sociological Review*, 45(5), 802–820.

Hall, Stuart (1973) Determination of New Photographs, in Stanley Cohen and Jock Young (eds), *The Manufacture of News*. London: Constable, pp.176–90.

Hall, Stuart (1996) Drifting into a Law and Order Society, in John Muncie, Eugene McLaughlin and Mary Langan (eds), *Criminological Perspectives*. London: Sage, pp. 257–70.

Hall, Stuart, Critcher, Chas, Jefferson, Tony, Clarke, John and Roberts, Brian (1979) *Policing the Crisis*. London: Macmillan.

Halliday, Terence C. (1994) Politics and Civic Professionalism: Legal Ethics and Cause Lawyers, *Law and Social Inquiry*, 24, 1013–53.

Handler, Joel F. (1992) Postmodernism, Protest, and the New Social Movements, *Law and Society Review*, 26(4), 697–740.

Harding, Richard (1997) *Private Prisons and Public Accountability*. Buckingham: Open University Press.

Harris, David (1993) The Appearance of Justice: Court TV, Conventional Television, and Public Understanding of the Criminal Justice System, *Arizona Law Review*, 35, 785–837.

Harris, Sandra (1984) Questions as a Mode of Control in Magistrates' Courts, *International Journal of the Sociology of Language*, 49, 5–27.

Hart, H. L. A. (1958) Positivism and the Separation of Law and Morals, *Harvard Law Review*, 71, 593–629.

Hart, H. L. A. (1961) *The Concept of Law*. Oxford: Clarendon Press.

Hart, H. L. A. (1980) Positivism and the Separation of Law and Morals, in Joe Feinberg and Hyman Gross (eds), *Philosophy of Law*. Belmont, CA: Wadsworth.

Hay, Douglas (1975a) *Albion's Fatal Tree*. New York: Partner Books.

Hay, Douglas (1975b) Property, Authority and the Criminal Law, in Douglas Hay (ed.), *Albion's Fatal Tree*. New York: Partner Books, pp. 17–64.

Held, David (1984) *Political Theory and the Modern State*. Stanford, CA: Stanford University Press.

Henham, Ralph J. (1990) *Sentencing Principles and Magistrates' Sentencing Behavior*. Avebury: Aldershot.

Hobbes, Thomas (1991 [1651]) *Leviathan*. Cambridge: Cambridge University Press.

Hofrichter, Richard (1987) *Neighborhood Justice in Capitalist Society: The Expansion of the Informal State*. Westport, CT: Greenwood Press.

Holdaway, Simon (1983) *Inside the British Police Force*. Oxford: Basil Blackwell.

Holmes, Malcolm D., Daudistel, Howard C. and Taggart, William A. (1992) Plea Bargaining and State District Court Case Loads: An Interrupted Time Series Analysis, *Law and Society Review*, 26(1), 139–59.

Holmes, Malcolm D., Hosch, H., Daudistel, Howard, Perez, D., Graves, J. (1996) Ethnicity, Legal Resources, and Felony Dispositions in Two Southwestern Jurisdictions, *Justice Quarterly*, 13, 11–30.

Howarth, Joan W. (2000) Women Defenders on Television: Representing Suspects and the Racial Politics of Retribution, *Gender, Race and Justice*, 3, 475–520.

Hunt, Alan (1990) The Big Fear: Law Confronts Postmodernism, *McGill Law Journal*, 35, 507–40.

Hutchinson, A. C. (1992) Doing the Right Thing? A Postmodern Politics, *Law and Society Review*, 26, 773–87.

Israel, Mark (1998) Ethnic Bias in Jury Selection in Australia and New Zealand, *International Journal of the Sociology of Law*, 26(1), 35–54.

James, Adrian L., Bottomley, Keith, Liebline, Alison and Clare, Emma (1997) *Privatizing Prisons: Rhetoric and Reality.* London: Sage.

James, Steve and Polk, Ken (1996) Police and Young Australians, in Duncan Chappell and Paul Wilson (eds), *Australian Policing: Contemporary Issues.* Melbourne: Butterworths, pp. 180–200.

Jenkins, Phillip (1994) The Ice Age: The Social Construction of a Drug Panic, *Justice Quarterly*, 13, 7–31.

Johnson, Robert (1990) *Death Work: A Study of the Modern Execution.* Pacific Grove, CA: Brooks/Cole.

Johnson, Terence (1972) *Professions and Power.* London: Macmillan.

Kalven, Harry and Zeisel, Hans (1966) *The American Jury.* Boston: Little, Brown and Company.

Katz, Jack (1988) *Seductions of Crime.* New York: Basic Books.

Kautt, Paul and Spohn, Cassia (2002) Crack-ing Down on Black Drug Offenders? Testing for Interactions Among Offenders' Race, Drug Type and Sentencing Strategy in Federal Drug Sentences, *Justice Quarterly*, 19, 1–36.

Keil, Thomas J. and Vito, Gennaro F. (1989) Race, Homicide Severity and the Application of the Death Penalty, *Criminology*, 27, 511–35.

Kelling, George, Pate, Tony, Dieckman, Duane and Brown, Charles (1974) *The Kansas City Preventive Patrol Experiment.* Washington, DC: Police Foundation.

Kelsen, Hans (1967) *The Pure Theory of Law.* Berkeley: University of California Press.

Kennedy, Helen (1992) *Eve Was Framed: Women and British Justice.* London: Vintage Books.

King, Nancy Jean (1999) The American Criminal Jury, *Law and Contemporary Problems*, 62, 41–70.

Kingdom, E. (1985) Legal Recognition of a Woman's Right to Choose, in Julie Brophy and Carol Smart (eds), *Women in Law.* London: Routledge and Kegan Paul.

Kinsey, Richard, Lea, John and Young, Jock (1986) *Losing the Fight Against Crime.* Oxford: Blackwell.

Kleck, Gary (1981) Racial Discrimination in Sentencing: A Critical Evaluation of the Evidence with Additional Evidence on the Death Penalty, *American Sociological Review*, 46(6), 783–805.

Klein, K. J. (1989) Woman Justice: Does She View the Law Differently? *Court Review*, 26, 18–23.

Lakoff, Robin (1975) *Language and Women's Place.* New York: Harper and Row.

Landsman, Stephan (1983) A Brief Survey of the Development of the Adversary System, *Ohio State Law Journal* 44, 713–47.

Larson, Magali Sarfatti (1977) *The Rise of Professionalism.* Berkeley, CA: University of California Press.

Laws, Sophie (1983) The Sexual Politics of Pre-menstrual Tension, *Women's Studies International Forum*, 6(1), 19–31.

Lee, R. G. (1992) From Profession to Business: The Rise and Rise of the City Law Firm, *Journal of Law and Society*, 19, 31–48.

Levensen, Laurie (1999) Working Outside the Rules: The Undefined Responsibilities of Federal Prosecutors, *Fordham Urbana Law Journal*, 26, 553–71.

Lindgren Alves, Jose A. (2000) The Declaration of Human Rights in Postmodernity, *Human Rights Quarterly*, 22(2), 478–500.

Lipkin, Robert Justin (1994) Can American Constitutional Law be Postmodern? *Buffalo Law Review*, 42, 317–94.

Lippman, M. (1979) Magistrates' Courts: A Game for Several Players, *Legal Services Bulletin*, 4(3), 109–12.

Lloyd, Dennis (1973) *The Idea of Law.* Harmondsworth: Penguin.

Lloyd-Bostock, Sally and Thomas, Cheryl (1999) Decline of the 'Little Parliament': Juries and Jury Reform in England and Wales, *Law and Contemporary Problems*, 62, 7–45.

Lobel, Jules (ed.) (1988) *A Less Than Perfect Union.* New York: Monthly Review Press.

Locke, John (1936 [1690]) *Two Treatises on Government.* London: J.M. Dent.

Lombroso, Cesare and Ferrero, William (1895) *The Female Offender.* London: Fisher Unwin.

Lopez, Ian F. Haney (1994) The Social Construction of Race: Some Observations on Illusion, Fabrication, and Choice, *Harvard Civil Rights-Civil Liberties Law Review*, 29, 1–62.

Luchjenbroers, June (1997) 'In Your Own Words …': Questions and Answers in a Supreme Court Trial, *Journal of Pragmatics*, 27, 477–503.

Lyotard, Jean-François (1984) *The Condition of Postmodernity: A Report on Knowledge*. Minneapolis: University of Minnesota Press.

MacDonald, Keith M. (1995) *Sociology of the Professions*. London: Sage.

MacKinnon, Catherine (1987) *Feminism Unmodified: Discourses on Life and Law*. Cambridge, MA: Harvard University Press.

MacKinnon, Catherine (1989) *Toward a Feminist Theory of the State*. Cambridge, MA: Harvard University Press.

MacKinnon, Catherine (2000) Some Points Against Postmodernism, *Chicago-Kent Law Review* 75, 687–712.

MacPherson, William (1999) *The Stephen Lawrence Inquiry*. London: The Stationery Office.

Maguire, Mike, Morgan, Rod and Reiner, Robert (1994) *The Oxford Handbook of Criminology*. Oxford: Clarendon Press.

Manning, Peter K. (1987) Ironies of Compliance, in Clifford D. Shearing and Philip C. Stenning (eds), *Private Policing*. Newbury Park, CA: Sage, pp. 293–316.

Manning, Peter K. (1989) Occupational Culture, in William G. Bailey (ed.), *The Encyclopedia of Police Science*. New York and London: Garland, pp. 360–4.

Manning, Peter K. and Van Maanen, John (1978) *Policing: A View from the Streets*. Santa Monica, CA: Goodyear Publishing Company.

Marshall, T. H. [1950] (1992) Citizenship and Social Class, in T. H. Marshall and Tom Bottomore (eds), *Citizenship and Social Class*. London: Pluto.

Marshall, T. H. and Bottomore, Tom (eds) (1992) *Citizenship and Social Class*. London: Pluto.

Martin, Susan Ehrlich and Jurik, Nancy C. (1996) *Doing Justice, Doing Gender*. Thousand Oaks, CA: Sage.

Martinson, Robert (1974) What Works? Questions and Answers about Prison Reform, *The Public Interest*, 35, 22–34.

Marx, Gary T. (1987) The Interweaving of Public and Private Police in Undercover Work, in Clifford D. Shearing and Philip C. Stenning (eds), *Private Policing*. Newbury Park, CA: Sage, pp. 172–93.

Marx, Karl (1962) *Capital*. London: Dent.

Marx, Karl and Engels, Friedrich (1964) *The German Ideology*. Moscow: Progress Publishers.

Matthews, R. and Young, Jock (1986) *Confronting Crime*. London: Sage.

Mathiesen, Thomas (2001) Television, Public Space and Prison Population, in David Garland (ed.), *Mass Imprisonment: Causes and Consequences*. London. Sage, pp. 28–34.

Matoesian, Gregory (1993) *Reproducing Rape: Domination Through Talk in the Courtroom*. Chicago: University of Chicago Press.

Matoesian, Gregory (1997) 'You Were Interested in Him as a Person?': Rhythms of Domination in the Kennedy Smith Rape Trial, *Law and Social Inquiry*, 22(1), 55–93.

Mauer, Marc (2001) The Causes and Consequences of Prison Growth in the United States, in David Garland (ed.), *Mass Imprisonment: Causes and Consequences*. London: Sage, pp. 4–14.

McBarnet, Doreen J. (1981) *Conviction: Law, the State and the Construction of Justice*. London: Macmillan.

McCormick, Peter and Job, Twyler (1993) Do Women Judges Make a Difference? An Analysis by Appeal Court Data, *Canadian Journal of Law and Society/Revue Canadienne de Droit et Société*, 8(1), 135–48.

McCulloch, J. (1988) Women in Prison, *Legal Service Bulletin*, 13(2), 60–1.

McKay, Jim and Smith, Philip (1995) Narrating the Hero: Media Frames in the O. J. Simpson Story, *Media Information Australia*, 4(1–2), 57–66.

Menkel-Meadow, Carrie (1984) Towards Another View of Legal Negotiation: The Structure of Problem Solving, *UCLA Law Review*, 31, 754–842.

Menkel-Meadow, Carrie (1985) Portia in a Different Voice: Speculations on a Women's Lawyering Process, *Berkley Women's Law Journal*, 1, 39–63.

Menkel-Meadow, Carrie (1999) The Sense and Sensibilities of Lawyers: Lawyering in Literature, Narratives, Film and Television, and Ethical Choices Regarding Career and Craft, *McGeorge Law Review*, 31, 1–28.

Merry, Sally Engle (1997) Global Human Rights and Local Social Movements in a Legally Plural World, *Canadian Journal of Law and Society/Revue Canadienne de Droit et Société*, 12(2), 247–71.

Messmer, H. and Otto, H. U. (eds) (1994) *Restorative Justice on Trial: Pitfalls and Potentials of Victim-Offender Mediation: International Research Perspectives.* Dordrecht and Boston: Kluwer.

Miller, Damien (1998) Knowing Your Rights: Implications of the Critical Legal Studies Critique of Rights for Indigenous Australians, *Australian Journal of Human Rights*, 5(1), 48–79.

Mills, C. Wright (1975) *The Sociological Imagination.* Harmondsworth: Pelican.

Morash, Merry, Haar, Robin N. and Rucker, Lila (1994) A Comparison of Programming for Women and Men in U.S. Prisons in the 1980s, *Crime and Delinquency*, 40(2), 197–221.

Morris, Norval and Rothman, David J. (eds) (1994) *The Oxford History of the Prison.* New York: Oxford University Press.

Moulds, Elizabeth F. (1980) Chivalry and Paternalism: Disparities of Treatment in the Criminal Justice System, in Susan Dateman and Frank R. Scarpatti (eds), *Women, Crime, and Justice.* New York: Oxford University Press.

Mulcahy, A. (1994) The Justifications of 'Justice': Legal Practitioners' Accounts of Negotiated Case Settlements in Magistrates' Courts, *British Journal of Criminology*, 34, 411–30.

Muncie, John, McLaughlin, Eugene and Langan, Mary (1996) *Criminological Perspectives.* London: Sage.

Mungham, Geoff and Bankowski, Zenon (1976) The Jury as Process, in Pat Carlen (ed.), *The Sociology of Law.* Keele: University of Keele.

Murphy, W. T. (1997) *The Oldest Social Science? Configurations of Law and Modernity.* Oxford: Clarendon Press.

Naffine, Ngaire (1986) Women and Crime, in Duncan Chappell and Paul Wilson (eds), *Australian Criminal Justice Systems: The Mid 1980s.* Sydney: Butterworths.

Naffine, Ngaire (1990) *Law and the Sexes: Explorations in Feminist Jurisprudence.* Sydney: Allen and Unwin.

Naffine, Ngaire (1997) *Feminism and Criminology.* Sydney: Allen and Unwin.

Nagel, Ilene and Johnson, Barry L. (1994) The Role of Gender in a Structured Sentencing System: Equal Treatment, Policy Choices, and the Sentencing of Female Offenders under the United States Sentencing Guidelines, *Journal of Law and Criminology*, 85, 181–221.

Nagin, Daniel S. and Paternoster, Raymond (1991) The Preventive Effects of the Perceived Risk of Arrest: Testing an Expanded Conception of Deterrence, *Criminology*, 29, 561–87.

Niederhoffer, Arthur and Blumberg, Abraham S. (eds) (1973) *The Ambivalent Force.* New York: Rinehart.

Nussbaum, Martha C. (1994) Skepticism About Practical Reason in Literature and Law, *Harvard Law Review*, 107, 714–744.

O'Barr, William (1982) *Linguistic Evidence: Language, Power and Strategy in the Courtroom.* New York: Academic Press.

O'Donovan, Katherine (1985) *Sexual Divisions in Law.* London: Weidenfeld and Nicholson.

Okin, Susan Miller (1979) *Women in Western Political Thought.* Princeton, NJ: Princeton University Press.

Olsen, Frances (1985) The Myth of State Intervention in the Family, *Journal of Law Reform* 18, 835–61.

O'Malley, Pat (1983) *Law, Capitalism and Democracy.* Sydney: Allen and Unwin.

Omatsu, Maryka (1997) The Fiction of Judicial Impartiality, *Canadian Journal of Women and the Law*, 9, 1–24.

Otto, Dianne (1998) Everything is Dangerous: Some Post-structural Tools for Rethinking the Universal Knowledge Claims of Human Rights Law, *Australian Journal of Human Rights*, 5(1), 17–45.

Owen, Barbara (1998) *In the Mix: Struggle and Survival in a Women's Prison.* Albany, NY: State University of New York Press.

Padavic, Irene and Orcutt, James D. (1997) Perceptions of Sexual Harassment in the Florida Legal System: A Comparison of Dominance and Spillover Explanations, *Gender and Society*, 11(5), 682–98.

Padgett, John F. (1990) Plea Bargaining and Prohibition in the Federal Courts, *Law and Society Review*, 24(2), 413–50.

Papke, Davis Ray (1999) Conventional Wisdom: The Courtroom Trial in American Popular Culture, *Marquette Law Review*, 82, 471–88.

Parsons, Talcott (1939) The Professions and Social Structure, *Social Forces*, 17, 457–67.

Parsons, Talcott (1954) *Essays in Sociological Theory*. New York: Free Press.

Parsons, Talcott (1967) Evolutionary Universals in Society, in *Sociological Theory and Modern Society*. New York: Free Press, pp. 490–520.

Parsons, Talcott (1970) *The Social System*. London: Routledge and Kegan Paul.

Pateman, Carole (1988) *The Sexual Contract*. Cambridge: Polity Press.

Patterson, Dennis (2003) From Postmodernism to Law and Truth, *Harvard Journal of Law and Policy*, 26(1), 49–65.

Petersilia, Joan (1999) Parole and Prisoner Reentry, in Michael H. Tonry and Joan Petersilia (eds), *Prisons*. Chicago: University of Chicago Press, pp. 479–529.

Phillips, Timothy and Smith, Philip (2000) Police Violence Occasioning Citizen Complaint: An Empirical Analysis of Time-Space Dynamics, *British Journal of Criminology*, 40(3), 480–96.

Piliavin, Irving and Briar, Scott (1964) Police Encounters with Juveniles, *American Journal of Sociology*, 49, 206–14.

Podlas, Kimberlianne (2001) Please Adjust Your Signal: How Television's Syndicated Courtrooms Bias Our Juror Citizenry, *American Business Law Journal*, 39, 1–24.

Pratt, John (2002) *Punishment and Civilization*. London: Sage.

Preis, Ann-Belinda (1996) Human Rights as Cultural Practice: An Anthropological Critique, *Human Rights Quarterly*, 18(2), 286–315.

Pritchard, Sarah (1995) The Jurisprudence of Human Rights: Some Critical Thought and Developments in Practice, *Australian Journal of Human Rights*, 2(1), 3–38.

Punch, Maurice (1985) *Conduct Unbecoming: The Social Construction of Police Deviance and Control*. London: Tavistock.

Putnis, Peter (1996) Police-Media Relations – Issues and Trends, in Duncan Chappell and Paul Wilson (eds), *Australian Policing: Contemporary Issues*. Melbourne: Butterworths, pp. 210–18.

Quinney, Richard (1977) *Class, State and Crime: On the Theory and Practice of Criminal Justice*. New York: Longman.

Reichman, Nancy (1987) The Widening Webs of Surveillance: Private Police Unravelling Deceptive Claims, in Clifford D. Shearing and Philip C. Stenning (eds), *Private Policing*. Newbury Park, CA: Sage, pp. 247–65.

Reiner, Robert (1985) *The Politics of the Police*. London: Harvester Wheatsheaf.

Reiner, Robert (1989) The Politics of Police Research in Britain, in Mollie Weatheritt (ed.), *Police Research; Some Future Prospects*. Aldershot: Avebury, pp. 3–20.

Reiner, Robert (1992) Policing a Postmodern Society, *The Modern Law Review*, 55(6), 761–81.

Reiner, Robert (1994) Policing and Police, in Mike Maguire, Rod Morgan and Robert Reiner (eds), *The Oxford Handbook of Criminology*. Oxford: Clarendon Press, pp. 705–72.

Reiss, Albert J. (1973) Police Brutality, in Arthur Niederhoffer and Abraham S. Blumberg (eds), *The Ambivalent Force*. New York: Rinehart, pp. 321–31.

Resnik, Judith (1996) Asking About Gender in Courts, *Signs*, 21(4), 952–90.

Reynolds, Christopher and Wilson, Paul (1996) Private Policing: Creating New Options, in Duncan Chappell and Paul Wilson (eds), *Australian Policing: Contemporary Issues*. Melbourne: Butterworths, pp. 219–32.

Roach Anleu, Sharyn (2000) *Law and Social Change*. London: Sage.

Robertson, Roland (1992) *Globalization: Social Theory Global Culture*. London: Sage.

Robinson, Dawn T., Smith-Lovin, Lyn and Tsaudis, Olga (1994) Heinous Crime or Unfortunate Accident? Effects of Remorse on Responses to Mock Criminal Trials, *Social Forces*, 73(1), 175–90.

Rose, Jonathan (1998) The Legal Profession in Medieval England: A History of Regulation, *Syracuse Law Review*, 48, 1–119.

Rothman, David J. (1995) Perfecting the Prison: United States 1789–1865, in Norval Morris and David J. Rothman (eds), *The Oxford History of the Prison*. New York: Oxford University Press, pp. 100–16.

Rousseau, Jean-Jacques (1968 [1762]) *The Social Contract*. Harmondsworth: Penguin.

Rowland, Robyn (1995) Human Rights Discourse and Women: Challenging the Rhetoric with Reality, *Australian and New Zealand Journal of Sociology*, 31(2), 8–24.

Rusche, Georg and Kirchheimer, Otto (1939) *Punishment and Social Structure*. New York: Columbia University Press.

Sarre, Rick (1996) The State of Community Based Policing in Australia, in Duncan Chappell and Paul Wilson (eds), *Australian Policing: Contemporary Issues*. Melbourne: Butterworths, pp. 26–41.

Savelsberg, Joachim J. (1994) 'Knowledge, Domination and Criminal Punishment' *American Journal of Sociology*, 99(4), 911–943.

Savelsberg, Joachim, King, Ryan and Cleveland, Lara (2002) Politicized Scholarship? Science on Crime and the State, *Social Problems*, 49(3), 327–48.

Schanck, Peter C. (1992) Understanding Postmodern Thought and its Implications for Statutory Interpretation, *Southern California Law Review*, 65, 2505–88.

Seidman, Steven (ed.) (1994) *The Postmodern Turn: New Perspectives on Social Theory.* Cambridge: Cambridge University Press.

Sellers, Martin (1993) *The History and Politics of Private Prisons: A Comparative Analysis.* London: Associated University Presses.

Shearing, Clifford D. and Stenning, Philip C. (1987a) *Private Policing.* Newbury Park: Sage.

Shearing, Clifford D. and Stenning, Philip C. (1987b) Reframing Policing, in Clifford D. Shearing and Philip C. Stenning (eds), *Private Policing.* Newbury Park, CA: Sage, pp. 9–18.

Shearing, Clifford D. and Stenning, Philip C. (1987c) Say Cheese! The Disney Order that is Not So Mickey Mouse, in Clifford D. Shearing and Philip C. Stenning (eds), *Private Policing.* Newbury Park, CA: Sage, pp. 317–24.

Sherman, Lawrence and the National Advisory Commission on Higher Education of Police Officers (1978) *The Quality of Police Education.* Washington, DC: John Wiley and Sons.

Sherry, Suzanna (1986) Civic Virtue and the Feminine Voice in Constitutional Adjudication, *Virginia Law Review*, 72, 543–606.

Simon, Rita, and Landis, Jean (1991) *The Crimes Women Commit, The Punishments They Receive.* Lexington, MA: Lexington Books.

Skolnick, Jerome (1975) *Justice Without Trial.* New York: Wiley.

Skolnick, Jerome and Bayley, David (1986) *The New Blue Line: Police Innovation in Six American Cities.* New York: Free Press.

Smart, Carol (1989) *Feminism and the Power of the Law.* London and New York: Routledge.

Smith, Philip (1996) Executing Executions, *Theory and Society*, 25(2), 235–61.

Smith, Philip (1999) The Elementary Forms of Place, *Qualitative Sociology*, 22(1), 13–36.

Smith, Philip (2001) *Cultural Theory: An Introduction.* Oxford: Blackwell.

Smith, Philip (2003) Punishment Technology as Cultural Expression, *Theory, Culture and Society*, 20(5), 27–51.

Songer, Donald and Crews-Meyer, Kelly (2000) Does Judge Gender Matter? Decision Making in State Supreme Courts, *Social Science Quarterly*, 81(3), 750–62.

Sparks, Richard (1994) Can Prisons be Legitimate? *British Journal of Criminology*, 34(1), 14–27.

Spierenburg, Pieter (1984) *The Spectacle of Suffering.* New York: Cambridge University Press.

Spitze, David (2000) Heroes or Villains? Moral Struggles Vs. Ethical Dilemmas: An Examination of Dramatic Portrayals of Lawyers and the Legal Profession, *Nova Law Review* 24, 725–59.

Spohn, Cassia, Welsh, Susan and Gruhl, John (1985) Women Defendants in Court: the Interaction Between Sex and Race in Convicting and Sentencing, *Social Science Quarterly*, 66(1), 178–85.

Spohn, Cassia (2000) Thirty Years of Sentencing Reform: The Quest for a Racially Neutral Sentencing Process, *Criminal Justice*, 3, 427–501.

Stark, Steven D. (1987) Perry Mason Meets Sonny Crocket: The History of Lawyers and the Police as Television Heroes, *University of Miami Law Review*, 42, 229–76.

Steffensmeier, Darrell and Demuth, Stephen (2000) Ethnicity and Sentencing Outcomes in U.S. Federal Courts: Who is Punished More Harshly? *American Sociological Review*, 65(4), 705–29.

Steffensmeier, Darrell, Ulmer, Jeffery and Kramer, John (1998) The Interaction of Race, Gender, and Age in Criminal Sentencing: The Punishment Cost of Being Young, Black, and Male, *Criminology*, 36(4), 763–98.

Sterling, Joyce (1993) The Impact of Gender Bias on Judging: Survey of Attitudes Toward Women Judges, *Colorado Lawyer* 22(February), 257–58.

Strang, Heather (2000) The Future of Restorative Justice, in Duncan Chappell and Paul Wilson (eds), *Crime and the Criminal Justice System in Australia: 2000 and Beyond.* Sydney: Butterworths, pp. 22–33.

Sykes, Gresham (1958) *The Society of Captives*. Princeton, NJ: Princeton University Press.

Taylor, Ian, Walton, Paul and Young, Jock (1973) *The New Criminology*. London: Routledge and Kegan Paul.

Thornton, Margaret (1996) *Dissonance and Distrust: Women in the Legal Profession*. Oxford: Oxford University Press.

Tilly, Charles (2000) *Stories, Identities and Political Change*. New York: Rowman and Littlefield.

Tobias, John J. (1972) Police and the Public in the UK, *Journal of Contemporary History*, 7(1), 201–20.

Toch, Hans (1977) *Police, Prisons and the Problem of Violence*. Rockville, MD: National Institute of Mental Health.

Tonry, Michael H. (1995) *Malign Neglect: Race, Crime, and Punishment in America*. New York: Oxford University Press.

Tonry, Michael H. (1996) *Sentencing Matters*. New York: Oxford University Press.

Tonry, Michael H. and Petersilia, Joan (1999) *Prisons*. Chicago: University of Chicago Press.

Tribe, Laurence (1985) *Constitutional Choices*. Cambridge, MA: Harvard University Press.

Turnbull, Colin (1961) *The Forest People*. London: Jonathan Cape.

Turner, Bryan S. (1993) Outline of a Theory of Human Rights, *Sociology*, 27(3), 489–512.

Turner, Bryan S. (1997a) Citizenship Studies: A General Theory, *Citizenship Studies*, 1(1), 5–18.

Turner, Bryan S. (1997b) A Neo-Hobbesian Theory of Human Rights: A Reply to Malcolm Waters, *Sociology*, 31(3), 565–71.

Tushnet, Mark (1984) Symposium: A Critique of Rights: An Essay on Rights, *Texas Law Review*, 62, 1363–95.

Umbreit, Mark (1992) Mediating Victim-Offender Conflict: From Single Site to Multi-Site Analysis in the U.S., in H. Messmer and H. U. Otto, (eds), *Restorative Justice on Trial: Pitfalls and Potentials of Victim-Offender Mediation: International Research Perspectives*. Dordrecht and Boston: Kluwer.

Van Maanen, John (1978) The Asshole, in Peter K. Manning and John Van Maanen, (eds), *Policing: A View from the Streets*. Santa Monica, C.A.: Goodyear Publishing Company, pp. 34–46.

Wacquant, Loïc (2001) Deadly Symbiosis: When Ghetto and Prison Meet and Mesh, in David Garland (ed.), *Mass Imprisonment: Causes and Consequences*. London: Sage, pp. 82–120.

Walker, L. (1984) Sex Differences in the Development of Moral Reasoning: A Review, *Child Development*, 55, 667–91.

Walker, Samuel, Spohn, Cassia and DeLone, Miriam (1999) *The Color of Justice: Race, Ethnicity and Crime in America*. Belmont, CA: Wadsworth.

Ward, David A. and Kassebaum, Gene G. (1965) *Women's Prison: Sex and Social Structure*. Chicago: Aldine.

Waters, Malcolm (1996) Human Rights and the Universalisation of Interests: Towards a Social Constructionist Approach, *Sociology*, 30(3), 593–600.

Weatheritt, Mollie (1989) *Police Research: Some Future Prospects*. Aldershot: Avebury.

Weber, Max (1978) *Economy and Society*. Berkeley, CA: University of California Press.

Western, John, Makkai, Toni and Natalier, Kristin (2001) Professions and the Public Good, *Law in Context*, 19, 21–44.

White, Rob and Alder, Christine (1994) *The Police and Young People in Australia*. Cambridge: Cambridge University Press.

White, Rob and Perrone, Santina (1997) *Crime and Social Control: An Introduction*. Oxford: Oxford University Press.

Wilbanks, William (1987) *The Myth of a Racist Criminal Justice System*. Monterey, CA: Brooks/Cole Publishing Company.

Wilczynski, Ania (1997) Mad or Bad? Child-Killers, Gender and the Courts, *British Journal of Criminology*, 37(3), 419–36.

Williams, Patricia J. (1988) Alchemical Notes: Reconstructing Ideals from Deconstructed Rights, in Jules Lobel (ed.), *A Less Than Perfect Union*. New York: Monthly Review Press.

Williams, Patricia J. (1991) *The Alchemy of Race and Rights: Diary of a Law Professor*. Cambridge, MA: Harvard University Press.

Willis, Evan (1995) *The Sociological Quest: An Introduction to Social Life*. St Leonards, NSW: Allen and Unwin.

Wilson, James Q. (1968) *Varieties of Police Behavior*. Cambridge, MA: Harvard University Press.

Wilson, James Q. and Kelling, George L. (1982) Broken Windows, *The Atlantic Monthly*, 249(3), 29–38.

Woodbury, Hanni (1984) The Strategic Use of Questions in Court, *Semiotica*, 48(3–4), 197–228.

Wright, S. (1992) Economic Rights and Social Justice: A Feminist Analysis of Some International Human Rights Conventions, *Australian Yearbook of International Law*, 12, 241–64.

Wundersitz, Joy (2000) Juvenile Justice in Australia: Towards the New Millennium, in Duncan Chappell and Paul Wilson (eds), *Crime and the Criminal Justice System in Australia: 2000 and Beyond.* Sydney: Butterworths, pp. 102–18.

Yeatman, Anna (1994) *Postmodern Revisionings of the Political.* New York: Routledge.

Young, Jock (1986) The Failure of Criminology: The Need for Radical Realism, in R. Matthews and Jock Young (eds), *Confronting Crime.* London: Sage, pp. 9–30.

Zatz, Marjorie S. (1987) The Changing Forms of Racial/Ethnic Bias in Sentencing, *Journal of Research in Crime and Delinquency*, 24, 69–72.

Zdenkowski, George (2000) Sentencing Trends: Past, Present and Prospective, in Duncan Chappell and Paul Wilson (eds), *Crime and the Criminal Justice System in Australia: 2000 and Beyond.* Melbourne: Butterworths, pp. 161–202.

Zimbardo, Philip (1972) The Pathology of Imprisonment, *Society*, 9, 4–8.

Zingraff, Matthew and Thomson, Randall (1984) Differential Sentencing of Women and Men in the U.S.A., *International Journal of the Sociology of Law*, 12(4), 401–13.

Index

Aborigines
    in court 125–126, 127, 128
    imprisonment rate of 175
    laws 57
Abortion 70–71
Abstraction 63
Adversarial proceedings 49
Agency capture 111, 118
Alternative adjudication 154–159
    characteristics 155
    experiences of 156
    family conferencing 155, 190
    victim offender mediation 155
Althusser, Louis 24
Anomie 14, 43
Appadurai, Arjun 205
Arpaio, Sheriff Joe 171–172
Asylums (Goffman) 27
Auburn System (prisons) 170, 193
Azande, the (an African culture) 10–11

'Back end' (of criminal justice system)
    185, 193
Base/superstructure model 19, 43
Battered Woman Syndrome 67–68
Baudrillard, Jean 88, 203
Bauman, Zygmunt 203
Bayley, David 110
Beccaria, Cesare 167, 170
Beck, Allen J. 176
Beck, Ulrich 204
Becker, Howard 26–27, 40
Beckett, Katherine 17
Bentham, Jeremy 29
Berger, Peter 196
'Biopower' (Foucault) 30, 43
Bittner, Egon 86, 91
Black, Donald 11, 105
Blumstein, Alfred 176–177
Body, the 29, 38–39
Boundary Maintenance 16–17, 43
Bowker, Lee 181

Boyle, Raymond 117
Braithwaite, John 155, 157, 189–190
Broderick, John 96
Brogden, Mike 110
'Broken Windows' theory (policing) 101
Brown, Michael 96

'Carceral city' (Foucault) 30, 43
'Carceral continuum', the (Foucault)
    30, 43
Carlen, Pat 39
Cashmore, Ellis 110
Chambliss, William 21
Chan, Janet 90, 104–105, 108
Chivalry effect 40, 43, 134
Civilizing Process, The (Elias) 37–38
Class relations and class conflict 19–24
Code of silence 107, 118
Community corrections 185, 193
Class, State and Crime (Quinney) 21
Cohen, Albert 181
Cohen, Stanley 17, 187–188
Collective conscience, the 14, 43
Colonialism 56–57, 87
Common law system 18, 47–48
Colquhoun, Patrick 85
Compliance systems 111, 118
Conflict theory 8–9, 43
Connell, R.W. 77
Consensus theory 8–9, 43
Contract theory 12–13
Cotterrell, Roger 2
Courts
    and alternative dispute resolution 157
    and language 125–128
    rationalization 122–123
    role of 121–122
Crews-Meyer, Kelly 147
Criminalization 21, 26, 43
Critical legal studies 61–62
    critique of rights 75–76
Cultural relativism 35, 74

Daly, Kathy 157
Danzig, Richard 154
Das Kapital (Marx) 19
Davies, Margaret 35
Davis, Sue 148
Death Penalty 188–189
Deterrence, philosophy of 167–8, 193
Difference 34, 43, 64–66, 151
Different voice 146–147
Differentiation 85, 119
Dinovitzer, Ronit 175
'Disciplinary power' 29, 43
Discipline and Punish (Foucault) 28–30
Discourse 30–31, 33, 43
Discretion
    executive 193
    minimizing judicial 136–139
    police 83, 94
    prosecutorial 124–125
Discrimination
    direct 129
    indirect 130–131
    contextual 131
    police and 104–106
Division of Labour in Society, The
    (Durkheim) 13–15, 17, 18
Dobash, Russell et al. 173, 174
'Docile body' (Foucault) 29, 43
Domestic violence 25, 67–68, 71
Dominant class 19, 43
Donzelot, Jaques 71
Doubly deviant 135
Durkheim, Emile 13–16, 77
Dworkin, Ronald 58

Economic determinism 19, 43
Elementary Forms of Religious Life,
    The (Durkheim) 17
Elias, Norbert 37–39, 172
Emotions 14, 16, 38–39, 130
Engels, Friedrich 20
Enlightenment 51, 197, 202–203
Equality
    feminist approaches to 63–66
    formal 62
    substantive 62
Erikson, Kai 16–17
Erlich, Eugen 52
Esteal, Patricia 185
Evans-Pritchard, E.E. 11

Family conferencing 155, 189–190
Feminism and feminist perspectives
    critiques of equality 63–66
    critiques of rights 76
    empiricism 41, 43

Feminism and feminist perspectives *cont.*
    left realism and 25
    liberal 40, 44
    radical 40, 44
    prisons, about 173–174, 183–185
    postmodern 41
    public private dichotomy 70–71
    rape trials 139–141
    socialist 40, 45
    standpoint 41, 45
    theoretical overview 39–42
Fielding, Nigel 109
Findlay, Mark 152–153
Fines 186
Focal concerns theory 131
Folk Devils and Moral Panics (Cohen) 17
Foucault, Michel 28–32, 169, 172, 203
'Front end' (of criminal justice system)
    185, 193
Fuller, Lon 59–60
Functionalism 13–14, 18, 44

Garfinkle, Harold (degradation
    ceremonies) 125
Garland, David 174, 177, 204
Gender
    alternative dispute resolution 158
    chivalry 134
    different voice
    equality 63–66
    feminism on 39–42
    lawyers 144–146
    judges 146–149
    juries 151
    Madonna- whore dichotomy 134–135
    objectivity 67
    and the police 89–90
    in prisons 173–174, 183–185
    rape 134–141
    sentencing 133–136
    violence 67–68
German Ideology, The (Marx and Engels) 20
Giallombardo, Rose 184
Giddens, Anthony 36–37
Gilligan, Carol 146–147
Girshick, Lori 184
Globalization 56, 87, 205
Goffman, Erving 27
Greer, Kimberly 184

Hagan, John 175
Hall, Stuart 23–24,103–104, 116
Hart, H.L.A 58, 59–60
Hay, Douglas 22–23
Henman, Ralph 148
History of Sexuality, The (Foucault) 30

Hobbes, Thomas 12
Holdaway, Simon 88
Hofrichter, Richard 157–158
Hunt, Alan 33

Incapacitation 168, 174, 193
Ideology, law and criminal justice
    and 19–24, 44
Intermediate Sanctions 185–188, 193

Job, Twyler 148
Johnson, Robert 188
Judges
    activism 48
    critiques of 67, 139–140
    focal concerns theory 140
    gender 146–149
    independence 48
    liberation hypothesis 132
Juries
    empanelling 151–152
    history of 149–150
    nullifications 153–154
    role 150–151
    understanding of 153
Juvenile justice 190

Kansas City Preventive Patrol
    Experiment 98–99
Kelling, George 99, 101
Kelsen, Hans 57–58
Kirchheimer, Otto 20–21, 177

Labelling theory 26–27, 44, 173
'Law and order society' (Hall) 103, 119
Lawyers
    in court 144–146
    gender 144–146
    ideal of service 142–143
    media representations of, 161–152
    professionals 55, 142–143
Left realism 25, 44, 106
Legal realism 61
Legal subject, the 34
Legal systems
    civil law 49
    common law 47–48
    emergence and evolution of 10–15,
        18, 52–55
Legislation 48
Leviathan (Hobbes) 12
Liberal legal philosophy 50–51
Liberation hypothesis 132
Locke, John 12
Lombroso, Cesare 135
Lyotard, Jean Francois 203

MacKinnon, Catherine 39, 65–66
Macpherson Report, The 106

Macquarie Harbour Penal
    Settlement 183
'Mad' women 135–136
Madonna–whore dichotomy
    134–135, 139–140
Mandatory sentencing 138, 177
Manning, Peter 88
Marshall, T.H. 72
Marx, Gary 114
Marx, Karl 19, 77
Marxist and Neo-Marxist criminology
    19–24, 177–178
    critique of 24–26
Master status 27, 44
Mathiesen, Thomas 177
Matoesian, Gregory 126, 140
Mbuti, the (an African culture) 10
McCormick, Peter 148
Media, the
    mass imprisonment and 177
    moral panic and 17, 23–24
    police and 88, 115–117
    popularity 160–161
    reality T.V. 162–163
    representations of law 159–163
    significance of 159–160
Menkle-Meadow, Carrie 147
Methodology 199–200
Mills, C. Wright 2
Minow, Martha 39
Modernity, influence of on criminal
    justice system 11, 14–15, 18–19,
    30, 36, 38, 52–55, 73, 85–86,
    172, 188, 200–202
Moral entrepreneurs 27, 44
Moral panic 17, 23–24, 44
Multiculturalism 87

Naffine, Ngaire 39, 41, 63, 202
Nation State and Violence, The
    (Giddens) 36–37
Natural law 58–61
Negotiated order 182–183, 193
Net widening 187, 193
New Blue Line, The (Skolnick and
    Bayley) 110
New Criminology, The (Taylor
    et al.) 21, 24
Nietzsche, Friedrich 30
Norms 9–10, 51–52
'Nothing works' (prisoner rehabilitation)
    174, 193
Nullifications 153–154

Objectivity 66–68
O'Malley, Pat 122–123
Outsiders (Becker) 26–27, 40
Owen, Barbara 184

Panopticon, the 29, 44
Parole 137–138, 185
Parsons, Talcott 18, 36
Patriarchy 39, 44
Pensylvania System (prisons) 170, 193
Phillips, Timothy 108
Plea bargaining 123
Police
  as gatekeepers 83
  culture 88–95, 107, 119
  deviance 107
  discretion 83, 94, 119
  and guilty pleas 123–124
  history of 84–87
  importance of 84
  media and 84, 115–117
  media representation of 160–162
  modernity and 86
  politics and 84, 103
  postmodernity and 87, 108
  reform of 108–110
Policing
  by consent 86, 119
  community 100–101, 118
  evidence based 98, 119
  private 112–115
  problem oriented 98, 119
  race/racism and 104–106
  reactive 96–97, 119
  routine patrolling 95–97
  styles and strategies 95–102
  zero tolerance 101–102, 119
Policing the Crisis (Hall et al.) 23–24
Policy regime 177, 193
Postmodernism 32–35, 44
  critique of rights 74–75
Postmodernity 55–57, 87, 202–204, 206
Positivism 57–58
Poststructuralism 30, 44
Power
  in alternative dispute resolution 156–157
  disciplinary 29, 43
  in families 69–70
  Foucault on 28–30
  gender and 39–42
  language and 125–128
  Marxism on 19–24
  microphysics of 29, 44
  prisons, in 181–183
  race control and 177
  sovereign 29, 45

Prisons
  correctional programs in 173–174, 184
  costs of 174–175
  culture of and life in 178–182, 184–185
  history and models of 169–172
  evaluation and efficiency of 172–175
  negotiated order in 182–183
  growth of 175–178
  population characteristics in 175
  private 190–192
  women in 174, 183–185
Private sphere (family) 69–72
Probation 185
Professionalization 85, 119, 142–143
Prosecutors 124–125
Public-private dichotomy 69–72

Question and answer format 126
Quinney, Richard 21

Race
  and juries 151–152
  and policing 104–106
  and prisons 176–177, 179
  and sentencing 129–133
  and the death penalty 189
Radical criminology 21, 44
Rape, 67, 126, 139–140, 141, 181
Rationalization
  of court processes 122–123, 154
  of criminal justice systems 36–37, 200
  of law 54–55
Recidivism 173, 175, 193
Reichman, Nancy 113
Reiner, Robert 88, 93–94, 95, 108, 115
Reintegrative shaming 189–190, 193
Rehabilitation, philosophy of 168, 193
  (see also Prisons, correctional
    programs in)
Reiss, Albert 92
Relativism 35, 74
Religion, influence on criminal justice
    system 170
Restorative Justice 190, 193, 154–159
Retribution, philosophy of 167, 194
Rights
  citizenship rights 72–73
  critical legal studies critiques of 74–76
  feminist critiques of 76
  foundationalist approach to 78
  human rights 73–74
  postmodern critiques of 74–75
  sociological approaches to 77–78
Risk and risk society 87, 204–205, 206
Rite of Passage 27, 45
Ritual 17–18

Robertson, Roland 205
Rousseau, Jean-Jacques 12
Rule of Law 51
Rusche, Georg 20–21, 177

Sanctions (positive and negative) 9–10, 44
'Sanctioning systems' 111, 119
Scutt, Jocelyn 39
Selective incapacitation 174, 194
Self, the 27, 38
Scarman Report, The 106
    history of 84–87
Sentencing
    chivalry 134
    ethnicity 129–133
    focal concerns theory 130
    gender 133–136
    liberation hypothesis 132
    mandatory 138
    minimizing judicial discretion 136–139
    organizational perspective 132
    philosophies behind 167–168
    three strikes legislation 138
    truth in 138
Separation of powers 48
Shearing, Clifford 110, 113–114
Sherman, Lawrence 109
Sherry, Suzanna 147
Simpson, O.J. 145–146, 189
Simulation 203, 206
Skolnick, Jerome 88, 92, 110
Smart, Carol 39
Smith, Philip 17–18, 108
Socialization 9, 45, 148
Social contract, the 12–13, 45
Social Contract, The (Rousseau) 12
Social control, forms of 9–11
Social order
    problem of 9, 44
    in traditional societies 10–11
Society of Captives, The (Sykes) 182
Sociological perspective (advantages and
    characteristics of) 1–4, 8, 196–200
Solidarity
    'mechanical' 14, 44
    'organic' 15
Songer, Donald 147
'Sovereign power' (Foucault) 29, 45
Spectacle of Suffering, The
    (Spierenberg) 38–39
Spierenberg, Pieter 38–39
State, the 12, 20–21, 24, 36–37, 86, 87,
    103, 113, 177, 187–188
Status offences 135
Stenning, Philip 113–114

Stereotyping 92, 119
Structuralism 30, 45
Subculture of violence 181, 194
Subordinate class 19, 45
Sykes, Gresham 178–179, 182
Symbolic interactionism 26–28

Taylor, Ian 21, 24
Three strikes legislation 138, 176
Tilly, Charles 198
Total institution 27, 45
Truth commissions 158–159
Truth in sentencing 138, 177
Turnbull, Colin 10
Turner, Bryan 78

Umbreit, Mark 156
van Gennep, Arnold 27
van Maanen, John 93
Varieties of Police Behaviour (Wilson) 95–96
Victimization
    in prison 180–182
    Three strikes legislation 138
Victim offender mediation 158

Wacquant, Loic 177–178
Walton, Paul 21, 24
Wayward Puritans (Erikson) 16–17
Weber, Max 18, 36–37, 54–55, 77–78, 86, 172
Western, Bruce 177
Wilczynski, Ania 136
Wilson, James Q. 95–96, 101
Women
    alternative dispute resolution 158
    chivalry 134
    in criminological theory and
        research 39–42
    different voice
    equality 63–66
    judges 146–149
    juries 151
    lawyers 144–146
    Madonna–whore dichotomy 134–135
    in the police 89–90
    in prison 174, 183–185
    and the police 89–90
    in prisons 173–174, 183–185
    rape 134–141
    sentencing 133–136
    violence towards 67–68

Young, Jock 21, 24, 25

Zero tolerance 101–102, 119
Zimbardo, Philip 180